PRINCIPLES OF LEGISLATIVE AND REGULATORY DRAFTING

Principles of Legislative and Regulatory Drafting provides a succinct guide to an area of law and practice which has previously been poorly served by English textbooks. It explains how drafters can convert legislative and regulatory policy into a form which has the desired effect in the most direct and accessible way.

On the basis that those who seek to communicate must be conscious of how their words will be read, it includes a chapter on interpretation. Other chapters include the nature of drafting instructions (including ethical considerations), the general principles of drafting, the protection of human rights, the creation of statutory corporations and schemes of licensing, subordinate legislation and the creation of criminal offences.

The principles and skills of drafting are very largely common to both the legislative and regulatory fields, but the book draws attention to areas in which significant differences arise.

Extracts from the Interpretation Act 1978 and the European Convention on Human Rights are included as Appendices.

The book provides an invaluable introduction for those engaged in legislative and regulatory drafting, while also being useful to anyone who is interested in the creation and interpretation of legislative and regulatory texts.

Principles of Legislative and Regulatory Drafting

Ian McLeod

·HART·
PUBLISHING

OXFORD AND PORTLAND, OREGON
2009

Published in North America (US and Canada) by
Hart Publishing
c/o International Specialized Book Services
920 NE 58th Avenue, Suite 300
Portland, OR 97213-3786
USA
Tel: +1 503 287 3093 or toll-free: (1) 800 944 6190
Fax: +1 503 280 8832
E-mail: orders@isbs.com
Website: http://www.isbs.com

Hart Publishing Ltd, 16C Worcester Place, Oxford, OX1 2JW
Telephone: +44 (0)1865 517530 Fax: +44 (0)1865 510710
E-mail: mail@hartpub.co.uk
Website: http://www.hartpub.co.uk

British Library Cataloguing in Publication Data
Data Available

ISBN: 978-1-84113-772-8

Typeset by Hope Services, Abingdon, Oxford
Printed and bound in Great Britain by
TJ International Ltd, Padstow, Cornwall

Preface

This book introduces, and puts into context, the principles which apply to the drafting of both legislation (whether primary or subordinate) and regulations made by a whole host of institutions such as professional bodies, trade associations, sporting organisations and universities.

As well as being useful to those who are coming to legislative or regulatory drafting for the first time, it provides a convenient source of reminders for those who undertake such work only occasionally. It may also interest anyone engaged in policy-making processes which result in the drafting of legislative and regulatory instruments, anyone who instructs drafters and anyone who wishes to develop their understanding of why legislative and regulatory instruments take the form they do.

The fact that I have been writing for two readerships has given me a significant problem of terminology. I have solved this difficulty by the simple expedient of referring to all legislative and regulatory documents as *instruments* and their contents as *provisions*—except, of course, where it seems to me that the context otherwise requires. Although this usage will no doubt upset some purists, the resulting ease of reading seems to me to outweigh the reduction in technical accuracy.

The fact of two readerships has also given me a problem of content. More particularly, by no means all regulatory instruments are drafted by lawyers, so I have had to be particularly careful in the assumptions I have made about my readers' pre-existing knowledge. However, my experience leads me to believe that for every reader who feels patronised by being told something he or she already knows, there are many more who are grateful for being told about (or reminded of) precisely the same thing. In any case, I am confident that regulatory drafters who are not lawyers will have no difficulty in translating into their own practical terminology those matters which they find conceptually relevant, even if I have expressed them legalistically.

Also, but less problematically, I have generally used the term *drafting* (and its variants) to apply to both legislative and regulatory contexts, thus avoiding the need for constant qualification. However, I most certainly do not intend the absence of qualification to suggest that the principles discussed in this book necessarily apply to drafting in other contexts, such as the preparation of conveyancing and commercial documents.

The real statutory provisions I have cited are all taken from Westminster legislation, and I have indicated their reality by providing their dates. Where I have found it convenient to make up a named example in order to illustrate a point as clearly and briefly as possible, I have used an obviously false date such as 20XX.

The whole of this book must be read as being based on the drafting practices developed within the unified jurisdiction of England and Wales (except, of course, where the context otherwise requires). However, I am confident that readers in other common law jurisdictions will be able to apply much of what I have written without any modification, and even more with only minor modifications. More particularly, my experience of being the main lecturer on the Intensive Course for Commonwealth Legislative Drafters in London University's Institute of Advanced Studies for a number of years, has given me a particular insight into the needs of under-resourced drafting offices in developing countries. Therefore, where it has seemed to me to be appropriate to do so, I have commented on the distinctive difficulties that members of such offices face.

I am grateful to Sir Edward Caldwell, formerly First Parliamentary Counsel, and Dr David Murray, Professor Emeritus of Government in the Open University, both of whom very generously read this book in draft. Their comments were invaluable but neither of them saw the final text and neither of them must be assumed to agree with everything I have said.

I am, as always, grateful to my wife, Jacqui, for her editorial assistance and her patience.

Finally, I have failed to resist the temptation to quote the following comment, even though it comes from a legal theorist rather than a drafter:

> I will venture to affirm, that what is called the *technical* part of legislation is incomparably more difficult than what may be styled as the *ethical*. In other words, it is far easier to conceive justly what would be useful law, than so construct that same law that it may accomplish the design of the law giver. (original emphasis)

John Austin, *Jurisprudence*, Vol 2, 4th edn, 1873, 1136.

Ian McLeod
25 January 2009

UPDATE ON THE WEBSITE OF THE OFFICE OF THE PARLIAMENTARY COUNSEL

Readers who wish to pursue the recommendations of the Drafting Technique Group of the Office of the Parliamentary Counsel should note that, between the date of this Preface and the date of this Update, the Office's web address became www.cabinetoffice.gov.uk/parliamentarycounsel.aspx/ (References to the old address appear on pages 67, 69, 79, 92, 94, 107 and 134.) The recommendations of the Drafting Technique Group are still accessed through the *drafting techniques* tab, but the scope of those recommendations has been substantially developed.

Ian McLeod
22 July 2009

Contents

Preface v
Table of Cases xv

1 Drafting and Communication 1

Introduction 1
The Imprecision of Language 2
Oral and Written Uses of Language 2
Clarity in Written Language 3
Introduction 3
Does *Clarity* have a Single Meaning and can Drafters Make Everything *Clear*? 3
How Objective is Clarity? 4
Introduction 4
Identifying Potential Readerships 5
The Fallacy of Assuming a Co-operative Readership 8

2 Principles of Interpretation 11

Introduction 11
Matters of Fact and Matters of Law 12
Introduction 12
The Leading Cases 12
The Myth of Literal Meaning 14
The Contextual Approach 15
Introduction 15
Purpose as Part of the Context 16
Introduction 16
Purposivism in Action 17
Reading Provisions and Instruments as a Whole 20
Introduction 20
Preambles and Long Titles 23
Short titles 23
Headings and Marginal Notes 24
Schedules, Definition Sections and Commencement Sections 24
Extrinsic Materials as Part of the Context 25
Introduction 25
Legal textbooks 25

Dictionaries 26
Pre-parliamentary Materials 26
Parliamentary Materials: the Use of Hansard 27
Post-parliamentary Materials 27
Presumptions 28
Introduction 28
The Presumption against Injustice 28
The Presumption against Absurdity 29
Updating Construction 29
Introduction 29
The Problem of Social Change 30
The Problem of Technological Change 32

3 Drafting Instructions 33

Introduction 33
The Nature of Drafting Instructions 34
The Content of Drafting Instructions 35
The Form of Drafting Instructions 38
The Ethical Dimension of Drafting 39
Introduction 39
Ethical Considerations 39

4 Constitutional Considerations and the Protection of Human Rights 43

Introduction 43
Interpreting Constitutions 44
Introduction 44
The Constitutional Context of Drafting 44
The Protection of Human Rights 46
Introduction 46
The Legal Protection of Human Rights before the Human Rights Act 1998 46
The Human Rights Act 1998 48
Introduction 48
The European Convention on Human Rights 48
Convention Rights under the Human Rights Act 49
How the Courts must approach Convention Rights 50
Interpretation and Validity of Legislation 50
Declarations of Incompatibility 52
The Duty imposed on Public Authorities 52
Statements of Compatibility 53
Is the HRA Retrospective as to Matters of Fact? 53

ECHR Concepts and their Interpretation 54
The Presumption of Compliance with International Law 57
Paving Legislation 58
The Reallocation of Executive Functions and Titles 60

5 General Principles of Drafting 61

Introduction 61
The Nature of The General Principles of Drafting 61
Introduction 61
The Mongoose Principle 61
Is Drafting an Art or a Science? 62
The Range of Drafting Techniques 63
Plain Language Drafting 63
Introduction 63
Plain Language Drafting in its Historical Context 64
An Inevitable Limitation on the Usefulness of Plain Language Drafting 64
Structuring an Instrument 65
Introduction 65
The Value of Uniformity 66
Thring's Five Rules 67
Introduction 67
The Text of the Rules 67
The Essence of the Rules 68
The Placing of Subordinate Provisions in Practice 69
Layout 71
Introduction 71
Sentence Length 72
Matters Requiring Particular Care and Attention 73
Using Words Consistently 73
Using the Active rather than the Passive 73
Drafting Positively 74
Constructing Legislative Sentences 75
Introduction 75
Following Conventional Sentence Structure 75
Gender-Neutral Drafting 76
Introduction 76
Some Drafting Techniques 76
Being Careful with Modifiers 78
Using Past, Present and Future Tenses 79

Using *And*, *Or* and *And/Or* 79
Is a Body Corporate Singular or Plural? 80
Avoiding Nominalisations 80
Using Ordinary Words 81
Introduction 81
Using Plain Language Guides 83
Provisos 83
Ranges of Items 84
Punctuation 85
Introduction 85
Round Brackets (or Parentheses) and Square Brackets (or Brackets Properly So-called) 87
Apostrophes 88
Commas 88
Restrictive and Non-restrictive Phrases and Clauses 89
Enacting Formulas, Titles and Preambles 90
Introduction 90
Enacting Formulas 91
Titles and Preambles 91
Amending Provisions 92
Introduction 92
Textual Amendment 92
Non-textual Amendment 92
Amending by Repeal and Re-enactment 93
Amending Provisions and Gender-neutral Drafting 94
Numbering Newly-inserted Provisions 94
Commencement (*or* Coming into Force) 94
Application and Extent 96
Savings and Transitional Provisions 98
Introduction 98
Some Examples of Savings and Transitional Provisions 98
Consequential Amendments and Repeals 99
Definition Sections 100
Introduction 100
Matters of Fact and Matters of Law 100
'*Means*' and '*Includes*' 100
Typography 101
Disapplying Definitions 102
Interpretation Acts 102

6 **Powers and Duties** 103

Introduction 103
The Distinction Between Powers and Duties 103
Introduction 103
May and *Shall* in the Context of Powers and Duties 104
Introduction 104
Enforcing Duties by Judicial Review 107
Introduction 107
Damages for Breach of Statutory Duty 110
Introduction 110
Two Specific Problems 112
Introduction 112
Does a Statute which imposes a Duty and also specifies a Penalty for Breach of that Duty, impliedly exclude all Other Remedies? 112
Does a Statute which creates a Right and Specifies a Remedy to Enforce that Right, impliedly exclude all other Remedies? 113
The Drafting Solution to Both Problems 113
Where Breach of Statutory Duty gives rise to a Claim in Damages, do the Normal Principles of Vicarious Liability apply? 113
Continuity of Powers and Duties 113
Anticipatory Exercise of Powers 114

7 **Licensing and Registration** 115

Introduction 115
Designing the Legislative Scheme 115
Application Procedures 116
Introduction 116
Standard Application Forms 116
Fees 117
Requirements as to Giving Notice of Applications 117
Requirements as to Consultation 118
First-time Applications, Renewals, Revocations and Appeals 120
Criteria for Granting or Withholding Licences 121
Conditional Licences 122
Duration of Licences 125
Enforcement 127
Transitional Provisions (Including Grandparenting) 130

The Status of Qualifications From Other Jurisdictions 130

8. Statutory Corporations 133

Introduction 133
The Nature of Statutory Corporations 133
Creating Statutory Corporations 134
Introduction 134
Common Provisions 134
Introduction 134
The Name 134
The Objects 135
Members 135
Meetings 136
Employees 137
Dissolution 137
Miscellaneous Matters 138
Paving Legislation 138

9. Penal Provisions 139

Introduction 139
The Nature of Criminal Liability 139
Introduction 139
Penalties and their Enforcement 140
Drafting Techniques for Creating Criminal Offences 143
Introduction 143
Techniques for Creating Criminal Offences 143
Continuing Offences 145
Introduction 145
Offences which continue before Conviction 146
Offences which continue after Conviction 146
Standards of Proof 147
Interpretation 147
Introduction 147
The Presumption that *Mens Rea* is a Necessary Element of Statutory Offences 148
Introduction 148
Expressions creating the Need for *Mens Rea* 149
Rebutting the Presumption of the Need for *Mens Rea* by Express Language 150
Rebutting the Presumption of the Need for *Mens Rea* by reference to the Subject Matter of the Offence 150

Mens Rea and Consent 154
Mens Rea and Offences Committed by Corporations 155
The Standard Scale of Fines 156

10 Subordinate Legisation 159

Introduction 159
The Doctrine of Ultra Vires 162
Introduction 162
The Drafters' Responsibilities 162
Classifying the Bases of Ultra Vires Action 167
Introduction 167
Jurisdictional Error 168
Wednesbury Irrelevance 168
Wednesbury Unreasonableness 169
Breach of Procedural Fairness at Common Law 170
Breach of Express Procedural Requirements under Statute 171
Excluding and Restricting Challenges to The Validity of Subordinate Legislation 171
Introduction 171
The Leading Cases 172
Introduction 172
Total Ouster Clauses 172
Time-limited Ouster Clauses 173
Finality Clauses 174
Henry VIII Clauses 174
Provisions containing Subjective Tests 175

Appendix 1 Extracts from the Interpretation Act 1978 177
Appendix 2 Extracts from the European Convention for the Protection of Human Rights and Fundamental Freedoms 187
Appendix 3 The Better Regulation Executive's Code of Practice on Guidance on Regulation 193

Index 199

Table of Cases

Ackers v Taylor [1974] 1 All ER 771 122
Agricultural, Horticultural and Forestry Industry Training Board v Aylesbury Mushrooms Ltd [1971] 1 WLR 190 119
Anisminic v Foreign Compensation Commission [1969] 2 AC 147 ....65, 172
Arrowsmith v Jenkins [1963] 2 QB 561..149
Artico v Italy [1980] 3 EHRR 1 48
Assam Railways and Trading Co v Commissioners of Inland Revenue [1935] AC 445 26
Associated Provincial Picture Houses Ltd v Wednesbury Corporation [1948] 1 KB 223 ....7, 168
Atkinson v Newcastle and Gateshead Waterworks Co (1877) 2 ExD 441 111
Attorney-General v Antigua Times [1976] AC 16 107
Attorney-General v Great Eastern Railway (1880) 5 App Cas 473......135, 163
Attorney-General v Lamplough (1878) 3 ExD 224..................................22, 66
Attorney-General v Prince Ernest Augustus of Hanover [1957] AC 436..23
Attorney-General v Wilts United Dairies Ltd (1921) 37 TLR 884...............161
B (A Minor) v Director of Public Prosecutions [2000] 2 AC 428................153
Backhouse v Lambeth London Borough Council (1972) 116 SJ 802 170
Baker, Re (1890) 44 ChD 262...104
Barker v Wilson [1980] 1 WLR 884 32
Barraclough v Brown [1897] AC 615...113
Bastin v Davies [1950] 2 KB 579 25
Bellinger v Bellinger [2003] UKHL 21, [2003] 2 AC 467 51
Black-Clawson International Ltd v Papierwerke Waldhof-Aschaffenburg AG [1975] AC 591 ....20, 23
Boaler, Re [1915] 1 KB 21 24
Boddington v British Transport Police [1999] 2 AC 143 172
Bonitto v Fuerst Bros & Co Ltd [1994] AC 75, 82 80
Bourne v Norwich Crematorium Ltd [1967] 1 WLR 691 20
Brown v Allweather Mechanical Grouting Co Ltd [1954] 2 QB 443 141
Brownsea Haven Properties Ltd v Poole Corporation [1958] Ch 574 22
Brutus v Cozens [1973] AC 854 ....12, 14, 100
Bugg and Greaves v Director of Public Prosecutions (1993) 157 JP 675......170
Burgess v McCracken (1986) 150 JP 509 18
Burmah Oil Co Ltd v Lord Advocate [1965] AC 75 46
Carter v Bradbeer [1975] 1 WLR 1204...16, 19

Casher v Holmes (1831) 109 ER 1263 21
Cassell & Co Ltd v Broome [1972] AC 1027 140
Castioni, In re [1891] 1 QB 149 .... 8, 16
Chief Constable of Essex v Germain (1991) 156 JP 109 122
Coltman v Bibby Tankers Ltd [1986] 1 WLR 751 (HCt), [1987] 2 WLR 1098 (CA), [1988] 1 AC 276 (HL) 28, 29
Commission for the New Towns v Cooper (GB) Ltd [1995] Ch 259 25
Cordell v Second Clanfield Properties Ltd [1969] 2 Ch 9 26
Cotterill v Penn [1936] 1 KB 53 149
Council of Civil Service Unions v Minister for the Civil Service [1985] AC 374 .... 167, 170
Courtauld v Legh (1869) LR 4 Exch 126 .... 22, 73
Customs and Excise Commissioners v Top Ten Promotions Ltd [1969] 1 WLR 1163 26
Cutler v Wandsworth Stadium [1949] AC 398 .... 110, 111
Davidson v Scottish Ministers [2004] UKHL 34, [2004] UKHRR 1079 121
de Freitas v Permanent Secretary of Ministry of Agriculture, Fisheries, Lands and Housing [1999] 1 AC 69 55
Derbyshire County Council v Times Newspapers Ltd [1992] 3 WLR 28 (CA), [1993] AC 534 (HL) 58
Dickenson v Fletcher (1873) LR 9 CP 1 147
Director of Public Prosecutions v Collins [2006] 4 All ER 602 13
Director of Public Prosecutions v Schildkamp [1971] AC 1 24
Director of Public Prosecutions v Hutchinson and Smith [1990] 2 AC 783 164
Dudgeon v United Kingdom (1982) 4 EHRR 149 54
Eastman Photographic Materials Co Ltd v Comptroller of Patents [1898] AC 571 26
Edwards v Bairstow [1956] AC 14 .... 13, 14
Energy Conversion Devices Incorporated's Applications, Re [1982] FSR 544 13
Evans v Amicus Healthcare Ltd [2004] EWCA 72, [2005] Fam 1 57
Federal Steam Navigation Co Ltd v Department of Trade and Industry [1974] 1 WLR 505, 523 80
Fisher v Bell [1961] 1 QB 394 7
Fitzpatrick v Sterling Housing Association [1998] Ch 304 (CA), [2001] 1 AC 27 (HL) 30, 32, 47
Foster v Diphwys Casson Slate Co (1887) 18 QBD 428 21
Gammans v Ekins [1950] 2 KB 328 30
Gammon (Hong Kong) Ltd v Attorney-General for Hong Kong [1985] AC 1 .... 150, 151
GCHQ – see *Council of Civil Service Unions v Minister for the Civil Service* *Ghaidon v Godin-Mendoza*, [2004] UKHL 30, [2004] 2 AC 557 .... 31, 50, 52, 73

Gilmore's Application, Re [1957] 1 QB 574 174
Gough and Another v Chief Constable of the Derbyshire Constabulary [2002] EWCA Civ 351, [2002] QB 1217 50
Groves v Lord Wimborne [1898] 2 QB 402 112
Halford v Brookes [1991] 3 All ER 559 147
Handyside v United Kingdom (1979–80) 1 EHRR 737 ....54, 56, 57
Hanlon v Law Society [1981] AC 124 87
Harrogate Borough Council v Simpson [1980] 3 All ER 647 ....30, 31
Henty v Wrey (1882) 21 ChD 332 25
Hodgetts v Chiltern Rural District Council [1983] 2 AC 120 146
Inland Revenue Commissioners v Hinchy [1960] AC 748 86
Institute of Patent Agents v Lockwood [1894] AC 347 174
Island Records Ltd, Ex parte [1978] Ch 122 111
Jones v Conway & Colwyn Bay Joint Water Supply Board [1893] 2 Ch 603 29
Julius v Lord Bishop of Oxford (1880) 5 App Cas 214 104
Kammins Ballrooms Co Ltd v Zenith Investments (Torquay) Ltd [1971] AC 850 ....7, 17, 18, 65, 106
Kruse v Johnson [1898] 2 QB 91, 99 167
Lawal v Northern Spirits Ltd [2003] UKHL 35, [2003] ICR 856 121
Letang v Cooper [1965] 1 QB 232 26
Lim Chin Aik v R [1963] AC 160 ....148, 154
London & Clydeside Estates Ltd v Aberdeen District Council [1980] 1 WLR 182 116
London County Council v Central Land Board [1958] 1 WLR 1296 27
M v Newham London Borough Council [1995] 2 AC 633 112
Madzibamuto v Lardner-Burke [1969] 1 AC 645 41
Magnhild SS v McIntyre Bros & Co [1920] 3 KB 321 (HCt), [1921] 2 KB 97 (CA) 21
Magor & St Mellons Rural District Council v Newport Corporation [1952] AC 189 45
Majrwoski v Guy's & St Thomas's NHS Trust [2006] UKHL 34, [2007] 1 AC 224 113
Malone v Metropolitan Police Commissioner (No 2) [1979] Ch 344 46
Manuel v Attorney-General [1983] Ch 77 46
Marshall v Cottingham [1982] 2 Ch 82 86
McDonald v Howard Cook Advertising Ltd [1972] 1 WLR 90 9
McInnes v Onslow-Fane [1978] 1 WLR 1520 ....120, 126
Minister of Health v R ex parte Yaffé [1931] AC 494 174
Moberly v Allsop (1996) 156 JP 514 137
Myles v Director of Public Prosecutions [2004] EWHC 594 (Admin), [2004] 2 All ER 902 50
Newman v Lipman [1951] 1 KB 333 18

Northern Ireland Trailers Ltd v County Borough of Preston [1972] 1 All ER 260 ....140, 143
Nottingham City District Council v Newton [1974] 1 WLR 923 114
Olsson v Sweden (1988) 11 EHRR 259 54
Padfield v Minister of Agriculture, Fisheries and Food [1968] AC 997 ....105, 169
Pepper v Hart [1993] AC 593 ....27, 53
Pharmaceutical Society of Great Britain v Storkwain Ltd [1986] 1 WLR 903 152
Pilling v Abergele Urban District Council [1950] 1 KB 636 169
Porter v Magill [2002] UKHL 67, [2002] AC 357 121
R (Alconbury Developments Ltd) v Secretary of State for the Environment, Transport and the Regions [2001] UKHL 23, [2003] 2 AC 295 50
R (Anderson) v Secretary of State for the Home Department [2002] UKHL 46, [2003] 1 AC 837 ....50, 51
R (Daly) v Secretary of State for the Home Department [2001] UKHL 26, [2001] 2 AC 532 55
R (G) v Barnet London Borough Council and Other Cases [2003] UKHL 57, [2004] 2 AC 208 108
R (Richards and Another) v Pembrokeshire County Council [2005] LGR 105 168
R (Rusbridger) v Attorney-General [2003] UKHL 38, [2004] 1 AC 357 51
R (Shrewsbury & Atcham Borough Council) v Secretary of State for Communities and Local Government [2008] EWCA Civ 148, [2008] 3 All ER 548 59
R v A (No 2) [2001] UKHL 25, [2002] 1 AC 45 ....51, 52, 53
R v Allen (1872) LR 1 CCR 367 21
R v Allen [1985] 1 AC 1029 26
R v Army Board of the Defence Council ex parte Anderson [1992] QB 169 121
R v Casement [1917] 1 KB 98 87
R v Cleworth (1864) 122 ER 707 22
R v Commissioner for Local Administration ex parte Eastleigh Borough Council [1998] QB 855 37
R v Cuthbertson and Others [1981] AC 470 22
R v Galvin [1987] QB 862 23
R v Hillingdon London Borough Council ex parte Royco Homes Ltd [1974] QB 720 123
R v Inner London Education Authority ex parte Ali and Another (1990) 2 Admin LR 822 107
R v Inner London Education Authority ex parte Westminster City Council [1986] 1 WLR 28 169
R v Inland Revenue Commisioners ex parte Rossminster [1980] AC 952 175

R v K [2002] 1 AC 462 153
R v Kansal (No 2) [2001] UKHL 62, [2002] 2 AC 69 54
R v Lambert [2001] UKHL 37, [2002] 2 AC 545 53
R v Local Government Election Commissioner ex parte Mainwaring [1992] 1 WLR 1059 147
R v Lord Chancellor ex parte the Law Society (1994) 6 Admin LR 833 171
R v Lord Chancellor ex parte Witham [1998] QB 575 47
R v Minister of Health ex parte Davis (1929) 93 JP 49 175
R v Ministry of Defence ex parte Smith [1996] QB 517 ....31, 55, 56
R v Ndhlovu (1968) 4 SA 515 41
R v Reading Borough Council ex parte Quietlynn (1987) 85 LGR 387 121
R v Richmond-upon-Thames London Borough Council ex parte McCarthy & Stone (Developments) Ltd [1992] 2 AC 48 ....161, 163
R v Secretary of State for Social Security ex parte Joint Council for the Welfare of Immigrants [1997] 1 WLR 275 47
R v Secretary of State for Social Services ex parte Association of Metropolitan Authorities [1986] 1 WLR 1 118
R v Secretary of State for the Environment ex parte Norwich City Council [1982] QB 808 176
R v Secretary of State for the Environment ex parte Ostler [1977] QB 122 174
R v Secretary of State for the Environment, Transport and the Regions ex parte Spath Holme Ltd [2001] 2 AC 349 20
R v Secretary of State for the Home Department and Another ex parte Norney and Anothers (1995) 7 Admin LR 861 58
R v Secretary of State for the Home Department ex parte Brind [1991] 1 AC 696 ....56, 57
R v Secretary of State for the Home Department ex parte Fire Brigades Union [1995] 2 AC 513 96
R v Secretary of State for Transport ex parte Factortame Ltd (No 2) [1991] 1 AC 603 45
R v Secretary of State for Transport ex parte Greater London Council [1986] 1 QB 556 166
R v Sheppard [1981] AC 394 149
R v St Margaret's Trust Ltd [1958] 1 WLR 522 151
R v Tithe Commissioners (1849) 14 QBD 459 105
R v Tower Hamlets London Borough Council ex parte Chetnik Developments Ltd [1988] AC 858 105
R v Wandsworth London Borough Council ex parte Beckwith [1996] 1 WLR 60 27
R v Wells Street Magistrate ex parte Westminster City Council [1986] 1 WLR 1046 152
Read v Croydon Corporation [1938] 4 All ER 631 111
Robinson v Barton-Eccles Local Board (1883) App Cas 798 101

S, Re [2002] UKHL 10, [2002] 2 AC 291 51
Salomon v Salomon [1897] AC 22 ....80, 133
Saunders, Re [1997] Ch 60 106
Secretary of State for Education and Science v Tameside Metropolitan Borough Council [1977] AC 1014 176
Secretary of State for Trade and Industry v Langridge [1991] Ch 402 ....106, 107
Sherras v de Rutzen [1895] 1 QB 918 148
Sigsworth, Re [1935] Ch 89 7
Siu Yin Kwan v Eastern Insurance Co Ltd [1994] 1 All ER 213 23
Smith v East Elloe Rural District Council [1956] AC 736 174
Stephens v Cuckfield Rural District Council [1960] 2 QB 373 24
Sweet v Parsley [1970] AC 132 ....152, 154
Utah Construction and Engineering Pty Ltd v Pataky [1966] AC 629 163
Vacher & Sons v London Society of Compositors [1913] AC 107 91
Wanstead Local Board of Health v Hill (1863) 32 LJMC (NS) 135 22
Ward v Holman [1964] 2 QB 580 23
Watson v Lucas [1986] 2 FLR 91 30
Watson v Thomas S Witney & Co Ltd [1966] 1 WLR 57 25
Wemhoff v Federal Republic of Germany (1979–80) 1 EHRR 55 48
Westminster City Council v Croyalgrange Ltd [1986] 1 WLR 674 150
White & Collins v Minister of Health [1939] 2 KB 838 168
Wings Ltd v Ellis [1985] AC 272 151

1

Drafting and Communication

Introduction

In the simplest of terms, the drafter's task is to convert policies into provisions which comply with the relevant formal conventions and are capable of being applied effectively in practice. Complying with the relevant formal conventions is seldom, if ever, problematic; but creating provisions which can be interpreted in only one way is another matter. In introductory terms—and without wishing to pre-empt the extended discussion of this topic which permeates the rest of this book—the essence of the problem flows from that aspect of the constitutional ideal of the rule of law which requires that the law should be predictable. Viewed in this way, the task of drafters in an ideal world would be to create provisions which not only have single and unequivocal meanings but which also communicate those meanings unfailingly to every reader.

Unfortunately, the imperfections of the real world often prevent drafters from performing this task as fully as they, and everyone else involved, would wish, with the result that the best that can often be achieved is the creation of instruments which are capable of supporting the smallest possible number of interpretations. The factors which give rise to this rather gloomy conclusion include the nature of language, the fallibility of drafters, the realities of the political process, the complexity of the subject-matter with which legislation deals and the fact that many of the aspects of life, commerce and technology to which law relates are constantly evolving, which means that drafters may be trying to hit moving targets. If it is thought that the instruments should also be accessible to the public at large without the benefit of expert advice, it becomes necessary to add the further constraint of the limited literacy of many people.

The rest of this chapter expands on some of the principal difficulties which flow from the fact that drafting is essentially an exercise in communication. In doing so, it comments on the imprecision of language in general and the differences between oral and written uses of language in particular, as well as emphasising the problem of clarity and the range of possible readerships.

The Imprecision of language

Legislative and regulatory instruments may have many purposes but in general terms most of their provisions are intended to facilitate, prohibit or regulate human conduct. However, the diversity of human conduct means that drafters have to try to deal with an unforeseeably wide range of future possibilities by creating forms of words which achieve sufficient clarity while retaining intelligibility. More particularly, the challenge facing the drafter has three aspects.

First, language is necessarily a relatively imprecise medium of communication compared with, say, mathematics. Understandably, therefore, inexperienced drafters may be tempted to try to cover all possible eventualities by creating very complex provisions. However, their more experienced colleagues will be well aware that drafting and interpretation are opposite sides of the same coin, which in turn means that everything must be drafted in the light of the principles of interpretation which will be used in order to identify their meaning. The possible meanings of *clarity* are discussed at page 3 and the scope for interpretation which flows from the imprecision of language is amply illustrated in chapter two, but for the moment all that need be said is that a sound knowledge of the relevant interpretative principles will often enable drafters to produce shorter, but no less effective, provisions than they would produce if they yielded to the temptation to pursue 'the perfection which . . . is usually in fact unattainable'.[1]

Secondly, the intrinsic imprecision of language is compounded by the fact that many provisions require concepts to be expressed at a high level of abstraction, while at the same time being capable of being applied to a wide range of highly specific individual instances.

Thirdly, the inevitable delay in resolving ambiguities once they have occurred makes it all the more important to avoid them whenever it is possible to do so.

> In conversation, ambiguity . . . is quickly removed by question and answer; in legislation, it may take the House of Lords by a three to two majority.[2]

Oral and Written Uses of Language

Except when speaking from a script or after effective rehearsal, speakers suffer from the disadvantage (compared with writers) of having to choose their

[1] N Hutton, 'The Mechanics of Law Reform' (1961) 24 *Modern Law Review* 18, 19. (Hutton was First Parliamentary Counsel.)

[2] GC Thornton, *Legislative Drafting* 4th edn (London, Butterworths, 1996) (subsequently transferred to Tottel) 96.

words more or less spontaneously, which will often have an obvious and adverse impact on the degree of precision with which they manage to express themselves. More positively, however, they have the advantage of having access to many techniques and devices, such as body language, tone of voice and variation in speed of delivery, which are simply unavailable to writers.

Writers, on the other hand, have greater opportunities to choose their words carefully, as well as having access to more sophisticated grammatical structures than most speakers can manage to create and deliver. These structures may include forward and backward references within a single sentence, as well as cross-references to both other instruments and other parts of the same instrument. Writers can also rely on devices such as footnoting, indentation, paragraphing, punctuation and a range of typographical variations, such as italicising and emboldening text and using different levels of headings, in order to support, clarify, refine or emphasise the meaning of their words and the structure of their instruments.

Clarity in Written Language

Introduction

It is obvious that drafters should use techniques which enhance clarity rather than those which do not do so. On closer analysis, however, it is equally obvious that this proposition is based on a number of assumptions.

First, it assumes both that *clarity* has a single meaning and that drafting techniques are, when competently deployed, capable of enabling even the most complex concepts and schemes to be reduced to the desired state of clarity.

Secondly, it assumes that clarity is an objective quality, rather than being in the mind of the reader.

Thirdly, it assumes that all readers will be content to identify a single meaning for each provision.

Each of these assumptions requires consideration.

Does *Clarity* have a Single Meaning and can Drafters make Everything *Clear*?

According to Kent, a former parliamentary counsel:

> There are two main objects that the draftsman aims at, and they are not easy to reconcile. First and foremost, to get the Bill right. The test is that when it is passed, and a trained lawyer or judge has mastered its intricacies, the meaning is clear (in the sense of unambiguous) and the intention carried out. Subject to this, the second object is to make the Bill as intelligible as possible to Parliament and the general public.[3]

[3] J Anderson, *In on the Act: Memoirs of a Law Maker* (London, Macmillan, 1979) 97.

This 'proper distinction between clarity (intelligibility) and clarity (unambiguity)',[4] may be illustrated by the response of Sir John Anderson, the minister responsible for the Bill which became the Civil Defence Act 1939, when told that the drafter was trying to simplify the following provision:

> For the purposes of this Act, the number of persons who work in or about a mine shall be deemed to be a number ascertained as follows, that is to say
>
> (a) by having regard to all the people employed in or about the mine and ascertaining how many of them are from time to time simultaneously present in or about the mine otherwise than below the surface, and
> (b) if the numbers so ascertained fluctuate, by ascertaining the highest figure below which throughout any consecutive period of fifteen minutes the numbers do not fall.

Anderson's response was that no further work was required because 'it's perfectly clear, when you understand it'.[5] Further insight into the two-fold nature of clarity is provided by Sir John Rowlatt's famous, if somewhat acerbic, comment that 'the intelligibility of a Bill is in inverse proportion to its chances of being right'.[6] These comments show that, in many cases, a drafter who is charged with obscurity need do no more than reply that drafting often involves striking a balance between the competing needs of *intelligibility* and *unambiguity* and that the outcome of this balancing exercise in each individual instance is inevitably a matter of professional judgment.

In short, if clarity is seen as a single concept, it must also, in all but the simplest of instances, be seen as a compromise between competing interests.

How Objective is *Clarity*?

Introduction

The assumption that clarity is an objective quality which a provision either does or does not possess (or which it possesses to a greater or lesser extent) would be sound if clarity could be defined by reference to entirely objective criteria. While some relatively objective criteria do exist (see much of the content of chapter five), the fact that drafting is intended to achieve communication (rather than simply expression), emphasises that the objective qualities of a provision are only part of the story. More particularly, since effective communication depends to a significant extent on the capacity of the recipient to understand what has been written, it follows that the effectiveness of communication may well vary substantially from one reader to another. Any genuinely useful discussion of the clarity of drafting must, therefore, seek to identify the range of potential readerships.

[4] *Ibid*, 118.
[5] *Ibid.*
[6] *Ibid*, 97. Rowlatt was First Parliamentary Counsel.

Identifying Potential Readerships

Drafters always have more than one readership, with four, five or six being typical and a seventh being possible. The first three readerships are relevant to all legislative, and many regulatory, instruments. (The regulatory instruments in question are those which may come before the courts either by way of judicial review or because they exist within the context of contractual relationships.)

The first readership in point of time is the client. In the case of legislation, the client may be identified as being either an instructing department (in the form of either or both its civil servants and its ministerial head) or Parliament, or both may be regarded as joint clients. Although each Bill concerns this readership for only a relatively short time (when compared with the lifespan of a typical statute), gaining its approval is obviously of truly basic importance. (But see page 71 for the Renton Committee's view on establishing the appropriate priority between the interests of users of Bills and the interests of users of Acts; and page 34 for the fact that some regulatory drafters may be, in effect, their own clients.)

The second readership is the courts, whose constitutional role is to provide authoritative statements as to the meaning of legislation and to adjudicate on disputes which are placed before them. Even regulatory provisions which cannot come before a court are likely to be subject to interpretation and application by domestic tribunals, whose functions may be seen as analogous to, if not identical with, those of the courts. Furthermore, many of those tribunals will, as a matter of practice, tend to give considerable weight to any principles of legislative interpretation which come to their attention.

The third readership is members of the legal profession, whose clients may legitimately expect to receive reasonably accurate advice whether they are involved in, or are contemplating, litigation, or when they are arranging their affairs in such a way as to avoid the possibility of litigation (so far as it is possible to do so). Legal representation may or may not be permitted before any specific domestic tribunal, but even if it is not permitted, nobody can prevent the parties from obtaining legal advice as to how the relevant instruments are likely to be interpreted and applied.

The identities of the fourth, fifth and sixth readerships will vary from context to context, but in general terms they will be as follows.

The fourth readership consists of public officials (such as inspectors of taxes and planning officers), as well as employees of professional bodies, trade unions and other interest groups which are required to administer legislative and regulatory schemes.

The fifth readership consists of members of other professions (such as accountants, architects, dentists, doctors and surveyors) whose relations with, and advice to, those who consult them may well be affected by legislative and regulatory considerations.

The sixth readership consists of those members of the public who may wish to understand their legal and regulatory position without recourse to professional, or other specialist, advisers.

The remaining possible readership consists of academic lawyers. In the nature of their work, academics will always examine new legislation in their specialist fields with particular rigour, but drafters may be particularly interested in their reactions to Bills which have come into being as the result of academic criticism of the existing law.

Some people may argue that the listing of readerships in this way gives the impression that there is a hierarchy of importance and that this impression is misleading because different instruments may have different principal readerships. Arguments of this sort would typically proceed on the basis that, for example, farmers would be the principal readership for a piece of subordinate legislation dealing with technicalities relating to the use of agricultural pesticides. However, these arguments give too little weight to the fact that, as a matter of constitutional doctrine, only the courts can provide authoritative rulings on the interpretation of legislation. Furthermore, any court which becomes involved will have to apply the accepted principles of legislative interpretation, which may well be inappropriate for identifying the meaning of instruments which have been composed less formally because they are intended for another readership. On the other hand, if an instrument is composed in order to be read according to the established principles of interpretation, there is no doubt that other people, who possess the necessary technical expertise, will prepare user-friendly guides based on their understanding of what it means. Of course, these guides will necessarily be unauthoritative but so will the understandings which members of the target readership may glean through their own unaided efforts. (See page 83 for guides to legislative and regulatory instruments.)

Returning to the main point of multiple potential readerships, there will often be wide variations between readerships in terms of both their interpretative skills and their levels of technical knowledge of the subject-matter of the instruments in question. Furthermore, these variations will also be present even within each readership, with these variations being likely to become wider and wider as consideration moves through the readerships in the order in which they are presented in the previous paragraphs. This raises a particular difficulty in relation to instruments which impact on the day to day affairs of people who have been spared the rigours of a legal education. This difficulty may be considered in two parts. First, most instruments are part of a larger, patchwork fabric, which, in the case of legislation, includes the common law, equity, European Community law and the law of the European Convention for the Protection of Human Rights and Fundamental Freedoms (which is usually shortened to the *European Convention on Human Rights* or simply the *ECHR*). Secondly, there are limitations stemming from substantial variations in the level of adult literacy.

Taking these topics in turn, even provisions which appear to be perfectly plain on a word-by-word basis may still convey practically nothing of any use to the reader. Stating this aspect of clarity at the level of general principle, the problem becomes one of knowing what must be made explicit and what may be safely left to implication. For example, section 38(6) of the Planning and Compulsory Purchase Act 2004 contains a presumption that applications for planning permission will be determined according to certain specified types of approved policies 'unless material considerations indicate otherwise'. However, the provision contains no guidance as to how the materiality of considerations is to be identified. This means it conveys nothing to lay readers and is, therefore, effectively meaningless from their point of view. Readers who happen to be lawyers with any basic competence in public law will recognise the provision as being neither more nor less than a statutory application of the principle of *Wednesbury* relevance.[7] On the other hand, readers with no prior knowledge of public law will be none the wiser; nor even, perhaps more importantly, better informed.

There are many cases in which the true interpretation of a provision has been held to depend on some common law doctrine which could not reasonably be thought to be within the likely knowledge of non-lawyers. Taking three examples at random (all of which are counter-intuitive), shopkeepers do not offer goods for sale;[8] a provision which prohibits a court from entertaining a particular kind of application, unless a specified condition is fulfilled, does not necessarily prevent a court from entertaining an application of that kind even though the condition is not fulfilled;[9] and a provision which states that the property of someone who has died without leaving a will *shall* be inherited by certain people does not mean that murderers can inherit from their victims.[10]

When considering the extent to which lay people are likely to be able to understand legislative and regulatory provisions, the question of average levels of adult literacy becomes important. According to the Adult Literacy Trust,[11] only the top 44 per cent of adults (taking the definition of *adult* as being anyone within the age range of 16–65) equals or exceeds the level of literacy which is necessary to obtain a General Certificate of Secondary Education (GCSE) at grades A–C (which together constitute the former General Certificate of Education (GCE) Ordinary Level 'pass' range.) The next 40 per cent have a level of attainment equivalent to GCSE grades D–G (which together constitute the former GCE Ordinary Level 'fail' range.) The remaining 16 per cent span a variety of lower literacy levels, none of which

[7] See *Associated Provincial Picture Houses Ltd v Wednesbury Corporation* [1948] 1 KB 223, discussed further at p 168.

[8] *Fisher v Bell* [1961] 1 QB 394.

[9] *Kammins Ballroooms Co Ltd v Zenith Investments (Torquay) Ltd* [1971] AC 850, discussed further at p 17.

[10] *Re Sigsworth* [1935] Ch 89.

[11] See www.literacytrust.org.uk

exceeds the level expected of an 11-year-old. Beneath the raw percentages attaining each level, there lurks the fact that the averages conceal substantial regional variations. For example, in the United Kingdom, in the more prosperous South East and the less prosperous North East, 51 per cent and 37 per cent respectively reached the highest level of attainment. (All these figures are based on government figures from 2003.)

While nothing in these statistics detracts from the desirability of communicating as plainly as the subject-matter allows, they do suggest that drafting provisions which the majority of the adult population will be able to understand may be an unattainable objective in the case of all but the most straightforward statutes.

The Fallacy of Assuming a Co-operative Readership

Literary writers compose their works as a matter of choice. Similarly, their potential readers choose whether to become actual readers. In other words, literary writers and their readers have a shared understanding that the rules of engagement allow dissatisfied readers to withdraw at any time.

Drafters, by way of contrast, act on instructions. Similarly, their readers (or at least those readers whose work requires them to do so) will persevere with their reading until they are satisfied that they have acquired a credible understanding and are able to argue for or against varying applications of the provision which is in issue. An important consequence flows from this. In *In re Castioni*,[12] Stephen J, who had had experience of legislative drafting before he became a judge, expressed the matter thus:

> It is not enough [for the drafter] to attain to a degree of precision which a person reading in good faith can understand, but it is necessary to attain if possible to a degree of precision which a person reading in bad faith cannot misunderstand. It is all the better if he cannot pretend to misunderstand it.

By way of contrast, it would be perverse for readers of literature to persist in their reading for the sole purpose of constructing a meaning which no ordinary person would think the words could bear (unless, perhaps, the readers in question are literary critics with professional axes to grind). However, lawyers' duties to their clients mean that they must be skilled at subjecting provisions to this sort of analysis. There may, after all, be more than a grain of truth in Jonathan Swift's description of lawyers as

> a society of men . . . bred up from their youth in the art of proving by words multiplied for the purpose, that white is black, and black is white, according as they are paid.[13]

[12] *In re Castioni* [1891] 1 QB 149, 167.
[13] J Swift, *Gulliver's Travels: A Voyage to the Country of the Houyhnhnms* (London, 1726) ch 5.

The possibility of imaginative arguments may be illustrated by the decision in *McDonald v Howard Cook Advertising Ltd*,[14] where subordinate legislation made under the Town and Country Planning Act 1971 required consent to be obtained for the display of outdoor advertisements which included, among other things, letters and figures exceeding 0.75 metres in height. The High Court held that a figure of a man which exceeded this height was not caught by the provision. However, there must be room for doubting whether the drafter had contemplated the possibility that it could be held to do so, because substituting *numerals* for *figures* would have been a simple way of putting the matter beyond doubt.

Even some readers who are not lawyers (the officers of organisations such as trade unions and interest groups being prime examples) will have substantial experience of the principal instruments which are relevant to their activities. One result of this is that they may well bring to the task of interpretation at least something of a lawyerly cast of mind. Drafters who understand and apply the principles of interpretation (see chapter two) may be able to avoid creating some problems, while readers who understand and apply the same principles may be able to achieve negotiated solutions to many of the problems which remain, thus avoiding the need for litigation. However, when a dispute does come to court there is likely to be at least some argument which can be advanced, more or less credibly, on each side (unless, of course, the dispute is confined entirely to matters of fact). This likelihood comes close to certainty in cases that reach those appellate courts which are accessible only through the grant of leave to appeal. In the words of the editor of the current (though not particularly recent) edition of *Maxwell on the Interpretation of Statutes*:

> It is . . . not taking too cynical a view of statutory interpretation . . . to express the hope that counsel putting forward diverse interpretations of some statutory provision will each be able to find in *Maxwell* dicta and illustrations in support of his case.[15]

As with literary writers and readers, therefore, the relationship between drafters and both judges and members of the legal profession can be said to be based on a shared understanding of the rules of engagement. (The same may also be true, albeit perhaps to a lesser extent, in respect of readers falling within the third and fourth readerships in the scheme outlined at page 5.) However, in these situations the use of the military metaphor is calculated to convey the (at least potentially) antagonistic nature of the relationship between drafters and their readers. Moreover, the drafter may be skirmishing on a number of fronts at the same time, since a single fact-situation may give rise to a dispute involving a number of parties, with each seeking the outcome which best serves its interests. (The potential for achieving various meanings by means of imaginative interpretation is discussed in chapter two.)

[14] *McDonald v Howard Cook Advertising Ltd* [1972] 1 WLR 90.

[15] P St J Langan, *Maxwell on the Interpretation of Statutes* 12th edn (London, Sweet & Maxwell, 1966) *v*.

2

Principles of Interpretation

Introduction

Communicating, rather than merely stating the law, means that the relevant principles of interpretation must always be at the forefront of the drafter's mind. This chapter, therefore, discusses the principles of interpretation (or construction) which are applied to the final product of the drafting process. Describing the topic in this way does, of course, raise a question of basic terminology, namely what, if anything, is the difference between *interpretation* and *construction*?

The short answer is that although various distinctions have been drawn between the two concepts,[1] in practice the terms are almost always used interchangeably. Even the Interpretation Act 1978 refers throughout to *construction*, despite its own title. On the other hand, at an instinctive level, there may be something in Bennion's assertion that 'it is natural to speak of "interpreting" a single word or phrase and "construing" an extended passage'.[2] Ultimately, perhaps the only truly sound conclusion is that the two terms appear to reflect a distinction without a difference. Nevertheless, considerations of stylistic consistency require every writer on the topic to follow a preferred usage, which in this book is *interpretation*, unless either the context or established usage otherwise requires. (The phrase 'updating construction'—see page 29—is an example of deviant but established usage.)

Returning to the outline of the content of this chapter, there is one preliminary question which must be answered before any sensible discussion of interpretation can take place, namely is the meaning of a word or provision a matter of fact or a matter of law? Having considered that question, the next stage is to emphasise the mythical nature of the idea of literal meaning, as well as the importance of reading words in their context (with the purpose for which they were written being an essential element of that context). The chapter concludes by considering the basic presumptions of interpretation and the

[1] For a short survey, see F Bennion, *Bennion on Statutory Interpretation* 5th edn (London, LexisNexis Butterworths, 2008) 23–24.

[2] *Ibid*, 23.

practice of applying updating constructions when significant changes have occurred in either technology or social attitudes between the time of enactment and the time of interpretation.

Matters of Fact and Matters of Law

Introduction

The distinction between matters of fact and matters of law may have at least three major consequences.

First, where the tribunal as a whole consists of two elements, one of which is a tribunal of law and the other a tribunal of fact (with a judge and jury being the most obvious example), it is important to know who has to decide which questions.

Secondly, the possibilities of challenge often differ according to whether the decision being challenged is a matter of law or a matter of fact, with, for example, rights of appeal on points of law often being more extensive than rights of appeal on matters of fact.

Thirdly, the doctrine of binding precedent applies only to matters of law, which fall to be determined in the light of legal argument, while matters of fact fall to be determined in the light of the evidence given (or the admissions made) in each case.

The Leading Cases

In *Brutus v Cozens*,[3] a number of anti-apartheid demonstrators, who had disrupted play at the Wimbledon tennis tournament, were charged with insulting behaviour whereby a breach of the peace was likely to be occasioned. The magistrates acquitted the defendants on the ground that their behaviour had not been insulting. The House of Lords refused to interfere with this finding, on the basis that its jurisdiction was limited to matters of law and the issue in this case concerned a matter of fact. Lord Reid stated the principle thus:

> The meaning of an ordinary word of the English language is not a question of law. The proper construction of a statute is a question of law . . . It is for the tribunal which decides the case to consider, not as law but as fact, whether in the whole circumstances the words of the statute do or do not as a matter of ordinary usage of the English language cover or apply to the facts which have been proved.[4]

[3] *Brutus v Cozens* [1973] AC 854.
[4] *Ibid*, 861.

However, three points must be made.

First, the question of whether something is an ordinary word of the English language is itself a matter of law.[5]

Secondly, in some cases at least, the meaning of an ordinary word of the English language must be identified in the light of contemporary standards. In *Director of Public Prosecutions v Collins*,[6] a constituent repeatedly telephoned his Member of Parliament and either spoke to members of the MP's staff or left recorded messages. In the course of these calls, the constituent, who felt strongly about immigration, spoke in terms of *Pakis*, *wogs* and *black bastards*. The magistrates acquitted him of sending grossly offensive messages by means of a public telecommunications system (contrary to section 127(1)(a) of the Communications Act 2003) on the ground that although his language was offensive, the statutory requirement that it must be *grossly* offensive had not been satisfied.

The High Court agreed with the magistrates' conclusion and dismissed the DPP's appeal, but the House of Lords allowed his further appeal. Lord Bingham said the purpose of the statute was not to protect the recipients of messages from being offended (the Malicious Communications Act 1988 did that) but was 'to prohibit the use of a service provided and funded by the public for the benefit of the public for the transmission of communications which contravene the basic standards of our society'.[7] He went on to say:

> It is for the justices to determine as a question of fact whether a message is grossly offensive . . . [and] . . . in making this determination the justices must apply the standards of an open and just multi-racial society, and that the words must be judged taking account of their context and all relevant circumstances. There can be no yardstick of gross offensiveness otherwise than by the application of reasonably enlightened, but not perfectionist, contemporary standards to the particular message sent in its particular context. The test is whether a message is couched in terms liable to cause gross offence to those to whom it relates.[8]

Thirdly, in *Re Energy Conversion Devices Incorporated's Applications*,[9] which involved the Patents Rules 1978, the House of Lords cautioned against using the distinction between fact and law to undermine the rule of law. Expressing the unanimous opinion of the House of Lords, Lord Diplock said:

> Your Lordships should, however, in my view, take this opportunity of stating once again the important constitutional principle that questions of construction of all legislation, primary or secondary, are questions of law to be determined authoritatively by courts of law . . . [and that] . . . no tribunal and no court of law has any discretion to vary the meaning of the words of primary or secondary legislation

[5] *Edwards v Bairstow* [1956] AC 14; and see Bennion, *Bennion on Statutory Interpretation*, above n 1 at 1222–23.

[6] *Director of Public Prosecutions v Collins* [2006] 4 All ER 602.

[7] See [7].

[8] See [9].

[9] *Re Energy Conversion Devices Incorporated's Applications* [1982] FSR 544, 560.

> from case to case in order to meet what the tribunal or court happens to think is the justice of the particular case. Tempting though it might sound, to do so is the negation of the rule of law. If there are cases in which the application of the Patents Rules leads to injustice, the cure is for the Secretary of State to amend the Rules. If what is thought to be the injustice results from the terms of the Act itself, the remedy is for Parliament to amend the Act.[10]

However, the dividing line between fact and law remains problematic. For example, in the income tax law case of *Edwards v Bairstow*,[11] the House of Lords held that the issue of whether a particular transaction was an 'adventure in the nature of trade' was a matter of law. It is difficult to see why 'insult' is an ordinary word of the English language (see *Brutus v Cozens*),[12] while 'trade' is not; but since the House of Lords deals only with appeals on points of law, this question of classification must itself be a matter of law.

In practice, drafters are almost always content that the general principles relating to the nature and effect of the distinction between matters of fact and matters of law should be left to operate in the usual way. However, subject only to the contents of the relevant drafting instructions and the impracticability of creating a doctrine of binding precedent in relation to matters of fact, it is always open to any drafter to specify that a particular matter must be treated as either a matter of law or a matter of fact, or to vary the consequences which would ordinarily flow from classifying a particular matter in accordance with the general principles.

The Myth of Literal Meaning

The traditional view, on which far too many generations of law students have been brought up, is that the process of interpretation starts with identifying the *literal* meaning of the enacted words. In fact, however, this approach is fundamentally defective, because it proceeds on the false assumption that a word, or a group of words, will always have a single, plain meaning. The truth of the matter is that many words have a variety of meanings and their meaning on particular occasions cannot be identified without reference to the context within which they are used.

If a poster in a shop window says *Last Week—Everything Half Price*, the plain meaning is that this is the last week of the sale. Nevertheless, purely as a matter of language, there is no reason why it should not mean that *last* week everything was half price, with the clear implication that *this* week the sale is over and that prices are back to their normal level. On the other hand, stating that George VI was the *last king of England*, cannot (without more) be

[10] *Ibid*, 560.
[11] [1956] AC 14.
[12] [1973] AC 854.

reasonably understood as an assertion that a republic will be established as a result of which neither Prince Charles nor one of his male heirs will succeed to the throne.[13] The plain meaning of the statement is, therefore, that George VI was the *most recent* king of England. It follows that the word *last* does not have a plain meaning at all, but rather at least two potential meanings, with the plain one being incapable of identification until a specific context has been identified.

It is not, therefore, surprising that Bennion summarises the modern approach to interpretation by saying that 'nowadays, a legislative drafter . . . never intends the literal rule to be adopted',[14] and that

> it is taken to be the legislator's intention that an enactment shall be construed according to the numerous general guides laid down for that purpose by law; and that where these conflict (as they often do) the problem shall be resolved by weighing and balancing the interpretative factors concerned.[15]

He proceeds to emphasise the *weighing and balancing* part of this formulation by saying:

> Contrary to what is often said, the court does not select any one of these many guides and then apply it to the exclusion of the rest. What the court does (or should do) is to take an overall view, weigh all the relevant interpretative factors, and then arrive at a balanced conclusion.[16]

Although Bennion devotes a 1600 page textbook to formulating, illustrating and commenting on the full range of interpretative criteria, it takes only a few words to say that particular importance is attached to the context within which a provision appears and that the purpose of a provision is a very important part of its context. Both context and purpose, therefore, require closer consideration.

The Contextual Approach

Introduction

Context is a multi-faceted concept and several of the facets overlap to the extent that studying the contextual approach to interpretation is more a question of absorbing the whole of the fabric of the topic than of pigeon-holing everything into a neat taxonomy. However, clarity of presentation requires the creation of some classificatory scheme. Accordingly, the rest of

[13] This passage must be read in the light of the fact that it was written in January 2009.
[14] F Bennion, *Understanding Common Law Legislation: Drafting and Interpretation* (Oxford, Oxford University Press, 2001) 44.
[15] *Ibid*, 84.
[16] *Ibid*.

this chapter begins by considering the purpose of a provision as part of the context within which it falls to be interpreted. It proceeds to deal with three other aspects of context, namely reading each provision and each instrument as a whole, the relevance of extrinsic materials and the relevance of the most basic presumptions of interpretation which the drafter is taken to know the courts are likely to apply. It concludes by considering the ways in which the courts are likely to deal with cases where social and technological developments mean that the context has changed between the time when provisions were drafted and the time when they are being interpreted.

Purpose as Part of the Context

Introduction

In 1975, Lord Diplock said:

> If one looks back to the actual decisions of this House . . . over the last thirty years one cannot fail to be struck by the evidence of a trend away from the purely literal towards the purposive construction of statutory provisions.[17]

Before considering this topic more closely, however, it is necessary to identify the relationship between the purpose underlying the use of specific words and the meaning of those words.

The purpose of a provision is the objective it is intended to achieve, while its meaning governs its application to the specific circumstances of individual cases. In the vast majority of cases, these two concepts overlap to such an extent that there is no need to dwell on the fact that there may be other cases in which they will not do so. However, either or both the difficulty of the drafter's task and the ingenuity of the lawyers whose function it is to argue their clients' cases (see *In re Castioni*[18] and Jonathan Swift's view of lawyers, both of which are noted at page 8) can be relied on to produce decisions in which the drafter's intentions are not reflected in the judicial outcomes.

The purposive approach to interpretation, therefore, requires that regard must be had to both the purpose behind the words and the meaning of the words, with the relationship between the two being that the purpose may inform (but not supplant) the meaning. Of course, this leaves open the question of how the purpose is to be identified.

Very briefly, the answer to this question lies in a number of sources, namely preambles, long titles, short titles, marginal notes and headings, pre-parliamentary materials, parliamentary materials and post-parliamentary materials.[19]

[17] *Carter v Bradbeer* [1975] 1 WLR 1204, 1206–0 7.
[18] *In re Castioni* [1891] 1 QB 149.
[19] See, respectively, pp 23, 23, 23, 24, 26, 27, 27.

Additionally, some statutes contain statements of purpose. For example, section 17(1) of the Courts and Legal Services Act 1990, which introduces Part II of the Act, provides:

> The general objective of this Part is the development of legal services in England and Wales (and in particular the development of advocacy, litigation, conveyancing and probate services) by making provision for new or better ways of providing such services and a wider choice of persons providing them, while maintaining the proper and efficient administration of justice.

However, statutory statements of purpose remain unusual in Westminster legislation. The Renton Committee on 'The Preparation of Legislation',[20] having taken evidence from, among others, parliamentary counsel from England, Scotland and New Zealand, noted that although judges, practitioners and academics tended to favour the use of statements of purpose, 'the draftsmen themselves are less enthusiastic',[21] on the grounds that such statements were either unnecessary, impracticable, or both. The Committee itself drew 'a distinction . . . between a statement of purpose which is designed to delimit and illuminate the legal effects of the Bill and a statement of purpose which is a mere manifesto'.[22] The Committee particularly noted the evidence of a distinguished American teacher of legislative drafting:

> Professor Reed Dickerson thinks that 'most purpose clauses are quite unnecessary'; that 'general purpose clauses tend to degenerate into pious incantations . . . such as . . . the one in a recent ecology Bill, which in substance said "*Hurray for Nature*"!' but that 'in prefatory language in individual sentences such as *For the purpose of this*, or *For the purpose of that*, or *In order to do this*, you may have an economic, focused purpose statement that is of some use'.[23]

Purposivism in Action

There are countless illustrations of purposivism in action but the following three cases provide particularly clear examples.

The first case, *Kammins Ballrooms Co Ltd v Zenith Investments (Torquay) Ltd*,[24] involved the scheme of security of tenure for business premises under Part II of the Landlord and Tenant Act 1954. Briefly, the statutory scheme requires that a tenant who wishes to retain the tenancy of premises on the expiry of the existing tenancy should ask the landlord to grant him a new one. If the landlord refuses to comply, the tenant can then apply to the court, which may then order the grant of a new tenancy. In the context of this procedure, section 29(3) of the Act provides that 'no application . . . shall be

[20] 'The Preparation of Legislation: Report of a Committee Appointed by the Lord President of the Council' (Cmnd 6053, 1975).

[21] *Ibid*, para 11.7.

[22] *Ibid*, para 11.8.

[23] *Ibid*, para 11.7.

[24] *Kammins Ballrooms Co Ltd v Zenith Investments (Torquay) Ltd* [1971] AC 850.

entertained unless it is made not less than two nor more than four months after . . . the making of the tenant's request for a new tenancy'. In *Kammins* the House of Lords held that the tenant's application to the court was not invalidated simply because it was made outside the statutory period. Lord Diplock acknowledged that

> Upon the literal approach, semantics and the rules of syntax alone could never justify the conclusion that the words '<u>No</u> application . . . <u>shall be</u> entertained <u>unless</u>' meant that some applications should be entertained notwithstanding that neither of the conditions which follow the word 'unless' was fulfilled.[25] (original emphasis)

However, he also said that a different conclusion could be reached by way of the *purposive* approach. In this case, purposivism involved recognising that the time limit in question had been enacted for the protection of landlords, by limiting the period within which they were at risk of an application being made. It followed that landlords were entitled to waive compliance with the time limit if they so wished. In other words, a court that finds that an application has been made out of time, must then consider whether the landlord has waived his right to rely on the time limit. (The fact that, in all the circumstances of the case, this particular landlord was held not to have waived compliance is irrelevant to the principle of interpretation.)

The following two cases illustrate what is perhaps the most important aspect of the purposive approach. Purposivism is concerned with identifying the meaning of words *for the purposes of the instrument in which they are used*, rather than seeking to attach some abstract or absolute meaning to those words. Turning to the cases themselves, in *Burgess v McCracken*,[26] a professional photographer was working in a public park. His method of business was to get people to agree to have their photographs taken. He took their photographs, they gave him their names and addresses and paid cash deposits. He subsequently sent them the photographs through the post and they sent him the balance of his fee. If his activities fell within the meaning of *trading in the park*, he was committing an offence.

A magistrates' court acquitted him on the basis that the earlier case of *Newman v Lipman*[27] had decided that exactly the same conduct in a street did not amount to the offence of *trading in the street*. The prosecution appealed to the High Court, which held that, in the context of these two cases, there was a relevant distinction between streets and parks. More particularly, the offence in relation to streets was intended to prevent obstructions of the kind that can arise when traders display their goods. Street photographers, on the other hand, do not do this and for all practical purposes they are indistinguishable from tourists, many of whom have cameras round their necks or in

[25] *Ibid*, 880.
[26] *Burgess v McCracken* (1986) 150 JP 509.
[27] *Newman v Lipman* [1951] 1 KB 333.

their hands. It follows that they do not commit the offence of trading in the street. On the other hand, people go into parks for relaxation and recreation. Therefore the offence in relation to parks has a wider purpose, which includes protecting people from annoyance caused by intrusive traders. It follows that, in the context of a park, the mere absence of obstruction does not justify an acquittal. These cases, therefore, provide a perfect illustration of Lord Diplock's comment, in *Carter v Bradbeer*:

> A question of statutory construction is one in which the strict doctrine of precedent can only be of narrow application. The *ratio decidendi* of a judgment as to the meaning of particular words or combinations of words used in a particular statutory provision can have no more than a persuasive influence on a court which is called upon to interpret the same word or combination of words appearing in some other statutory provision.[28]

The discussion so far has proceeded on the basis of the eminently reasonable assumption that there will always be a *purpose*, in the sense of an objective which the instrument is intended to achieve. (Any other assumption would involve supposing that the relevant provision had been enacted on an entirely arbitrary basis.) However, similar reasoning does not lead to the conclusion that there will always be a *legislative intention* if that phrase is understood to represent some pre-conception of the way in which a provision will be applied to the specific circumstances of individual cases (because the legislator cannot have envisaged all the possible circumstances which may arise). In the words of the American Realist, John Chipman Gray that there will often have been nothing which can realistically be called a *legislative intention*:

> The fact is that the difficulties of so called interpretation arise when the legislature had no meaning at all; when the question which was raised on the statute never occurred to it; when what the judges have to do is, not to determine what the legislature did mean on a point which was not present to its mind, but to guess what it would have intended on a point not present to its mind, if the point had been present.[29]

The interpretative process does, of course, disclose other sources of difficulty beyond that identified in this quotation, but this element of overstatement does not detract from the validity of Gray's essential point.

Although the courts can scarcely deny the cogency of Gray's point of view, they have devised a strategy which marginalises its significance by asserting, in effect, that the concept of legislative intention is safely within the keeping of the courts and therefore has very little to do with the legislature. In the words of Lord Reid:

> We often say that we are looking for the intention of Parliament, but that is not quite accurate. We are seeking the meaning of the words which Parliament used.

[28] [1975] 1 WLR 1204, 1206.

[29] JC Gray, *The Nature and Sources of the Law* 2nd edn (New York, Columbia University Press, 1921) 173.

> *We are seeking not what Parliament meant but the true meaning of what they said.*[30] (emphasis added)

Of course, this leaves open the question of how the courts should identify the true meaning of the words which the legislature has used. In *R v Secretary of State for the Environment, Transport and the Regions ex parte Spath Holme Ltd*,[31] Lord Nicholls sidestepped, rather than answered, this question when he described the *intention of Parliament* as

> a shorthand reference to the intention which the court *reasonably* imputes to Parliament in respect of the language used. It is not the subjective intention of the minister or other person who promoted the legislation. Nor is it the subjective intention of the draftsman, or of individual members or even of a majority of individual members of either House. These individuals will often have widely varying intentions. Their understanding of the legislation and the words used may be impressively complete or woefully inadequate. Thus, when courts say that such-and-such a meaning 'cannot be what Parliament intended', they are saying only that the words under consideration cannot *reasonably* be taken as used by Parliament with that meaning. (emphasis added)

In short, therefore, the only mind which is involved in formulating the intention of the legislature is that of the judge who undertakes the task of interpretation. Although this view is clearly now the established orthodoxy of the English common law, and although it works well enough in purely practical terms, it is difficult to avoid the conclusion that it reduces the phrase which it purports to explain to the status of a transparent fiction.

Reading Provisions and Instruments as a Whole

Introduction

The most obvious and immediate context of any words is the remainder of the sentence, provision or instrument within which they appear.

The classic judicial statement of the importance of the remainder of the sentence is found in *Bourne v Norwich Crematorium Ltd*,[32] where Stamp J said:

> English words derive colour from those which surround them. Sentences are not mere collections of words to be taken out of the sentence, defined separately by reference to the dictionary or decided cases, and then put back again into the sentence with the meaning which one has assigned to them as separate words so as to give the sentence or phrase a meaning which as a sentence or phrase it cannot bear without distortion of the English language. That one must construe a word or phrase in a section of an Act of Parliament with all the assistance one can from decided cases

[30] *Black-Clawson International Ltd v Papierwerke Waldhof-Aschaffenburg AG* [1975] AC 591, 613.

[31] *R v Secretary of State for the Environment, Transport and the Regions ex parte Spath Holme Ltd* [2001] 2 AC 349, 396.

[32] *Bourne v Norwich Crematorium Ltd* [1967] 1 WLR 691, 696.

> and, if you will, from the dictionary, is not in doubt; but having obtained all that assistance, one must not at the end of the day distort that which has to be construed and give it a meaning which *in its context* one would not think it can possibly bear. (emphasis added)

The decision in *R v Allen*,[33] which turned on section 57 of the Offences against the Person Act 1861, provides a clear illustration of the importance of the remainder of a sentence as the relevant context. The section deals with the offence of bigamy thus: 'Whosoever being married shall marry any other person during the life of the former husband or wife . . . shall be guilty of felony'. The court held that someone who is already married lacks the capacity to marry, and therefore *married* and *marry* cannot have the same meaning. More particularly, section 57 must mean something like *whosoever being validly married shall go through a ceremony of marriage with another person.*

Similarly, in *Foster v Diphwys Casson Slate Co*,[34] the relevant statute provided that explosives could be taken into a mine only if they were contained in a 'case or canister'. The court held that the context of that particular statute required all containers to be of the same strength and solidity as canisters and that, therefore, a cloth bag did not satisfy the requirement.

The general principle that the meaning of a word can depend on the company it keeps has spawned two specific principles which are, essentially, no more than illustrations of it, although they are usually discussed under their own names.

The first of these specific principles is that where general words follow a list of things of a certain rank, there is a presumption that the general words do not include things of a higher rank. Known for obvious reasons as the *rule of rank* (or the *rank principle*), this presumption may be illustrated by *Casher v Holmes*.[35] The court accepted that a provision imposing excise duties on 'copper, brass, pewter, and tin, and all other metals not enumerated' would not apply to gold and silver, because these are precious metals, and are, therefore, of a higher rank than the metals specified in the Act.

The second specific principle is that where general words follow particular words there is a presumption that the general words are limited to things of the same kind (or class) as those which are specifically mentioned. Despite the rapid decline of legal Latin, this proposition is still generally known as the *ejusdem generis principle* (or *rule*), because *ejusdem generis* is Latin for *of the same class*. In *Magnhild SS v McIntyre Bros & Co*,[36] McCardie J (whose view of the matter was approved by the Court of Appeal),[37] said:

[33] *R v Allen* (1872) LR 1 CCR 367.
[34] *Foster v Diphwys Casson Slate Co* (1887) 18 QBD 428.
[35] *Casher v Holmes* (1831) 109 ER 1263.
[36] *Magnhild SS v McIntyre Bros & Co* [1920] 3 KB 321, 330.
[37] [1921] 2 KB 97.

> The only test seems to be whether the specified things which precede the general words can be placed under some common category. By this I understand that the specified things must possess some common and dominant feature.

The application of this test may be illustrated by *Wanstead Local Board of Health v Hill*.[38] The Public Health Act 1848 provided that establishing certain businesses required the consent of the Local Board of Health. The businesses were 'blood-boiler, bone-boiler, fell-monger, slaughterer of cattle, horses, or animals of any description, soap-boiler, tallow-melter, tripe-boiler or other noxious or offensive business, trade or manufacture'. The court held that all the specified businesses involved the collection of large quantities of animal matter and, therefore, did not include a brick-works.

The drafter does not escape the application of the *ejusdem generis* principle by simply omitting the word *other* from the general words,[39] nor by including the word *whatsoever*.[40]

The final aspect of the potential relevance of other words contained in the same instrument is that 'it is a sound rule of construction to give the same meaning to the same words occurring in different parts of an Act'.[41] While busy practitioners no doubt see this as nothing more than a counsel of perfection in relation to substantial statutes (to take an extreme example, the Companies Act 2006 runs to 1300 sections and 16 schedules, which together occupy 760 pages of the Queen's Printer's copy) its validity as a matter of principle cannot reasonably be questioned. However, it would be more difficult for drafters to plead ignorance of any of the provisions of the instruments they were drafting. Before leaving the topic of reading instruments as a whole, it is important to notice that legislation which has been amended is to be read as a whole in its original form[42] and, therefore, the drafter of amending legislation should try to achieve consistency with the original.

In the cases outlined above, the immediate textual context consisted of the other words of the instrument which was being interpreted, but in some cases omissions from that instrument may be equally significant. In *R v Cuthbertson and Others*,[43] the appellants had been convicted of conspiracy to contravene the Misuse of Drugs Act 1971, one provision of which enabled a court to order the forfeiture of a defendant's property following conviction for 'an offence under this Act'. Although conspiracy to contravene the Act was undoubtedly an offence, it was not one which was created by the 1971 Act and, therefore, the appellants had not been convicted of an offence *under that Act*. The House of Lords declined to hold that the Act conferred power to make a forfeiture order.

38 *Wanstead Local Board of Health v Hill* (1863) 32 LJMC (NS) 135.
39 *Brownsea Haven Properties Ltd v Poole Corporation* [1958] Ch 574, 599.
40 *R v Cleworth* (1864) 122 ER 707.
41 *Courtauld v Legh* (1869) LR 4 Exch 126, 130.
42 *Attorney-General v Lamplough* (1878) 3 ExD 224.
43 *R v Cuthbertson and Others* [1981] AC 470.

Preambles and Long Titles

Preambles are not the same as long titles but it is not unknown for judges to confuse them with each other. (For example, in *Ward v Holman*[44] Lord Parker CJ used both terms interchangeably in one short judgment when referring to the Public Order Act 1936, even though the most cursory examination of the Act would have shown that it had only a long title.) More particularly, a preamble recites the reasons why the Act was passed, while a long title explains (even if very much in outline) what the Act is intended to do. There are, however, two reasons why the two categories may be confused.

The first reason is simply that both preambles and long titles come at the beginning of the Act.

The second reason is that, when it comes to interpreting the substance of the Act, there is an established principle that both can be used in order to resolve (but not to create) doubts arising from provisions contained in the body of the Act.

In *Attorney-General v Prince Ernest Augustus of Hanover*,[45] Lord Normand said:

> It is only when it conveys a clear and definite meaning in comparison with relatively obscure or indefinite enacting words that the preamble may legitimately prevail.
>
> The primacy of the words in the body of an Act was confirmed in *Siu Yin Kwan v Eastern Insurance Co Ltd*,[46] where the Privy Council declined to allow the preamble to an Act to be used in order to extend the ambit of perfectly plain words in the body of the Act; and in *R v Galvin*,[47] where the court declined to allow the long title to an Act to be used in order to restrict the scope of perfectly plain words in the body of an Act.

Finally, however, Lord Simon struck a discordant note in *Black-Clawson International Ltd v Papierwerke Waldhof-Aschaffenburg AG*,[48] by saying that where a long title provides the plainest of all guides to the general objectives of a statute, there can be no justification for restricting its use to cases of ambiguity.

Short Titles

The short title appears at the beginning of a statute but the English practice is for the section which creates it to come towards the end of the statute, along with the details relating to commencement, application and territorial extent. There is no doubt that the short title is part of the Act, and as such it can be used for the purpose of interpretation. The fact that it is, by definition, a *short*

[44] *Ward v Holman* [1964] 2 QB 580.
[45] *Attorney-General v Prince Ernest Augustus of Hanover* [1957] AC 436, 467.
[46] *Siu Yin Kwan v Eastern Insurance Co Ltd* [1994] 1 All ER 213.
[47] *R v Galvin* [1987] QB 862.
[48] [1975] AC 591.

title means that 'accuracy may be sacrificed to brevity,'[49] but wherever possible drafters should nevertheless do what they can to avoid confusion. For example, the Planning-gain Supplement (Preparations) Act 2007 (which is mentioned at page 58 as an example of paving legislation) provides for expenditure to be incurred in relation to preparations for the imposition of a tax on the increase in the value of land resulting from the grant of planning permission. Although the phrase *planning-gain* is understandable in this context, it is (albeit without a hyphen) already a well-established term of art in planning law, where it means some benefit to the community which a developer is willing to provide in return for being granted planning permission.

Headings and Marginal Notes

The traditional style of English statutory drafting has been to include *headings* (also known as *cross-headings*) between groups of sections, and *marginal notes* (also known as *side-notes* or *shoulder notes*) in the margin beside individual sections. From 2000 onwards, material which would previously have appeared in marginal notes has appeared in section titles, within the margins of the body of the text. This change clearly requires the introduction of some new terminology, but none appears to have been forthcoming. However, *group section headings* and *section headings* may be used as convenient formulations to describe what were previously known as headings and marginal notes respectively.

Historically, the interpretative value of headings and marginal notes has sometimes been questioned because both were—as group headings and section headings still are—inserted by the drafter, without being subject to debate in Parliament. However, two points are reasonably clear.

First, there is a judicial consensus that both are relevant to the process of interpretation 'provided that we realise that they cannot have equal weight with the words of the Act'.[50]

Secondly, the material which was previously contained in marginal notes (and which is now, of course, contained in section headings), can be a particularly useful aid to identifying the mischief at which a provision is aimed,[51] (or, in more modern terms, the purpose of the provision). As Upjohn LJ said:

> While the marginal note to a section cannot control the language used in the section, it is at least permissible to approach a consideration of its general purpose and the mischief at which it is aimed *with the note in mind.* (emphasis added)

Schedules, Definition Sections and Commencement Sections

Schedules, definition sections and commencement sections are all discussed in chapter five.

[49] *Re Boaler* [1915] 1 KB 21, 40.
[50] *Director of Public Prosecutions v Schildkamp* [1971] AC 1, 10.
[51] *Stephens v Cuckfield Rural District Council* [1960] 2 QB 373, 383.

Extrinsic Materials as Part of the Context

Introduction

The preceding paragraphs deal with points of interpretation (and, therefore, by inference, also of drafting) which arise from the instrument itself. However, it is also necessary to consider how far the context extends beyond the boundaries of the instrument. This is best done by analysing extrinsic materials into five different categories, namely legal textbooks, dictionaries, pre-parliamentary materials, parliamentary materials and post-parliamentary materials.

Legal Textbooks

Although lawyers tend turn to their textbooks when looking up the law, it is worth remembering that no textbook can be relied on as containing the law. All any textbook can ever do is to provide the author's view of what the law is, with the law itself remaining firmly located in the cases, the statutes and any other relevant primary sources. However, the courts recognise the realities of legal life and are willing to give considerable respect to statements contained in well-known textbooks. In the words of Sir George Jessell MR, 'although textbooks do not make law, they show more or less whether a principle has been generally accepted'.[52] But the essential point remains, and was nicely caught by Lord Goddard CJ in *Bastin v Davies*,[53] when speaking of *Bell's Sale of Food and Drugs*:

> This court would never hesitate to disagree with a statement in a textbook . . . if it thought fit . . . [but] . . . if a statement has appeared in a well-known textbook for a great number of years and has never been dissented from by a judicial decision, it would be most unfortunate to throw doubt on it after it had been acted on . . . for so long.

The authors and editors of even the most respected works are not beyond error—and, therefore, judicial correction—as cases involving *Halsbury's Laws of England*[54] and *Halsbury's Statutes of England*[55] demonstrate. Futhermore, the opinions of judges delivered extra-judicially must be read with caution:

> The process of authorship is entirely different from that of judicial decision. The author . . . has the benefit of a broad and comprehensive study of his chosen subject . . . But he is exposed to the perils of yielding to preconceptions and he lacks the . . . sharpening of focus which the detailed facts of a particular case bring to the judge. Above all, he has to form his ideas without the aid of the purifying ordeal of skilled argument on the specific facts of a contested case . . . and I would, therefore,

[52] *Henty v Wrey* (1882) 21 ChD 332, 348.
[53] *Bastin v Davies* [1950] 2 KB 579, 582–83.
[54] *Watson v Thomas S Witney & Co Ltd* [1966] 1 WLR 57.
[55] *Commission for the New Towns v Cooper (GB) Ltd* [1995] Ch 259.

> give credit to the words of any reputable author . . . as expressing tenable and arguable ideas, as fertilisers of thought, and as conveniently expressing the fruits of research in print . . . But I would expose those views to the testing and refining process of argument.[56]

Dictionaries

Dictionaries may seem to be the most obvious source of guidance as to the meanings of words, but in fact they seldom offer much assistance in either drafting or interpretation.

> It is highly dangerous, if not impossible, to attempt to place an accurate definition upon a word in common use; you can look up examples of its many uses if you want to in the *Oxford Dictionary* but that does not help on definition. The task of the court in construing statutory language . . . is to look at the mischief at which the Act is directed and then, in that light, to consider whether as a matter of common sense and everyday usage the known, proved or admitted or properly inferred facts of the particular case bring the case within the ordinary meaning of the words used by Parliament.[57]

The principal use of dictionaries in practice arises where it is necessary to identify the meaning of a word when an old provision was drafted. However, such cases are likely to be few and far between; and, even when they do arise, a contemporary dictionary of any substance is likely to offer a range of meanings for many of the words it defines.

Pre-parliamentary Materials

Pre-parliamentary materials, such as reports of official committees and royal commissions are useful because, in the words of Lord Halsbury LC, 'there is no more accurate source of information as to the mischief at which the Act was aimed'.[58] The express mention of *mischief* is significant: this dictum does not extend to using such sources to identify *meaning*.[59] Lord Hailsham LC maintained the relevance of this distinction when he described the use of reports to identify the *mischief only* as being 'the present practice'.[60] However, as Lord Denning MR pointed out, identifying the mischief 'does not help very much, for the simple reason that Parliament may, and often does, decide to do something different to cure the mischief'.[61]

A report of the Law Commission is likely to be a particularly useful guide to the mischief at which any ensuing legislation is aimed.

[56] *Cordell v Second Clanfield Properties Ltd* [1969] 2 Ch 9, 16.
[57] *Customs and Excise Commissioners v Top Ten Promotions Ltd* [1969] 1 WLR 1163, 1171.
[58] *Eastman Photographic Materials Co Ltd v Comptroller of Patents* [1898] AC 571
[59] *Assam Railways and Trading Co v Commissioners of Inland Revenue* [1935] AC 445
[60] *R v Allen* [1985] 1 AC 1029, 1035.
[61] *Letang v Cooper* [1965] 1 QB 232, 240.

Parliamentary Materials: the Use of Hansard

As a matter of first impression it may seem obvious that *Hansard*, as the official record of parliamentary proceedings, should be available to the courts when interpreting statutes, on the basis that the parliamentarians who debated a Bill before it became an Act may well have said what they intended it to mean. However, this was not the view which the English courts took until the watershed decision in *Pepper v Hart*.[62]

The case turned on a provision in the Finance Act 1976. The provision was ambiguous but when the Bill which became the Act was going through Parliament, the Financial Secretary to the Treasury had made it plain that the government intended the words to bear the meaning which was favourable to the taxpayer.

Delivering the leading speech, Lord Browne-Wilkinson with the agreement of five of the other six Law Lords hearing the case (Lord Mackay LC being the dissentient), said that the rule excluding reference to *Hansard* should no longer apply where:

> (a) legislation is ambiguous or obscure, or leads to an absurdity; (b) the material relied upon consists of one or more statements by a minister or other promoter of the Bill together if necessary with such other parliamentary material as is necessary to understand such statements and their effect; (c) the statements relied upon are clear.[63]

Post-parliamentary Materials

Government departments which administer (or supervise the administration of) particular areas of law often issue guidance to their own officials and to the public. At one time it was held that such guidance could not be cited in argument, on the basis that a judge who knows what the official view is, will then find it practically impossible to come to a conclusion on the law itself without being influenced by that view.[64] However, the modern practice gives judges more credit for being able to leave irrelevant matters out of account when making their decisions and official guidance is, therefore, citable, on the basis that it is to be given whatever weight (if any) that the court thinks is appropriate. For example, in *R v Wandsworth London Borough Council ex parte Beckwith*,[65] Lord Hoffmann referred to a circular in which central government purported to explain the statutory duty of local authorities to provide residential care for the elderly, before concluding that its statement of the law was 'simply wrong'.

The question is more difficult when it relates to interpretative practice in respect of regulation-making bodies' guidance as to the effect of their regulations.

62 *Pepper v Hart* [1993] AC 593.
63 *Ibid*, 640.
64 *London County Council v Central Land Board* [1958] 1 WLR 1296.
65 *R v Wandsworth London Borough Council ex parte Beckwith* [1996] 1 WLR 60, 65.

On the one hand, it can be argued that any information which may assist decision-makers should be capable of being admissible in principle, leaving the question of its admissibility in practice to be determined on a case-by-case basis. This argument is likely to be followed by another one, to the effect that when explanatory guidance is admitted, its weight (if any) should also be decided on a case-by-case basis.

On the other hand, there is always a danger that, in practice, the guidance will routinely become admissible, after which it will routinely be given substantial weight (probably on the basis that the guidance has created a legitimate expectation as to the meaning of the regulations). Additionally, where (as will very often be the case) decision-makers are not lawyers, there is much to be said for excluding explanatory guidance from their decision-making processes, on the basis that non-lawyers who are aware of something may experience difficulty in excluding it from their consideration. In other words, decisions are likely to be made on the basis of the guidance rather than on the basis of the regulations themselves. This distinction could be important if regulations are drafted more carefully and scrutinised more rigorously before adoption than guidance is.

If a regulation-making body does decide that its explanatory guidance should not be admissible in decision-making processes, both the regulations and the guidance should include express provisions to this effect.

Presumptions

Introduction

The courts routinely have regard to a number of principles of interpretation which they call *presumptions*. Although there is no universally accepted list of these presumptions, most of them—such as the presumption that the law should not be altered retrospectively—are very well established. Broadly speaking, the starting point is simply the presumption against injustice, together with one of its most widely applicable variants, namely the presumption against absurdity. Indeed, it is possible to argue that the presumption against injustice is the only presumption, with all the others—including the presumption against absurdity—being no more than examples of it.

The Presumption against Injustice

The most basic of all the presumptions, namely the presumption against injustice, may be illustrated by the case of *Coltman v Bibby Tankers Ltd*, which turned on the meaning of section 1(3) of the Employer's Liability (Defective Equipment) Act 1969. The section provided that, for the purposes of that Act,

' "equipment" includes any plant and machinery, vehicles, aircraft and clothing'. In the High Court,[66] Sheen J held that if a worker died as the result of the unseaworthiness of a ship due to defects in its hull, his estate was not prevented from seeking damages simply because ships are not mentioned in the statutory definition. In the context of the 1969 Act, it would be unjust to differentiate between harm suffered in (say) aircraft and harm suffered in ships. A majority of the Court of Appeal[67] reversed the decision, but the original decision was unanimously reinstated by the House of Lords,[68] where Lord Oliver said:

> The purpose of the Act was manifestly to saddle the employer with liability for defective plant of every sort with which the employee is compelled to work in the course of his employment, and I can see no ground for excluding particular types of chattel merely on the ground of their size or the element on which they are designed to operate.

As well as illustrating the application of the presumption against injustice, from the drafter's point of view this case carries what is perhaps an even more important message. The changing fortunes of the parties as this case progressed through the hierarchy of the courts shows that it is unwise tc rely on presumptions rather than express provisions.

The Presumption against Absurdity

While recognising that there are many competing views as to the ambit of justice, both conceptually and in its application to individual sets of circumstances, the presumption against absurdity is based on the commonsense proposition that it would be unjust for legislation to produce an absurd result.

The presumption against absurdity may be illustrated by *Jones v Conway & Colwyn Bay Joint Water Supply Board*.[69] A company which was supplying water had a statutory right to lay mains through other people's land. The court held that this right could be exercised before the water was supplied, because it would be absurd to say that water had to be supplied before the necessary mains had been laid.

Updating Construction

Introduction

The general principle is that the meaning of a provision can change with the passage of time (or, as it is sometimes put, *an updating construction* is

[66] *Coltman v Bibby Tankers Ltd* [1986] 1 WLR 751.
[67] [1987] 2 WLR 1098.
[68] [1988] 1 AC 276, 301.
[69] *Jones v Conway & Colwyn Bay Joint Water Supply Board* [1893] 2 Ch 603.

appropriate, or *the statute is always speaking*). The exceptional cases where this principle does not apply are sometimes called *fixed-time Act*s (or, in other words, Acts which are passed to deal with a particular state of affairs at a particular time), but these are very rare. The two main situations where updating constructions are appropriate arise where there has been either *social* or *technological* change since the statute was passed.

The Problem of Social Change

Since the Increase of Rent and Mortgage Interest (Restrictions) Act 1920, the law has protected certain people from eviction on the death of a tenant of residential property. More particularly, that Act and a number of its successors, have given security of tenure to a tenant's spouse, or a member of a tenant's family, who was residing with the tenant at the time of the tenant's death.

For many years, the courts held that the protection afforded by this principle did not extend to the survivors of unmarried relationships. For example, in *Gammans v Ekins*,[70] Asquith LJ said that

> to say of two people masquerading . . . as husband and wife (there being no children to complicate the picture) that they were members of the same family seems to be an abuse of the English language.

However, by the penultimate decade of the last century the Court of Appeal held that, in the present context, a family exists if the relationship looks like a marriage in the old sense of a lifelong union rather than one which is merely temporary or casual.[71] By that time, homosexual equality was firmly on the human rights agenda, so the next stage in the development of the law centred on whether the survivor of a same-sex relationship was entitled to security of tenure under the Act.

In *Harrogate Borough Council v Simpson*,[72] the Court of Appeal held that the survivor of a lesbian relationship was not entitled to succeed to her deceased partner's tenancy. The basis of this decision was two-fold. First, Parliament could have made express provision if it had wished such an entitlement to exist. Secondly, public opinion would not see a homosexual relationship in the same light as a heterosexual one.

In *Fitzpatrick v Sterling Housing Association*,[73] the Court of Appeal divided two against one on the question of whether the survivor of a male same-sex relationship was a member of the deceased's tenant's family and could, therefore, inherit security of tenure. All three judges were plainly sympathetic to the surviving partner, but both Roch LJ and Waite LJ felt the

70 *Gammans v Ekins* [1950] 2 KB 328, 331.
71 *Watson v Lucas* [1986] 2 FLR 91.
72 *Harrogate Borough Council v Simpson* [1980] 3 All ER 647.
73 *Fitzpatrick v Sterling Housing Association* [1998] Ch 304.

matter was one for Parliament rather than the courts. However, Ward LJ managed to overcome such constitutional qualms:

> To exclude same-sex couples from the protection of the [Rent Act 1977] proclaims the inevitable message that society judges their relationships to be less worthy of respect, concern and consideration than the relationship between members of the opposite sex. The fundamental human dignity of the homosexual couple is severely and palpably affected by the impugned distinction. The distinction is drawn on grounds relating to their personal characteristics, their sexual orientation. If the law is as my Lords state it to be, then it discriminates against a not insignificant proportion of the population who will justly complain that they have been denied their constitutional right to equal treatment under the law.[74]

He concluded his judgment thus:

> I have not reached this decision lightly. In truth, it has caused me a great deal of anxiety. I have worried that I have gone too far. If it is a matter for Parliament, and not for me, I hope that Parliament will consider it soon. I have endeavoured to reflect public opinion as I see it, but I am very conscious that public opinion on this topic is a continuum and it is not easy to see where the line is to be drawn. As Bingham MR said in *R v Ministry of Defence ex parte Smith* [1996] 1 All ER 257 at 263 [in which the Court of Appeal upheld the legality of excluding homosexuals from the armed forces], 'A belief which represented unquestioned orthodoxy in year X may have become questionable by year Y and unsustainable by year Z'.
>
> I have come to the clear conclusion that *Harrogate Borough Council v Simpson* was decided in year X; Waite and Roch LJJ, for reasons with which I could well have agreed, believe us to be in year Y, whereas I have been persuaded that the discrimination would be thought by the broad mass of the people to be so unsustainable that this must now be year Z. To conclude otherwise would be to stand like King Canute, ordering the tide to recede when the tide in favour of equality rolls relentlessly forward and shows no sign of ebbing. If I am to be criticised—and of course I will be—then I prefer to be criticised, on an issue like this, for being ahead of the times, rather than behind the times. My hope . . . is that I am in step with the times.[75]

In passing, it is interesting to note that Ward LJ[76] approved Dworkin's comment that the judge 'interprets not just the statute's text but its life, the process that begins before it becomes law and extends far beyond that moment . . . [the judge's] interpretation changes as the story develops'.[77] The House of Lords allowed an appeal by a 3:2 majority.[78]

Finally, in *Ghaidon v Godin-Mendoza*,[79] the House of Lords went all the way, and held that the surviving partner was the *spouse* of the deceased tenant for the present purposes.

[74] *Ibid*, 337.
[75] *Ibid*, 340.
[76] *Ibid*, 336.
[77] R Dworkin, *Law's Empire* (London, Fontana, 1986) 348 (reprinted by Hart Publishing, Oxford, 1998).
[78] [2001] 1 AC 27.
[79] *Ghaidon v Godin-Mendoza* [2004] UKHL 30, [2004] 2 AC 557.

The Problem of Technological Change

In some cases the changes in the meanings of words stem from technological considerations rather than social ones; but, from the point of view of statutory interpretation, the problem and the solution are substantially the same in both cases.

In *Barker v Wilson*,[80] the question was whether microfilm was a *bankers' book* for the purposes of the Bankers' Books Evidence Act 1879, which defined the phrase as including 'ledgers, day books, cash books, account books and all other books used in the ordinary business of the bank'. Holding that microfilm could be a bankers' book for the purposes of the Act, Bridge LJ said:[81]

> The Bankers' Books Evidence Act 1879 was enacted with the practice of bankers in 1879 in mind. It must be construed in 1980 in relation to the practice of bankers as we now understand it. So construing the definition of *bankers' books* and the phrase *an entry in a banker's book*, it seems to me that clearly both phrases are apt to include *any form of permanent record* kept by the bank of transactions relating to the bank's business, made by any of the methods which modern technology makes available, including, in particular, microfilm. (emphasis added)

A drafter who is wondering whether a court is likely to apply an updating construction, will find useful guidance in the approaches of Bridge LJ in *Barker v Wilson* and Ward LJ in the Court of Appeal in *Fitzpatrick v Sterling Housing Association*. Admittedly, the actual outcome of each case may well depend on the individual judge's perception of the constitutional propriety of judicial intervention, especially in cases, such as *Fitzpatrick*, involving moral judgments and their relevance to social policy. But this question will not even arise unless the principles of interpretation suggest that an updating construction may be appropriate. Constitutional sensitivities suggest, therefore, that in cases of substantial doubt it may be worthwhile to enact the updating in a subsequent statute. For example, section 1 of the Malicious Communications Act 1988 created an offence of sending 'letters and other articles with intent to cause distress or anxiety'. Although it might be thought that this kind of provision is a clear candidate for an updating construction, section 43 of the Criminal Justice and Police Act 2001 expressly amended the earlier provision by extending it to emails and text messages.

[80] *Barker v Wilson* [1980] 1 WLR 884.
[81] *Ibid*, 887.

3

Drafting Instructions

Introduction

The opening chapters of this book focus primarily on communication between drafters and their readers. However, before the rest of this book continues to explore how drafters try to achieve effective communication, it may be helpful to go one stage further back, in order to examine how policy makers communicate with drafters by way of drafting instructions. (It is, however, a useful preliminary to observe that the use of the word *instructions* may be misleading if taken too literally. As much of the rest of this chapter will show, the receipt of instructions begins a period of reciprocal consultation between the drafter and the instructing department, rather than containing orders which must be obeyed.)

Although this communicative process is, conceptually, the same in both legislative and regulatory drafting, at a purely practical level it will often be much less formal in the regulatory context, because bodies which have only an intermittent need for regulatory instruments are much less likely to employ specialist drafters. Where this is the case, the people who do the drafting will (unless they are employed on a part-time or casual basis specifically for this purpose) do other things as well. Therefore, their drafting work will be undertaken in the context of continuing working relationships which range much more widely (and are, therefore, likely to be correspondingly more complex) than those which arise from the simple model of a client instructing a lawyer to perform a single task.

More particularly, drafters who find themselves in this position are likely to have been involved in the development and formulation of policy before it gets to the stage where they have to express that policy in regulatory form. This has the obvious practical advantage that drafting considerations can be taken into account at an earlier stage than is often possible in the legislative context. On the other hand, the greater integration of many regulatory drafters into the fabric of their organisations may mean that they bring to bear a reduced level of objectivity when compared with their legislative counterparts. As Thornton says: 'Independence from the instructing officer or department . . . enables the drafter to see a legislative proposal in a wider and more balanced context than is possible for others'.[1] One important aspect of many regulatory drafters' lack of this kind of objectivity is that they are less likely than legislative drafters to be able to see all the less obvious ramifications of what they draft. They are similarly less likely to have previous relevant experience drawn from other drafting tasks, as well as less extensive knowledge of how other drafters have solved the problems with which they have to deal.

In some small regulation-making bodies, the people who lead the way in policy development and formulation may also be the ultimate drafters. There is nothing intrinsically objectionable about this state of affairs but, in practice, it can mean that regulatory drafters may be more easily satisfied than their legislative counterparts that they have all the information they need to produce effective instruments.

In short, any situation in which drafters are, in effect, their own clients, carries with it the risk of that extreme lack of objectivity which underlies the old saying that the lawyer who advises himself has a fool as a client.

All in all, therefore, some regulatory drafters may be tempted to ignore this chapter on the ground that it has nothing to offer them. However, even those regulatory drafters who fall into the extreme category of being, in effect, their own clients, will benefit from much of this chapter. More particularly, the discussion of what should go into instructions will serve as a useful indication of the kind of questions they should ensure they have asked themselves.

Most legislative drafters work on instructions in much the same way as other lawyers do. The exceptions are most likely to be those working in developing countries, who may even sometimes be instructed simply to draft a Bill on a specific topic, with issues of both policy and content being left entirely to them. The situation of these drafters may, therefore, be more akin to that of some regulatory drafters; but the general proposition that legislative drafters work on instructions remains sound.

The Nature of Drafting Instructions

In broad terms, drafting instructions should make clear both the policy which the proposal is required to implement and the details of the proposal itself.

Ideally, before the instructing department prepares instructions it should have a fully developed policy, on the basis of which it has formulated an equally fully developed set of legislative proposals. But the reality is often different. One particular source of difficulty is that developing a policy, and its associated legislative proposals, consumes a great deal of staff time, which the

[1] GC Thornton, *Legislative Drafting* 4th edn (London, Butterworths, 1996, subsequently transferred to Tottel) 134.

senior management of the instructing department may be unlikely to make available until a Bill is assured a place in the legislative programme. In practice, however, by the time the government has allocated places in the legislative programme for the forthcoming parliamentary session, there is likely to be insufficient time for the details of the policy and its associated legislative proposals to be fully worked out before the drafter needs to be instructed. The drafter, therefore, must often start work in the light of whatever is available, knowing that further development of the initial draft will become necessary as further instructions are received. Where this situation arises, it is hardly surprising if the ensuing Bill takes on the appearance of a house which, if not exactly built on sand, does show signs of having been built on foundations which shifted during the period of construction.[2]

However, the drafter is by no means a purely passive partner in relation to drafting instructions. Given the almost inevitable inadequacies and imperfections of initial drafting instructions, questions seeking clarification of some of their contents are only to be expected. Even the delivery of the first draft of the Bill to the instructing department is only one stage in an iterative process. The instructing department comments on the draft and the drafter responds with appropriate re-drafting. Furthermore, this process of comment and re-drafting may well continue for several more rounds and will often have the potential to continue for substantially longer than the time that is actually available for it to do so; the ensuing legislation would often be better if that additional time had actually been available.

Unfortunately, the confidential nature of the drafter's work ensures that very little detailed information about the precise nature of the drafter's interaction with the instructing department in individual cases ever enters the public domain. However, Thornton comments that 'in general terms . . . the rights and wrongs of the policy . . . are not the drafter's concern' before going on to say that 'the drafter has a professional duty to approach each task with objectivity', and that 'the proper discharge of the drafter's duty may require comment upon the implications of the policy behind the instructions in a way that may be unwelcome'.[3] A further, and important, aspect of the drafter's function is drawing attention to relevant matters which have escaped the notice of the policy makers.

The Content of Drafting Instructions

Drafting instructions should explain any foreseeable problems arising from the way in which the proposal will impact on existing statutory provisions or

2 George Engle, a former First Parliamentary Counsel, gives an insider's view of this in 'Bills are Made to Pass as Razors are Made to Sell' [1983] *Statute Law Review* 7; see especially 11–13.

3 *Legislative Drafting*, above n 1 at 134.

common law principles (or both), including any consequential repeals or amendments (or both) which will be necessary as a result of implementing the proposal. Any relevant international obligations should also be identified. Those with a taste for alliteration, therefore, may see the content of drafting instructions in terms of the policy, the proposal and any predictable problems arising from the wider legal context.

In addition to explaining the policy and the proposal and identifying any predictable problems arising from the wider legal context, good drafting instructions should draw attention to any official reports, judicial decisions and academic opinions which a prudent drafter would consider to be relevant. If the instructing department is in doubt as to the relevance of specific material, good practice suggests that it should be mentioned, thus leaving the question of relevance to the drafter's professional judgement.

For the purposes of managing staff resources, the head of the drafting office needs to know the degree of priority which the government attaches to the proposal.

Any issues of constitutional principle (such as interference with fundamental rights and freedoms) should be identified.

If the instructing department has any relevant information on how other jurisdictions have approached the same problem (and with what results) this should also be included (together with a commentary on the extent to which the other jurisdictions' experiences is likely to be replicated in the drafter's own jurisdiction).

If criminal offences are to be created, the issue of whether they should require *mens rea* should be addressed (see page 148), as should issues of application and extent in every case (see page 96).

If those who are instructing the drafter have undertaken an impact assessment, that assessment should be included. (*Regulatory impact assessment* was the standard terminology after the Regulatory Reform Act 2001, but after the Legislative and Regulatory Reform Act 2006 this became simply *impact assessment*, in order to reflect more accurately the scope of the concept).

Impact assessments are generally required when legislation affects the private sector, the third (*sc.* charitable and not-for-profit) sector and public services. They are intended to ensure that anyone with an interest in the proposed legislation can understand what is proposed and how it will impact on them, as well as the estimated costs and benefits. They also provide an opportunity for any affected parties to identify potential unintended consequences.[4]

Moving on from impact assessment, if the legislative proposal creates a decision-making function, the question of how (if at all) decisions can be challenged must be considered. There are three possibilities.

[4] See www.berr.gov.uk/whatwedo/bre/policy/scrutinising-new-regulations/

The first possibility is that people who are adversely affected by the exercise of the function may have the benefit of an existing right of appeal. Drafting instructions may contain a proposal to limit or exclude the existing right.

The second possibility is that there is no existing right of appeal, but there is an established type of appeal which is available in similar situations and which can easily be imported into the regime which is being created. A typical situation in which this is likely to be the case arises where an application for some sort of licence or other permission in relation to land use is either refused or granted subject to conditions. There is often a right of appeal to the relevant minister, with a further appeal (or an initial appeal if a minister is the initial decision-maker) to the High Court on a point of law (see page 173). In this sort of situation, drafting instructions should address the question of whether the existing type of appeal should be made available. If it is proposed that a right of appeal on an existing model should not be available in the new regime, drafting instructions should state the underlying rationale for its exclusion, since this enables the quality of the thinking which underlies the exclusion to be considered.

Limiting or excluding existing rights of appeal and failing to extend existing types of appeal to new situations, create no difficulty as a matter of drafting. However, in some jurisdictions each of these possibilities may raise constitutional issues which the instructing department should bring to the attention of the drafter, although it is the duty of the drafter to identify such issues in the absence of specific instructions. The performance of this duty is equally important whether there are grounds for believing that the relevant inclusion in, or omission from, the drafting instructions is the result of an oversight, or the consequence of a conscious decision.

The third possibility is that neither of the first two possibilities exists, in which case the question of providing an avenue of appeal must be approached as a matter of policy and with a completely open mind. While the creation of a specific right of appeal may cause resentment on the part of the decision-maker (and to this extent may be said to cause a political difficulty) it is very unlikely to cause any constitutional difficulty (at least within the context of a liberal democracy). However, it is unwise to assume that the absence of a right of appeal (irrespective of the way in which this absence comes about) will render the decision-maker immune from all legal challenge. In *R v Commissioner for Local Administration ex parte Eastleigh Borough Council*,[5] the High Court noted that when Parliament created the office of local ombudsman it did not also create a right of appeal. On the basis of this omission, the court concluded that Parliament should, therefore, be presumed to have intended that decisions of the local ombudsman were to be unchallengeable in the courts. In due course, however, the Court of Appeal said that the absence of a right

[5] *R v Commissioner for Local Administration ex parte Eastleigh Borough Council* [1998] QB 855.

of appeal justified the conclusion that judicial review was appropriate, because otherwise an aggrieved complainant to the local ombudsman would have no redress.

The fourth possibility is that the general law makes a decision-making process susceptible to judicial review but the instructing department wishes to exclude judicial review from the regime which is being created. In this case, drafting instructions should identify the reason underlying a provision to this effect, since barring access to justice always raises an issue of principle. (The extent to which various forms of words are effective to exclude judicial review is discussed in chapter ten.)

The Form of Drafting Instructions

An important aspect of the English common law practice of legislative drafting is that drafting instructions are prepared in narrative style, rather than in the form of draft Bills. This choice of style is, of course, a direct consequence of the tradition of having specialist legislative drafters, who have full responsibility for conceptualising the policy in legislative terms and consequently deciding how the Bill should be structured and drafted. Driedger explains why drafters object to drafting instructions taking the form of draft Bills:

> If he receives a draft, he must construe and interpret what may be an imperfect statement, and he may misunderstand what is intended. A draftsman who is presented with a draft measure would not be discharging his duties if he assumed that a proper legislative plan had been conceived and that proper provisions had been chosen to carry it out; he cannot be expected to confine himself merely to a superficial examination of the outward form of the measure. The drafting of legislation does not consist in polishing what others have written.
>
> As a rule, no time is saved by preparing a draft Bill for submission to the draftsman . . . Even assuming that a perfect Bill is submitted to the draftsman, he must still subject it to the complete drafting process, for how else can he discover that it is a perfect Bill and satisfy himself that it will give legislative effect to the intended policy? Draft measures prepared by inexperienced persons are usually defective, and then the draftsman must spend much time in undoing what has been done. This is particularly awkward where the draft has been circulated and discussed before submission to the draftsman, because those who have seen it expect that the final draft will closely resemble it and will resist any attempt to alter its fundamental structure.[6]

However, it is important to distinguish between, on the one hand, instructions which take the form of draft Bills and, on the other, instructions which are essentially narrative in form but which nevertheless contain specific

[6] EA Drieger, *The Composition of Legislation* 2nd revised edn (Ottawa, Department of Justice, 1957) xix–xx.

precedents that are known to have worked either well or badly in the past. Leaving drafters to decide whether to adopt, adapt or reject specific precedents is quite different from requiring them to evaluate, and perhaps re-draft, entire Bills and is not, therefore, open to the same objections.

Despite Driedger's strictures, it is not difficult to understand why drafters in short-staffed drafting offices (particularly, but not exclusively, in developing countries) may welcome instructions in the form of draft Bills. The drafting office's productivity can be maintained at a gratifyingly high level if its members are content to delegate all the structural work to lawyers (or even administrators) in the instructing departments and confine their own activities to refining and polishing. However, it would be unwise to pretend that such a division of labour can take place without compromising quality to a significant extent. An important part of the specialist drafters' expertise lies in conceptualising legislative policy in drafting terms, as well as in implementing that conceptualisation in the form of a draft Bill. Of course, there may be circumstances in which this compromise is necessary as a purely practical expedient and some drafters may even seek to justify it on the basis that perfection is never the natural condition of legislation, irrespective of the drafting procedure which produces it. Nevertheless, an office whose members gloss over the fact that quality has been compromised are undermining any case they may subsequently make for being resourced on a basis which would allow all legislation to be drafted from beginning to end by specialist drafters.

The Ethical Dimension of Drafting

Introduction

Subject to two exceptional cases (namely where either the law of a particular jurisdiction provides that legislative drafters are holders of public office or the government employs private practitioners to undertake legislative drafting—see page 40), the starting point must be that legislative drafters are government employees in the ordinary way.

Ethical Considerations

There are two views of the way in which legislative drafters may legitimately react if they are asked to draft something which they find ethically or constitutionally unacceptable. One is the mainstream view and the other is that of Seidman, Seidman and Abeysekere.

The mainstream view of the status of salaried legislative drafters begins with the basic proposition that they are government employees, from which it follows that, in respect of their obligation to accept and act on lawful instructions, they presumptively enjoy no special status. However, three glosses must be added to this basic proposition and its consequence.

First, legislative drafters will almost always be professionally qualified lawyers, from which it follows that their codes of professional conduct may contain relevant specific provisions. (In the regulatory context it will, of course, be far more common to find drafters who are neither professionally qualified lawyers nor subject to any other professional body's jurisdiction.)

Secondly, legislative drafters' terms of employment may contain specific relevant provisions. A provision that a lawyer–client relationship exists between drafters and the government is by no means universal but where it does exist it clearly gives drafters the right to decline instructions. (In practice, the exercise of this right may be tempered by the drafters' wish to preserve good working relationships in the longer term and may also be subject to any relevant rules of professional conduct.) On the other hand, drafters must remember that one consequence of terms of employment which give them lawyer–client status is that the government is no more bound to accept their advice than any other client is bound to accept his or her lawyer's advice. However, this aspect of the lawyer–client relationship can effectively be overridden by a ministerial edict that the drafters' advice on matters of law will be accepted in all cases. In any event, both drafters and their governments generally proceed on the basis that where a lawyer–client relationship does not exist in terms, in practice something very much akin to that relationship does, nevertheless, exist.

Thirdly, drafters may have the status of being holders of public office. While the effect of such status will vary in detail from one jurisdiction to another, in general terms it will give drafters a degree of guaranteed independence.

Having clarified the range of possible relationships between drafters and those who instruct them, it has become obvious that those who are neither holders of public office nor employed on a lawyer–client basis may find themselves in difficulty if they receive instructions to draft a Bill which they consider to be either morally repugnant, or unconstitutional, or both.

Taking these two situations in turn, drafters who are expected to draft a Bill which they find morally repugnant and whose conditions of service contain no relevant conscience clause, must pursue one of three courses of action. Either they persuade the head of their office to allocate that Bill to another drafter; or they resign; or they continue to work with a strained conscience. Drafters who find themselves in real personal difficulty but who nevertheless continue to draft a Bill which they consider to be offensive may derive some comfort from the way in which Wilfred Owen described himself (having combined intellectual pacifism with courageous service in the trenches) as 'a conscientious objector with a very seared conscience'.[7]

[7] In a letter to his mother in (1917).

Precisely the same alternatives arise where drafters object to proposed legislation on the basis of unconstitutionality rather than moral repugnance. At first sight it may seem odd to equate the two situations, but this conclusion is inescapable.

In a legal system which recognises the constitutional doctrines of the separation of powers and the rule of law, it is fundamental that the courts, and only the courts, can provide authoritative rulings on matters of law. Therefore, until a court rules on the constitutionality of a particular piece of legislation, the presumption of legality (more traditionally expressed as *omnia praesumuntur rite esse acta*) means that it must be regarded as being no more than allegedly, rather than actually, unconstitutional. Any other consequence would give legislative drafters the power to quash government decisions to bring forward specific legislative proposals, which would amount to the power to veto the enactment of any legislation which is, to the slightest degree, constitutionally controversial. The constitutional significance of such a veto would be so great that it is entirely reasonable to suggest that it would have to be expressly conferred by the constitution itself. (Additionally, the character of the British constitution as an amalgam of law and convention means that it is perfectly possible for something to be *unconstitutional* without being *unlawful*,[8] which makes it even less plausible that a lawyer's opinion should always be automatically privileged over anyone else's.)

If a disputed legislative proposal is plainly unconstitutional by any reasonable standards (for example, a statute authorising genocide), it may be argued that the position differs from the two situations outlined above. However, in such a case the legislative proposal is likely to be so far adrift from established moral and constitutional values that it may properly be classified as revolutionary. On this basis and in this context, it is relevant to compare the predicament of the legislative drafter with that of the judge who, having been appointed by a pre-revolutionary regime, is subsequently called on to recognise laws made by its post-revolutionary successors.

The most practical analysis of this situation comes from applying Kelsen's concept of the *grundnorm*, as applied in the Zimbabwean case of *R v Ndhlovu*.[9] On this basis, the judge who at this stage is still acting under the authority of the pre-revolutionary regime which appointed him or her, must inquire into the status of the legislature which has passed the law. If this inquiry leads the judge to conclude that the revolution has been successful, it follows that the pre-revolutionary regime no longer has any constitutionally recognised existence. It follows from this that the judge can no longer continue to act under the authority which that regime conferred on him or her. In other words, the judge must decide whether to continue to discharge the judicial function under the authority of the new regime, or to cease to act altogether.

[8] *Madzimbamuto v Lardner-Burke* [1969] 1 AC 645.

[9] *R v Ndhlovu* (1968) 4 SA 515.

By analogy, therefore, although the drafter clearly lacks the constitutional power of a judge to make authoritative decisions on the legitimacy of a regime, at the level of personal conscience he or she must go through the same Kelsenian intellectual process as a judge who does have that power. Then, having come to a decision, the drafter must either accept the legitimacy of the new regime or resign. Of course it can be argued that, in addition to the lack of any authority to give constitutionally legitimate answers to disputed questions of law, there is another and entirely practical factor which distinguishes drafters from judges for the present purposes. This factor is simply that the drafters' predicament arises before the law is made, rather than at the later, post-legislative stage, by which time it may well have become easier to assess the success or otherwise of the revolution. However, in terms of principle, precisely the same question arises, namely has the revolutionary government become legitimate?

In short, therefore, drafters who are caught up in revolutionary situations have two options of last resort, namely to resign or 'join the revolution'.

Turning to the alternative approach, Seidman, Seidman and Abeysekere assert that:

> Parliamentary counsel enjoys the same independence as a judge. Persuaded that a proposed bill would result in an unconstitutional law, a counsel may refuse instructions to draft that bill. *No-one can appeal that decision.*[10] (emphasis added)

Unfortunately, this assertion is so far out of line with conventional ideas of constitutionalism, as outlined above, that it cannot be taken seriously in the absence of either supporting authority, or at least supporting argument, neither of which the authors produce. Even in the relatively rare cases of drafters who are holders of public office, it is inconceivable that this status would carry with it the power to override government decisions. It seems, therefore, that their view can be discarded on the simple basis that it is wrong.

[10] A Seidman, RB Seidman and N Abeysekere, *Legislative Drafting for Democratic Change* (London, Kluwer Law International, 2001) 30.

4

Constitutional Considerations and the Protection of Human Rights

Introduction

Since the enactment of legislation is one of the most formal activities which a state can undertake, it is only to be expected that some constitutional principles will be relevant to the legislative process and the content of the ensuing legislation. It follows that legislation, and legislative drafting, must be seen in a constitutional context.

This chapter comments on interpreting constitutions and identifies the underlying doctrines of the British constitution which (apart from the doctrine of the legislative supremacy of Parliament) are common to the constitutions of most, if not all, liberal democracies. It then discusses the protection of human rights under both the common law and the joint regime of the Human Rights Act 1998 (HRA) and the European Convention on Human Rights (ECHR). It concludes by identifying the nature and constitutional significance of paving legislation and the way in which executive powers and titles may be reallocated under the Ministers of the Crown Act 1975 and suggests how the idea underlying that Act can be applied in regulatory contexts.

Drafters from common law jurisdictions in which the ECHR has no direct relevance may, nevertheless, find its concepts and their interpretation provide some interesting (and perhaps even transferable) insights.

Regulatory drafters, operating as they do within a different set of contexts, may initially feel that the explicitly constitutional orientation of this chapter means that it holds nothing of interest to them. On more mature consideration, however, many regulatory drafters will realise that they have to deal with many of the same problems as their legislative counterparts (with obvious examples including the need for legal—or, in their case, regulatory—certainty, proportionality and the protection of legitimate expectations). Furthermore, many regulatory regimes operate according to a basic body of rules which sets up (or constitutes) the regulatory regime itself. This body of rules may be contained in a statute, a royal charter or some other instrument and may be either externally imposed or voluntarily adopted; but whatever its origin and the nature of its authority, it may be regarded as being a form of constitution.

Interpreting Constitutions

Introduction

Goldsworthy offers a detailed comparative account of how constitutions can be interpreted,[1] but Barak provides[2] a particularly useful insight, based on his classification of legislative purposes into those which are objective and those which are subjective. According to this classification, objective purposes consist of those 'goals, interests and values' which a text is 'designed to actualise', while subjective purposes consist of 'the intention of the author of the text'. When interpreting constitutions, the objective purpose 'prevails in most cases' and the subjective purpose is 'relevant mainly where there are conflicting objective purposes'.

Drafters who are concerned with ensuring the constitutional propriety of their legislation (especially those who function within a context where the courts can strike down unconstitutional legislation) must be steeped in the case law of their own constitutions. But Barak's distinctions provide a more generalised conceptual framework which is also applicable in the case of the British constitution, whose incremental creation and uncodified nature are of its essence.

The Constitutional Context of Drafting

The decisions of the English courts are clearly informed by the constitutional doctrines of the rule of law, the legislative supremacy of Parliament and the separation of powers, all of which, therefore, impact on the drafter's work.

First, in its most basic form, the 'rule of law' simply means that people are entitled to be governed according to law rather than according to the exercise of arbitrary discretion. An important element of the rule of law is, therefore, predictability in the field of interpretation. However, in practice, decision-

[1] J Goldsworthy, *Interpreting Constitutions: A Comparative Study* (Oxford, Oxford University Press, 2006).

[2] The scheme is summarised as part of a one, unnumbered, page in app 3 of A Barak, *Purposive Interpretation in Law* (English translation, Princeton, Princeton University Press, 2005).

makers must have some scope for the exercise of judgement and discretion, which, in the present context, includes deciding on the meaning of the language which the drafter has used.

At a practical level, therefore, the rule of law is satisfied provided that the limits of any leeway in decision-making can be identified and the exercise of the decision-making power is subject to legal control. The drafter's contribution is to try to reconcile two competing objectives. On the one hand, instruments should be clearly structured and contain sufficient detail to promote adequate certainty in typical situations. On the other, governmental decision-makers and the courts need to be left with sufficient scope to apply the principles of interpretation in ways which produce appropriate outcomes in whatever cases come before them. (The principles of interpretation are discussed in chapter two.)

Secondly, when the courts are dealing with Acts of Parliament, the doctrine of the legislative supremacy of Parliament limits the courts' role to interpreting and applying whatever Parliament has enacted. The question of quashing simply cannot arise. (Even where a statute is incompatible with European Community law, the courts have no quashing power but can only disapply the offending provision.[3]) Admittedly, the judicial power of interpretation can be used very creatively in cases where the courts feel that such an approach is justified (see, for example, the cases on purposivism which are discussed at page 17) but the fundamental point remains that the courts never have any power, under any circumstances, to quash any Act of Parliament. Of course, subordinate legislation does not have the protection of the legislative supremacy of Parliament for the simple reason that it is not made by Parliament. Subordinate legislation can, therefore, be quashed (see chapter ten).

Thirdly, the doctrine of the separation of powers holds that the executive, legislative and judicial forms of state power should be exercised by different people or bodies. Although the courts do still make the common law, the separation of powers can have an inhibiting effect in cases involving legislative interpretation, where the courts can always fall back on the argument that Parliament should be left to amend or repeal that which it has created, rather than having the courts indulging in overly creative interpretation. In other words, the separation of powers can operate as a particularly potent constraint on the exercise of judicial power when coupled with the legislative supremacy of Parliament. More particularly, in some cases the combination of these two doctrines can lead the courts to recall Lord Simonds warning that even where statutory language is ambiguous,

> the power and duty of the court to travel outside them on a voyage of discovery are strictly limited . . . [and the courts should not be guilty of] a naked usurpation of the legislative function under the thin disguise of interpretation.[4]

[3] *R v Secretary of State for Transport ex parte Factortame Ltd (No 2)* [1991] 1 AC 603.

[4] Lord Simonds in *Magor & St Mellons Rural District Council v Newport Corporation* [1952] AC 189, 191.

Finally, it is worth noticing that an insistence on the importance of the separation of powers may be said to come from a desire that there 'may be a government of laws and not of men'.[5] However, this formulation overlooks the fact that laws are conceived, drafted, enacted and subsequently interpreted, by people. Furthermore, as many of the cases cited in chapter two show, the power of interpretation should not be underestimated when a court feels that robust decisions are required if the interests of justice are to prevail.

The Protection of Human Rights

Introduction

This section of this chapter discusses the protection of human rights and fundamental freedoms (which, for the sake of simplicity, is abbreviated here to 'human rights'). More particularly, the main focus will be on the HRA and its implications for drafters. However, a preliminary sketch of the constitutional fundamentals provides a useful overview of the context within which the HRA was enacted.

The Legal Protection of Human Rights before the Human Rights Act 1998

Written constitutions usually lend themselves to protecting human rights. By way of contrast, the British constitution's basic doctrine of the legislative supremacy of Parliament means that any provisions which attempt to entrench the protection of human rights could, from a purely legal point of view, be repealed or amended just as easily as they were enacted in the first place: 'As a matter of law the courts of England recognise Parliament as being omnipotent in all save the power to destroy its own omnipotence'.[6]

However, although the legislative supremacy of Parliament extends to overturning judicial decisions (even retrospectively),[7] in practice (if always subject to Parliament finding the time and the political will to reverse their decisions), the courts possess substantial power to protect human rights on a case-by-case basis. Admittedly, the courts' record in exercising this power has been variable, but a power which is not always exercised does not cease to be a power. Some case law is instructive.

In *Malone v Metropolitan Police Commissioner (No 2)*,[8] Sir Robert Megarry V-C held that it had been lawful for the police to tap the telephone of a suspected criminal because the law contained nothing to prevent them from doing so.

[5] Art XXX of the Massachusetts Constitution (1780).
[6] Sir Robert Megarry V-C, *Manuel v Attorney-General* [1983] Ch 77, 89.
[7] See, eg, *Burmah Oil Co Ltd v Lord Advocate* [1965] AC 75.
[8] *Malone v Metropolitan Police Commissioner (No 2)* [1979] Ch 344.

The decision of the High Court in *R v Lord Chancellor ex parte Witham*[9] arose from the introduction of new rules governing court fees. The rules were made by the Lord Chancellor (in exercise of powers conferred by the Supreme Court Act 1981) with the agreement of the Lord Chief Justice, the Master of the Rolls, the Vice-Chancellor and the President of the Family Division. The new rules not only substantially increased the fees but also removed an exemption which had benefited people who were receiving income support. They did, however, give the Lord Chancellor power to reduce or remit the fees in individual cases of undue financial hardship. Despite the possibility of reduction or remission of fees, the High Court upheld an argument that the Lord Chancellor had exceeded his statutory powers because the increases would effectively exclude many people from access to the courts.

Where multi-judge courts hear cases, the common occurrence of a split decision (even though all the judges are dealing with the same facts and have heard the same arguments) emphasises the fact that judicial outcomes are a kind of lottery, where the identity of the winner depends on which judges are sitting.

For example, *R v Secretary of State for Social Security ex parte Joint Council for the Welfare of Immigrants*[10] arose from certain regulations which the Secretary of State had made under the Social Security (Contributions and Benefits) Act 1992. Simon Brown LJ, with whom Waite LJ agreed, held the regulations to be unlawful because they would reduce some asylum seekers to 'a life so destitute that to my mind no civilised society can tolerate it'.[11] But Neill LJ dissented, having had regard to both the objectives of the legislation and the responsibility of the Secretary of State to balance competing considerations when allocating resources.

Similarly, in *Fitzpatrick v Sterling Housing Association*,[12] the House of Lords held (by 3:2) that the surviving partner of a same-sex relationship was entitled to inherit the tenancy of their home on the death of his partner, in whose name the tenancy had been held, although the Court of Appeal had divided by 2:1 the other way.

It is against the background of the impossibility of effective long-term protection by statute, coupled with the unreliability of effective protection by the common law that the HRA (as the only piece of Westminster legislation which deals with the protection of human rights in a comprehensive way) must be considered. However, even in the post-HRA era, it is worth saying that the courts may still look to the pre-HRA attitudes when dealing with human rights matters which do not fall within the scope of the ECHR as made relevant to national law by the HRA.

9 *R v Lord Chancellor ex parte Witham* [1998] QB 575.

10 *R v Secretary of State for Social Security ex parte Joint Council for the Welfare of Immigrants* [1997] 1 WLR 275.

11 *Ibid*, 292.

12 *Fitzpatrick v Sterling Housing Association* [1998] Ch 304 (CA), discussed more fully at p 31; and [2001] AC 27 (HL).

The Human Rights Act 1998

Introduction

The scheme of the HRA proceeds on the basis of accepting the constitutional doctrine that one Parliament cannot bind its successors, while seeking to minimise the practical uncertainties which flow from reliance on the common law as a means of protecting human rights. However, before examining the Act in more detail, it is necessary to consider the ECHR itself.

The European Convention on Human Rights

The ECHR functions under the auspices of the Council of Europe and disputes as to its interpretation and application come before the European Court of Human Rights (ECtHR), which sits at Strasbourg. In other words, and at the risk of labouring the point, it does not function under the auspices of the European Community (or Union as it is more commonly known), and so its cases do not go the European Court of Justice, which sits at Luxembourg. However, even more importantly in purely practical terms, while the doctrine of the supremacy of European Community law is firmly established, there is no doctrine of the supremacy of the law of the ECHR as interpreted by the ECtHR (which is known as *Strasbourg jurisprudence*) and so national law prevails.

A well-established principle of international law, currently contained in article 31 of the Vienna Convention on the Law of Treaties 1969, requires that a treaty 'shall be interpreted in good faith in accordance with the ordinary meaning to be given to the terms of the treaty in their context and in the light of its object and purpose'.

In accordance with article 33(4) of the Vienna Convention, the authentic texts (which in this case are in English and French) must be construed in such a way as to 'reconcile them as far as possible', but the ECtHR has held that where this is impossible in the case of the ECHR, the 'object and purpose' of the Convention must be decisive.[13] This brings two provisions of the preamble to the ECHR into play. First, its object and purpose are 'the maintenance and further realisation of Human Rights and Fundamental Freedoms'. Secondly, it is the contracting states' 'profound belief . . . [that] . . . Fundamental Freedoms . . . are . . . best maintained on the one hand by an effective political democracy and on the other by a common understanding and observance of the human rights upon which they depend'.

This purposive (or teleological) approach to interpretation may be illustrated by *Artico v Italy*,[14] in which the Court found there had been a breach of the right to legal assistance under article 6(3)(c) of the ECHR when a lawyer nominated to represent someone never actually did so because of

[13] *Wemhoff v Federal Republic of Germany* (1979–80) 1 EHRR 55.
[14] *Artico v Italy* (1980) 3 EHRR 1.

other professional commitments and ill-health. The ECtHR held that the right could be satisfied only by *effective* legal assistance.

Convention Rights under the Human Rights Act

The central concept in the HRA is Convention rights. However, this phrase does not mean all the rights protected by the Convention itself, but only those specified in section 1(1) of the Act, which defines the concept by reference to certain articles of, and protocols to, the Convention. The relevant article and protocols (which are reproduced in full in appendix two), may be summarised as follows:

article 2	the right to life;
article 3	prohibition of torture or inhuman or degrading treatment or punishment;
article 4	prohibition of slavery or forced labour;
article 5	the right to liberty and security of the person;
article 6	the right to a fair trial;
article 7	freedom from the imposition of retrospective criminal liability and punishment;
article 8	the right to respect for private and family life;
article 9	freedom of religion;
article 10	freedom of expression;
article 11	freedom of assembly and association;
article 12	the right to marry and found a family;
article 14	prohibition of discrimination in enjoyment of rights under the Convention.

First Protocol

article 1	the right to property;
article 2	the right to education;
article 3	the right to free elections.

Sixth Protocol

articles 1 & 2 prohibition of the death penalty

Section 1(2) of the Act makes the operation of these articles subject to derogations and reservations.

Neither the rights protected by article 1 (which imposes a duty on the state 'to secure to everyone within their jurisdiction the rights and freedoms' protected under the Convention) nor those protected by article 13 (which requires the state to provide effective domestic remedies for breaches of the Convention) are Convention rights under the HRA. The governments's reasoning for these omissions was that no specific provision was necessary because the HRA, taken as a whole, covers both these matters anyway.

How the Courts must approach Convention Rights

Section 2 of the Act provides that any court or tribunal which has to determine any question in relation to a Convention right 'must take into account' the relevant Strasbourg jurisprudence. The Act gives no guidance as to the weight which must be given to this jurisprudence, as against all the other interpretative factors which may arise in any given case. However, in *R (Alconbury Developments Ltd) v Secretary of State for the Environment, Transport and the Regions*,[15] Lord Slynn took a strict view:

> In the absence of some special circumstances it seems to me that the court should follow any clear and constant jurisprudence of the European Court of Human Rights. If it does not do so, there is at least a possibility that the case will go to that court, which is likely in the ordinary case to follow its own constant jurisprudence.

In *R (Anderson) v Secretary of State for the Home Department*,[16] Lord Bingham refined this proposition somewhat, by saying that the House of Lords would require a 'good reason' to 'depart from the principles laid down in a carefully considered judgment of the [European] Court [of Human Rights] sitting as a Grand Chamber'. (A sitting of the Court as a Grand Chamber consists of seventeen judges rather than the usual seven.) Nevertheless, the relationship is one of persuasiveness, not bindingness. As Laws LJ, with the concurrence of Poole J, emphasised in *Gough and Another v Chief Constable of the Derbyshire Constabulary*,[17] 'our duty is to take account of the Strasbourg jurisprudence, not necessarily to apply it'. On a related but not identical point, in *Myles v Director of Public Prosecutions*,[18] MacKay J, giving the judgment of the Divisional Court, said that where decisions of the courts of other Convention states conflict with those of domestic courts, the domestic authorities must be given decisive weight.

Interpretation and Validity of Legislation

Section 3(1) of the HRA imposes what has come to be known as 'the interpretative obligation', namely that 'so far as it is possible to do so, primary and subordinate legislation must be read and given effect in a way which is compatible with the Convention rights'. In *Ghaidon v Godin-Mendoza*,[19] Lord Rodger emphasised the dual nature of this obligation:

> [107] Section 3(1) contains not one, but two, obligations: legislation is to be read in a way which is compatible with convention rights, but it is also to be given effect in

[15] *R (Alconbury Developments Ltd) v Secretary of State for the Environment, Transport and the Regions* [2001] UKHL 23, [2003] 2 AC 295, [26].

[16] *R (Anderson) v Secretary of State for the Home Department* [2002] UKHL 46, [2003] 1 AC 837, [18].

[17] *Gough and Another v Chief Constable of the Derbyshire Constabulary* [2002] EWCA Civ 351, [2002] QB 1213, [32].

[18] *Myles v Director of Public Prosecutions* [2004] EWHC 594 (Admin), [2004] 2 All ER 902.

[19] *Ghaidon v Godin-Mendoza* [2004] UKHL 30, [2004] 2 AC 557.

> a way which is compatible with those rights. Although the obligations are complementary, they are distinct. So there may be a breach of one but not of the other. For instance, suppose that legislation within the ambit of a particular convention right requires a local authority to provide a service to residents in its area. The proper interpretation of the duty in the legislation may be straightforward. But, even if the local authority interprets the provision correctly and provides the appropriate service, if it provides the service only to those residents who support the governing political party, the local authority will be in breach of art 14 in relation to the other article concerned and, in terms of s 3(1), will have failed to give effect to the legislation in a way which is compatible with convention rights. So, even though the heading of s 3 is 'Interpretation of legislation', the content of the section actually goes beyond interpretation to cover the way that legislation is given effect.

Section 3(2) provides that section 3(1) applies to all legislation enacted at any time, and the provision is, therefore, retrospective to the extent that it does not apply merely to post-Act legislation. Pausing only to comment that the Act's retrospectivity in relation to matters of *fact* will be discussed below, it must be emphasised that section 3(2) also provides that section 3(1) does not affect the *validity* of any *primary* legislation, nor of *delegated* legislation made under a parent Act containing a provision to that effect. On the assumption that primary legislation made in exercise of the royal prerogative is unlikely to be encountered and that parent Acts containing exempting provisions will be extremely rare in practice, the practical effect of these provisions is, therefore, to introduce a new principle of interpretation while respecting constitutional orthodoxy in respect of both the legislative supremacy of Parliament and the quashability of delegated legislation. (In passing, it may be useful to recall that experience in relation to Community law has shown that English courts are generally able to construe legislation in such a way as to be compatible with some other scheme of things when they are required to do so.)

However, there remains the question of how far the courts can legitimately go when identifying 'possible' interpretations in order to achieve compliance with Convention rights. In *R v A (No 2)*,[20] Lord Steyn emphasised that 'the interpretative obligation . . . is a strong one. It applies even if there is no ambiguity in the language . . . It is an emphatic adjuration by the legislature'. Subsequently, however, both the House of Lords collectively and Lord Steyn personally resiled from this position on the basis that imposing a Convention compliant interpretation in the absence of ambiguity in the statute is to cross the boundary of interpretation and enter the constitutionally prohibited territory of amendment.[21]

[20] In *R v A (No 2)* [2001] UKHL 25, [2002] 1 AC 45, [44].

[21] See, eg, *Re S* [2002] UKHL 10, [2002] 2 AC 291; *R (Anderson) v Secretary of State for the Home Department* [2002] UKHL 46, [2003] 1 AC 837; *R (Rusbridger) v Attorney-General* [2003] UKHL 38, [2004] 1 AC 357; and *Bellinger v Bellinger* [2003] UKHL 21, [2003] 2 AC 467.

Assuming that compliance with the interpretative obligation is possible in any given case, it may take one of two forms. First, it may amount simply to giving a compatible interpretation in that case. Secondly, it may amount to a general statement as to how the provision in question should be interpreted. However, the second alternative will be relatively rare, because

> it would only be if there was a material risk of incompatibility . . . in all such cases that it would be appropriate to lay down a rule of general application as to how . . . [the incompatible provision] . . . ought to be read.[22] (original emphasis.)

Declarations of Incompatibility

Although the Act contains nothing to diminish the legislative supremacy of Parliament, section 4 does give a court at (or above) the level of the High Court the power to make declarations of incompatibility where primary legislation conflicts with Convention rights.

Declarations of incompatibility have no effect on the cases in which they are made, nor on the continuing validity and operation of the statutes in respect of which they are made. However, under section 10 of the Act, they may result in the provisions being amended or repealed by remedial orders. (Remedial orders will typically take the form of delegated legislation, in order to avoid the pressures on time which beset the government's legislative programme.) However, where the declaration of incompatibility relates to an Order in Council made in exercise of the royal prerogative, the remedial order may be in the form of a further Order in Council made in the same way. The section also provides that remedial orders may be made where the incompatibility of English law is identified by the ECtHR, as well as by an English court.

Finally, in *Ghaidan v Godin-Mendoza*,[23] the House of Lords emphasised that Parliament had intended the interpretative obligation to be the principal means of protecting Convention rights; and that declarations of incompatibility were intended to be used only as a last resort.

The Duty imposed on Public Authorities

Section 6 of the Act makes it unlawful for a public authority (which is defined as *excluding* both Houses of Parliament but as *including* courts and tribunals, as well as 'any person certain of whose functions are functions of a public nature') to act in a way which is incompatible with Convention rights. (The Act leaves the meaning of the phrase 'functions of a public nature' to be worked out on a case-by-case basis, in true common law style.) The effect of section 7 of the Act is that a person who wishes to establish that there has been a breach of the duty under section 6, may do so proactively by claiming

[22] Lord Hope, *R v A (No 2)* [UKHL] 25, [2002] 1 AC 45, [105].
[23] [2004] UKHL 30, [2004] 2 AC 557.

judicial review, or reactively by way of defence to proceedings brought by, or at the instigation of, the public authority.

Statements of Compatibility

Under section 19 of the Act, which came into force on 24 November 1999 (almost a year before the bulk of the Act came into force), Ministers who are in charge of Bills in either House of Parliament must, before the Second Reading of the Bill, state either that in their view there is no incompatiblity with Convention rights, or that they wish the House to proceed in the absence of such a statement. The latter alternative is likely to arise only very occasionally, but it did do so in the parliamentary proceedings which resulted in the passage of the Communications Act 2003. (Section 321 of that Act authorises the prohibition of political advertising on television, even though this breaches the Convention right to freedom of expression.)

While the courts may refer to a ministerial statement of compatibility when interpreting a statute,[24] they will do so only with caution. As Lord Hope said, in *R v A (No 2)*,[25] having commented approvingly on counsel's decision not to rely on a statement of compatibility:

> These statements may serve a useful purpose in Parliament. They may also be seen as part of the parliamentary history, indicating that it was not Parliament's intention to cut across a Convention right . . . No doubt they are based on the best advice that is available. But they are no more than expressions of opinion by the Minister. They are not binding on the court, nor do they have any persuasive authority.

Is the HRA Retrospective as to Matters of Fact?

Although, section 3(2) of the Act clearly provides that the interpretative obligation imposed by section 3(1) applies to pre-Act statutes, the Act makes only one express provision relating to its own retrospectivity as to matters of fact. More particularly, the combined effect of section 7(1)(b) and section 22(4) is that where a public authority acted in breach of a Convention right before the Act came into force and legal proceedings are subsequently brought by, or at the instigation of, that authority, the defence may rely on the breach of the Convention right even though the breach of the Convention right occurred before the 1998 Act came into force.

A particular problem in relation to retrospectivity arose in *R v Lambert*.[26] A majority in the House of Lords held that where both the facts and the hearing of any case arising from those facts, occurred before the Act came into force, any subsequent appeal against that decision which is heard now the Act is in force, must be determined in accordance with the pre-Act position.

[24] *Pepper v Hart* [1993] AC 593, 1 All ER 42, discussed at p 27.
[25] See n 22, [69].
[26] *R v Lambert* [2001] UKHL 37, [2002] 2 AC 545, [69].

Although this conclusion may be thought to be no more than an application of the presumption against retrospectivity in statutory interpretation, Lord Steyn dissented on the basis that public authorities (including the courts) are under a duty to act compatibly with Convention rights; and, therefore, the appellate court must do so in a case such as the present one. On this basis, the fact that the previous court was not subject to the duty is nothing to the point. The sequel to *Lambert* came quickly in the form of *R v Kansal (No 2)*,[27] where a majority of the House held that *Lambert* had indeed been wrongly decided but nevertheless decided to follow it, on the basis that it represented a possible view of the law and there were no particularly compelling reasons to depart from it.

ECHR Concepts and their Interpretation

With the exception of the prohibition of torture or inhuman or degrading treatment or punishment (article 3), all Convention rights are subject to some kind of limitation or qualification. Of particular interest in this respect are articles 8–11, which are all expressly capable of being restricted by law to such extent as is 'necessary in a democratic society' for the reasons set out in each of the articles. It is useful to notice, therefore, that in *Dudgeon v United Kingdom*,[28] where homosexual relationships were said to fall within the category of private life (rather than family life), the court identified 'tolerance and broad-mindedness' as two of the 'hallmarks' of a democratic society. What may 'be necessary in a democratic society' will, of course, be a question for the court in each case, but some indication of its scope can nevertheless be given.

In *Handyside v United Kingdom*,[29] the Court said, when upholding the domestic law relating to the forfeiture of obscene publications:

> While the adjective 'necessary' . . . is not synonymous with 'indispensable', neither has it the flexibility of such expressions as 'admissible', 'ordinary', 'useful', 'reasonable' or 'desirable'.

More positively, in *Olsson v Sweden*,[30] while finding that there was no basis in the current state of Swedish law for the practice of social workers of restricting parental access to children who were in the care of public authorities, the Court said:

> According to the court's established case-law, the notion of necessity implies that an interference corresponds with a *pressing social need* and, in particular, that it is *proportionate* to the legitimate aim pursued. (emphasis added)

[27] *R v Kansal (No 2)* [2001] UKHL 62, [2002] 2 AC 69.
[28] *Dudgeon v United Kingdom* (1982) 4 EHRR 149, 165.
[29] *Handyside v United Kingdom* (1979–80) 1 EHRR 737, 754.
[30] *Olsson v Sweden* (1989) 11 EHRR 259, 275.

In practice, this test clearly requires the application of both the doctrine of *proportionality* (to which it explicitly refers) and the doctrine of the *margin of appreciation*.

Taking these in turn, at its simplest, the doctrine of proportionality merely requires that the means which are used must be proportionate to the ends which are to be achieved. Addressing the matter at slightly greater length, in the Privy Council case of *de Freitas v Permanent Secretary of Ministry of Agriculture, Fisheries, Lands and Housing*,[31] Lord Clyde said that a court should ask itself:

> Whether: (i) the legislative objective is sufficiently important to justify limiting a fundamental right; (ii) the measures designed to meet the legislative objective are rationally connected to it; and (iii) the means used to impair the right or freedom are no more than is necessary to accomplish the objective.

In *R (Daly) v Secretary of State for the Home Department*,[32] Lord Steyn expressly approved these observations, before going on to say:

> The starting point is that there is an overlap between the traditional grounds of review and the approach of proportionality. Most cases would be decided in the same way whichever approach is adopted. But the intensity of review is somewhat greater under the proportionality approach.

He proceeded to offer 'a few generalisations':

> First, the doctrine of proportionality may require the reviewing court to assess the balance which the decision maker has struck, not merely whether it is within the range of rational or reasonable decisions. Secondly, the proportionality test may go further than the traditional grounds of review inasmuch as it may require attention to be directed to the relative weight accorded to interests and considerations. Thirdly, even the heightened scrutiny test developed in *R v Ministry of Defence ex parte Smith* . . . is not necessarily appropriate to the protection of human rights.[33]

More particularly:

> The intensity of review, in similar cases, is guaranteed by the twin requirements that the limitation of the right was necessary in a democratic society, in the sense of meeting a pressing social need, and the question whether the interference was really proportionate to the legitimate aim being pursued.[34]

The problem which this approach poses for the English courts is that one of their traditional bases for determining whether executive decision-making is lawful has been the test of whether the decision is so unreasonable that no reasonable decision-maker could have made it. In other words, the courts

[31] *de Freitas v Permanent Secretary of Ministry of Agriculture, Fisheries, Lands and Housing* [1999] 1 AC 69, 80.

[32] *R (Daly) v Secretary of State for the Home Department* [2001] UKHL 26, [2001] 2 AC 532.

[33] *Ibid*, [27].

[34] *Ibid.*

allow decision-makers a considerable degree of latitude, which, in turn, excuses the courts from adjudicating on the correctness of the decision. Although it is clear that, in practice, the overall test of unreasonableness may be applied with varying degrees of intensity (so that, for example, decisions which adversely affect human rights are more difficult to justify than those which do not do so, as evidenced by *R v Ministry of Defence ex parte Smith*[35] where homosexuals had been discharged from the armed forces simply because of their sexual orientation), it is equally clear that the test of proportionality makes it practically impossible for the courts to avoid making explicit judgments about the appropriateness of executive decisions.

The difficulty which this caused in the pre-HRA era was well captured in *R v Secretary of State for the Home Department ex parte Brind*,[36] where Lord Lowry said:

> There can be very little room for judges to operate an independent judicial review proportionality doctrine in the space which is left between the conventional judicial review doctrine and the admittedly forbidden appellate approach.

However, in the light of the HRA, it is clear that, in some cases at least, the judges have no option but to become involved in this way. This means that, by way of a fundamental deviation from the pre-HRA constitutional position, they have to work out the basis on which to do so. Two cases are particularly instructive.

Turning to the concept of the *margin of appreciation*, in *Handyside*[37] the ECtHR said:

> By reason of their direct and continuous contact with the vital forces of their countries, state authorities are in principle in a better position than the international judge to give an opinion on the . . . 'necessity' of a 'restriction' or 'penalty' . . . It is for the national authorities to make the initial assessment of the reality of the pressing social need.
>
> Consequently art 10(2) leaves to the contracting states a margin of appreciation. This margin is given both to the domestic legislator ('prescribed by law') and to the bodies, judicial amongst others, that are called upon to interpret and apply the laws in force.
>
> Nevertheless, [the Convention] does not give the contracting states an unlimited power of appreciation. The court, which . . . is responsible for ensuring those states' engagements, is empowered to give the final ruling on whether a 'restriction' or 'penalty' is reconcilable with [a Convention right or freedom] . . . The domestic margin of appreciation thus goes hand in hand with a European supervision. Such supervision concerns both the aim of the measure challenged and its 'necessity'; it covers not only the basic legislation but also the decision applying it, even one given by an independent court.

[35] *R v Ministry of Defence ex parte Smith* [1996] QB 517.

[36] *R v Secretary of State for the Home Department ex parte Brind* [1991] 1 AC 696, 767.

[37] (1979–80) 1 EHRR 737, 753–54.

In other words, the ECtHR recognises the existence of an area of discretion which it leaves entirely to national legal systems. Therefore the Court may be said to be exercising a supervisory jurisdiction, similar to that exercised by the English courts in judicial review.

Finally, although the meaning of the rather odd phrase 'margin of appreciation' has become clear, the phrase itself is 'a solecism originating in the literal rendering in the English text of the decision in *Handyside v UK* . . . of the French phrase *marge d'appréciation*, meaning margin of appraisal or judgment'.[38]

The Presumption of Compliance with International Law

There is a presumption that Parliament intends to legislate in accordance with the United Kingdom's international obligations and this clearly requires the courts to have regard to any relevant international conventions when seeking to resolve ambiguities of statutory wording. However, this presumption has had only limited success in protecting human rights.

In the pre-HRA case of *R v Secretary of State for the Home Department ex parte Brind*,[39] where the freedom of expression of television journalists was restricted by certain directives issued by the Secretary of State, the House of Lords refused to say that the presumption of statutory interpretation justified a finding that the Secretary of State had acted unlawfully in exercising an administrative discretion without having had regard to the ECHR. More particularly, Lord Bridge, having acknowledged the existence of the presumption, said:

> But where Parliament has conferred on the executive an administrative discretion without indicating the precise limits within which it must be exercised, to presume that it must be exercised within Convention limits would be to go far beyond the resolution of ambiguity. It would be to impute to Parliament an intention not only that the executive should exercise the discretion in conformity with the Convention, but also that the domestic courts should enforce that conformity by the importation into domestic administrative law of the text of the Convention and the jurisprudence of the European Court of Human Rights in the interpretation and application of it . . . When Parliament has been content for so long to leave those who complain that their Convention rights have been infringed to seek their remedy in Strasbourg, it would be surprising suddenly to find that the judiciary had, without Parliament's aid, the means to incorporate the Convention into such an important area of domestic law and I cannot escape the conclusion that this would be a judicial usurpation of the legislative function.[40]

However, some judges have been able to identify circumstances which justified disregarding the restrictive approach exemplified by *Brind*, even before

[38] See the joint judgment of Thorpe and Sedley LJJ in *Evans v Amicus Healthcare Ltd* [2004] EWCA 727, [2005] Fam 1, [63].

[39] [1991] 1 AC 696.

[40] *Ibid*, 748.

the HRA had been passed. The classic example is *R v Secretary of State for the Home Department and Another ex parte Norney and Others*,[41] where the administrative discretion in question had been conferred by a statute that had been passed to bring English law on prisoners' rights into line with the ECHR. Dyson J said that, despite the decision in *Brind*, in the instant case it would be perverse for the court to ignore the relevant Convention provision.

In *Derbyshire County Council v Times Newspapers Ltd*,[42] (and still in the pre-HRA era) both the Court of Appeal and the House of Lords agreed that a local authority cannot sue for libel, but differed in their opinion of the relevance of the Convention. Emphasising that the public interest in freedom of speech outweighed the local authority's interest in protecting its own reputation, Lord Keith, with whom the other Law Lords agreed, said:

> It is of the highest public importance that a democratically elected governmental body, or indeed any governmental body, should be open to uninhibited public criticism. The threat of a civil action for defamation must inevitably have an inhibiting effect on freedom of speech.[43]
>
> . . .
>
> The conclusion must be, in my opinion, that under the common law of England a local authority does not have the right to maintain an action of damages for defamation. That was the conclusion reached by the Court of Appeal, which did so principally by reference to art 10 of the European Convention on Human Rights.[44]
>
> My Lords, I have reached my conclusion upon the common law of England without finding any need to rely upon the European Convention.[45]

Paving Legislation

It is commonplace for a government which introduces a Bill into Parliament in order to create a new statutory scheme to wish to undertake preparatory work in connection with that scheme before the Bill becomes an Act or, once the Act has been passed, before it is intended to come into force. The problem which arises in each case is how to ensure that there is lawful authority for the preparatory work.

Taking the pre-enactment situation first, there is no doubt that an individual monarch (being the Crown for the time being), as well as an individual Secretary of State (acting in the name of the Crown) both have distinctive

[41] *R v Secretary of State for the Home Department and Another ex parte Norney and Others* (1995) 7 Admin LR 861.

[42] *Derbyshire County Council v Times Newspapers Ltd* [1992] 3 WLR 28 (CA), [1993] AC 534 (HL).

[43] [1993] AC 534, 547.

[44] *Ibid*, 550.

[45] *Ibid*, 551.

powers which are not shared by any other person, body or organisation (and which collectively constitute the royal prerogative). Similarly, there is no doubt that the monarch and an individual Secretary of State also possess the ordinary range of common law powers of the sort which any other legal person also has (because both are bodies corporate). The difficulty lies in identifying the precise scope of both ranges of powers.

Ultimately, each case must turn on its detailed facts, but in *R (Shrewsbury & Atcham Borough Council) v Secretary of State for Communities and Local Government*,[46] the Court of Appeal acknowledged that the formulation of new policies through legislation is a necessary and incidental part of the ordinary business of central government, from which it follows that a Secretary of State can lawfully take preparatory steps such as consulting on the relevant policies and issuing a White Paper. It is also clear that there is power to engage in informal processes (such as planning for the introduction of the new statutory scheme) which are not intended to have any legal consequences in themselves, even though they subsequently form the basis of post-enactment decisions which do have legal consequences.

The position is less clear if a Secretary of State wishes to engage in preparatory activities which do have legal consequences in themselves. In this case a choice has to be made. The government may rely on either the royal prerogative or the narrower range of ordinary common law powers on the one hand, or secure the enactment of legislation giving specific lawful authority to engage in preparatory activities in relation to, and thus paving the way for, the proposed legislation on the other hand. The second option, which is known, for the obvious reason, as *paving legislation*, is relatively rare, but the Planning-gain Supplement (Preparations) Act 2007 provides a straightforward example (even though the short title of the Act is not particularly well chosen—see page 24). Section 1(1) and (2) of the Act, when read together, authorise the Commissioners of Revenue and Customs, the Secretary of State and the Northern Ireland Department to

> incur expenditure for the purpose of or in connection with preparing for the imposition of a tax on the increase in the value of land resulting from the grant of permission for development.

Turning to the post-enactment situation, the solution lies in having one section come into force either immediately on the Act receiving the Royal Assent, or very soon afterwards. This section authorises the Secretary of State to undertake appropriate preparatory work before the rest of the Act comes into force and may also avoid any doubt as to the legality of pre-Royal Assent preparatory work by retroactively authorising it. It would be difficult for anyone to object to retroactive legislation in relation to anything done between

[46] *R (Shrewsbury & Atcham Borough Council) v Secretary of State for Communities and Local Government* [2008] EWCA Civ 148, [2008] 3 All ER 548.

publication of the Bill and the coming into force of the Act, since the Bill itself would have signalled the intention to proceed in this way.

The Reallocation of Executive Functions and Titles

Although governments tend to reorganise departmental responsibilities for administrative, managerial and political reasons rather than for legal ones, any significant reorganisation is likely to have legal consequences and, therefore, to require a legal basis. The most convenient way to deal with the legalities is to enact a single umbrella statute, providing for a scheme of subordinate legislation which can be relied on whenever reorganisations are required, without the necessity to draft, and find parliamentary time for, specific statutes. The Ministers of the Crown Act 1975, which provides that the Queen may, by Order in Council, make transfer of ministerial functions orders, is a useful model.

Broadly, transfer of functions orders may do one or more of the following: change the title of a minister; provide that a function previously performed by the Minister of X shall be performed by the Minister of Y; provide for a function of the Minister of X to be exercisable concurrently with the Minister of Y (or to cease to be so exercisable); change references in 'instruments' to specific ministers so that they apply to different ministers (the term 'instruments' being broad enough to cover contracts, leases, licences and so on, as well as legislative instruments); and provide for the dissolution of government departments and the redistribution of their functions. Transfer of functions orders may also make appropriate incidental, consequential and supplemental provisions for matters such as the transfer of property, rights and liabilities and for whatever adaptations of enactments relating to the functions which are being transferred as may be necessary to enable them to be exercised by the minister to whom they are transferred.

Essentially the same technique can be used in regulatory contexts by the simple expedient of including similar powers in the instrument (if any) which allocates functions to senior employees or committees. However, in the case of professional bodies, trade associations and similar organisations which are run on democratic lines, care must be taken to avoid (or remove) conflicts with any existing provisions which entitle the membership to vote on structural reorganisations.

5

General Principles of Drafting

Introduction

Although every instrument must be drafted on the basis that it is unique, many issues and tasks recur routinely. It is, therefore, not surprising that many drafting techniques are employed equally routinely to deal with these issues and tasks. These techniques may legitimately be called *general principles of drafting*.

The Nature of the General Principles of Drafting

Introduction

The body of general principles which, taken as a whole, constitutes a drafter's basic toolkit, equips competent drafters to demonstrate a variety of virtues, and enables them to avoid a multitude of vices, in relation to language, law and logic. They range from the macro level, dealing with the structure of an instrument as a whole, to the micro level, dealing with individual words, phrases and punctuation marks. But the need to become immersed in the general principles of drafting should never lead drafters to overlook one of the most important precepts of written communication as a whole, namely the mongoose principle.

The Mongoose Principle

The mongoose principle takes its name from an old story about a customer who wrote to a pet shop:

> Dear Sirs,
> Please send me two mongooses.
> Yours etc,
> *A. Customer.*

However, on reading over the letter before sending it, the writer felt some doubt as to whether the plural of *mongoose* was really *mongooses*. To be on the safe side, she tore the letter up and wrote the following:

> Dear Sirs,
> Please send me two mongeese.
> Yours etc,
> *A. Customer.*

However, on reading over this version of the letter, she felt that *mongeese* did not sound quite right either, so she tore this letter up as well, before writing the following:

> Dear Sirs,
> Please send me one mongoose.
> Yours etc,
> *A. Customer.*
> PS: On second thoughts, make it two.

The *mongoose principle*, therefore, states: *if in difficulty or doubt, rewrite it.* The principle provides a simple solution to many problems and drafters who are reluctant to apply it are likely to spend an excessive amount of time and energy engaged in unproductive work, before abandoning failed drafts and starting again.

Is Drafting an Art or a Science?

From time to time, the question arises of whether drafting is an art or a science, with drafters themselves usually coming down on the side of art. It is, of course, true that good drafting is seldom (if ever) entirely mechanistic or formulaic and that two drafters presented with identical instructions could well produce very different (but equally effective) instruments. Reliance on these facts tends to lead to the conclusion that drafting is not a science. However, the variability of drafting outcomes from a single set of instructions illustrates only that drafting is, or can be, a creative process, without saying anything about the nature of that creativity. More particularly, it does not establish that drafting is an art. Part of the reason is that the emphasis in the artistic endeavour tends to be on engaging the emotions, while the drafter's output engages the intellect. But there is an even more basic point.

Conceptualising a proposal and drafting an appropriate instrument is a two-stage process. The whole of this process is often described as *drafting*, but if this usage becomes the basis of the question 'is drafting a science or an art?' it becomes clear that neither term is adequate to describe such a complex process. In reality, if a single term has to be chosen to describe the second stage of the drafting process, that term could well be *craft* (using this word to signify a variety of skills which can be taught, learned, practised and developed). When craft skills are manual they may be perfected, or so nearly perfected as makes no difference. When craft skills are intellectual, such as those of the drafter, it may be that perfectibility, or even approximate perfectibility, is not attainable; but this shows only that the second stage of the drafting process is a difficult craft to master and not that it is not a craft at all.

In short, therefore, unless—as is very unlikely—imperfectibility is taken as the distinguishing mark of artistry rather than being merely a characteristic which it shares with other means of communication, the process of drafting, taken as a whole, cannot legitimately be called either an art or a science. However, chasing definitions tends to be an unrewarding activity for anyone who is not a lexicographer and what matters in the present context is what drafters do and how they do it. An important aspect of this is that styles of drafting may change. For example, Sir Geoffrey Bowman, a former First Parliamentary Counsel who comes down in favour of the *art* side of the debate, gives the following example of the development of his own style in relation to a very common type of provision:[1]

> The enactments specified in Schedule 9 to this Act are hereby repealed to the extent specified in the third column of that Schedule. (1980)
>
> The provisions mentioned in Schedule 5 are repealed to the extent specified in column 3. (1996)
>
> Schedule 11 contains repeals. (2000)

The Range of Drafting Techniques

The range of drafting techniques is too broad to be sensibly reduced to a few sentences but some indication can be given. Some issues involve the most appropriate structure for instruments. Others involve the way in which the layout of a page can contribute to good communication. Perhaps the most obvious ones involve the best use of language in order to convey meaning as clearly as possible. Finally, some involve the technical features of legislative and regulatory instruments. This chapter deals with each of these issues in turn, but before doing so it provides a short overview of the topic of plain language drafting.

Plain Language Drafting

Introduction

The application of plain language drafting techniques to legislative and regulatory instruments often provokes strong reactions, from evangelical zeal

[1] G Bowman, 'Why is there a Parliamentary Counsel Office?' [2005] *Statute Law Review* 69, 79.

at one end of the spectrum to total abhorrence at the other. However, this section of this chapter does not attempt to provide a full account of the topic, on the basis that all good drafting is as plain as it can reasonably be. Once this is accepted, it follows that the principles of plain language provide a sub-text to all effective guidance on good drafting, including that which is contained not only in this chapter, but in this book as a whole. Nevertheless, the high profile which discussion of plain language drafting enjoys, makes it desirable to offer some preliminary comment in order to place the topic in context.

Plain Language Drafting in its Historical Context

Although the idea of plain language drafting in the context of the law gained little prominence before the final quarter of the last century, there is nothing distinctively modern about emphasising the desirability of using plain language to improve the efficacy of communication generally.

For example, St Paul said 'except ye utter by the tongue words easy to be understood, how shall it be known what is spoken? for ye shall speak into the air.'[2] Similarly, in the very early eighteenth century, Alexander Pope, said:

> Words are like leaves, and where they most abound
> Much fruit of sense beneath is seldom found.[3]

Bringing the commentary firmly into both the realm of drafting and the modern age, Sir Carleton Kemp Allen neatly points out not only that obscurity in statutes is nothing new, but also that there is more than one way of achieving it:

> From the laconic and often obscure terseness of our earliest statutes, especially when in Latin, we swung in the sixteenth, seventeenth and eighteenth centuries to a verbosity which succeeded only in concealing the real matter of the law under a welter of superfluous synonyms.[4]

An Inevitable Limitation on the Usefulness of Plain Language Drafting

Without wishing in any way to detract from the desirability of legislative and regulatory language being as plain as it reasonably can be, it is worth identifying one inevitable limitation on its usefulness, namely that the words of an instrument mean only what they are authoritatively held to mean.

> It has been sometimes said that the Law is composed of two parts—legislative law and judge-made law, but in truth all the Law is judge-made law. The shape in which a statute is imposed on the community as a guide for conduct is that statute as interpreted by the courts. The courts put life into the dead words of the statute. To quote

[2] First Epistle to the Corinthians (14:9).
[3] A Pope, *An Essay on Criticism* (1711).
[4] CK Allen, *Law in the Making* 7th edn (Oxford, Oxford University Press, 1964) 482.

> . . . from Bishop Hoadley [an 18th century English clergyman]. . . 'Nay, whosoever hath an absolute authority to interpret any written or spoken laws, it is He who is truly the law Giver to all intents and purposes, and not the Person who first wrote or spoke them'.[5]

Despite an element of overstatement (especially under a constitution based on the doctrine of the legislative supremacy of powers, where the legislature wins with loaded dice), there can be little doubt that the essence of this comment is sound. But there is equally little doubt that its good sense is very easily overlooked. For example, Sir William Dale, arguing for the importance of legislation being understandable by non-lawyers, considers the best way to acquire knowledge of the contents of an Act is to read a Queen's printer's copy.[6] While this is true as far as it goes, it misses the point that the ability to acquire knowledge of the *meaning* of the contents of an Act requires a knowledge of the general principles of interpretation, together with (at least in many cases) a knowledge of the pre-existing law on the relevant topic and a knowledge of any relevant judicial decisions on the provisions which are being read. Nor is it an answer to the last part of this criticism, to say that if Acts were drafted in plain terms, there would be no need to depend on judicial interpretation. (For perfectly plain language being given unexpected meanings, see, for example, *Kammins Ballrooms Ltd v Zenith Investments (Torquay) Ltd* and *Anisminic v Foreign Compensation Commission* which are discussed at pages 17 and 172, respectively.

Structuring an Instrument

Introduction

Although drafters are likely to see the structure of an instrument as a coherent whole, for the purposes of analysis, discussion of structural matters falls naturally into two parts, dealing respectively with *principal* and *subordinate* provisions.

Principal provisions are designed to give effect to the policy of the instrument (including matters of both substance and procedure). Subordinate provisions appear in many (and sometimes in all) examples of a given type of instrument. Typical subordinate provisions in statutes deal with matters such as application and extent, commencement, definitions, and savings and repeals (all of which are discussed at pages 96–102.) However, although individual drafters may have their own preferred forms of words for provisions such as these (see, for example, the evolving preferences of one drafter in

[5] JC Gray, *The Nature and Sources of the Law* (New York, Columbia University Press, 1909) 119–120.

[6] W Dale, *Legislative Drafting: A New Approach* (London, Butterworths, 1977) 11.

relation to provisions which repeal earlier provisions), the functions performed by such provisions vary little (if at all) between instruments of the same type.

The distinction between principal and subordinate provisions is a useful aid to explanation, but it is not absolute. For example, a definition may either be included in a principal provision (which may confer a benefit, power or status, or impose a burden, disability or disqualification, or have any other legal effect) or it may be hived off to appear, together with other definitions, in a dedicated (but, for the purposes of the present classification, subordinate) provision elsewhere. Similarly, schedules usually contain matters of detail which the drafter thinks would be detrimental to the clarity of the main thrust of the instrument if they were interspersed among its principal provisions and therefore he or she places them at the end, rather than in the mainstream, of the instrument. However, the question of precisely which details should appear among the principal provisions and which should be relegated to a schedule, is a matter of professional judgement for the drafter as 'a mere question of drafting . . . The schedule is as much a part of the statute . . . as any other part'.[7]

The fact that provisions may be analysed into two categories in this way should not be allowed to distract attention from one of the most basic rules of structure, namely the desirability of uniformity between instruments of the same type.

The Value of Uniformity

Until the creation of the office of the Parliamentary Counsel to the Treasury in 1869, each government department was responsible for drafting its own Bills. That office was created in order to promote a degree of uniformity in the drafting of government legislation and Henry Thring (who was knighted in 1873 and created Baron Thring in 1886) was its first incumbent. (The title of the office remained unchanged until 1969, when some of the Treasury's functions—including those of the office of the Parliamentary Counsel—were transferred to the newly-created Civil Service Department and the final three words of the office's title were dropped. On the demise of the Civil Service Department in 1980, the office was—and remains—attached to the Cabinet Office.)

Thring's view was that 'uniformity in Acts of Parliament is of so much consequence that it is most desirable that some general rule of arrangement should wherever possible be adopted'.[8] Once something is identified as being desirable, the legal mind is immediately tempted to try to formulate a rule (or set of rules) which will ensure that the desired objective will be achieved in

[7] Brett LJ, *Attorney-General v Lamplough* (1878) 3 ExD 214, 229.

[8] Thring, *Practical Legislation* 2nd edn (London, John Murray, 1902) 41.

practice. However, it is a commonplace experience that rules of this sort run two risks.

The first risk is that they will be formulated at such a high level of generality that they will fail to be genuinely useful. Alternatively, they risk being formulated in such prescriptive terms that they become Procrustean beds that can accommodate the variety of material which they are supposed to make uniform only at the unattractive cost of distortion or mutilation (or an even less attractive combination of both). Although Thring errs on the side of yielding to the prescriptive temptation by formulating five rules, it is only fair to note that he tries to mitigate the danger inherent in doing so by readily acknowledging that they should be adopted only 'wherever possible'. More particularly, he acknowledges that his rules 'not only admit of considerable variation but sometimes require it: they will, however, serve as a guide to the draftsman in ordinary cases'.[9] Nevertheless, he defends their utility on the ground that 'any rule in so complicated a matter as legislation affords assistance to the draftsman, although it admits only of partial application'.[10]

It is interesting to note that Thring's insistence on the non-bindingness of 'rules' relating to drafting is still reflected (in Westminster at least, although some other jurisdictions are more prescriptively minded) in the output of the Drafting Technique Group of the Office of the Parliamentary Counsel. The introduction to the Group's recommendations, which are published on the internet and are noted in this book where appropriate, expressly acknowledge[11] that 'there will be times when drafters consider that, in the circumstances of the case, it would be appropriate to depart from a recommended approach'.

Despite their age, Thring's rules remain sufficiently useful to justify closer consideration.

Thring's Five Rules

Introduction

It cannot be emphasised too strongly that Thring himself clearly regarded his 'rules' as being more in the nature of *guidelines*.

The Text of the Rules

Rule I Provisions declaring the law should be separated from, and take precedence of [*sic*], provisions relating to the administration of the law.[12]

[9] *Ibid*, 46.
[10] *Ibid*.
[11] www.parliamentary-counsel.gov.uk/, *drafting techniques* tab, 1.
[12] *Ibid*, 38.

Rule II The simpler proposition should precede the more complex and in an ascending scale of propositions the less [*sic*] should come before the greater.[13]

Rule III Principal provisions should be separated from subordinate provisions. The latter should be placed towards the end of the Act, while the former should occupy their proper position in the narrative of the occurrence to which they refer.[14]

Rule IV (a) Local or exceptional provisions, (b) temporary provisions, and (c) provisions relating to repeal of Acts should be separated from the other enactments, and placed by themselves under separate headings.[15]

Rule V Procedure and matters of detail should be set apart by themselves, and should not, except under very special circumstances, find any place in the body of the Act.[16]

The Essence of the Rules

It is clear that the single principle which underlies all five rules is simply that different types of provision should be dealt with separately. The essence of this principle can be stated in the form of the first two of the following propositions.

First, provisions setting out substantive law should be separated from those setting out administrative and procedural matters. Although Thring's commentary indicates that the substantive provisions should ordinarily come first, he does acknowledge that there are cases where 'the law would seem to be an emanation from the authority, rather than the authority an institution established for administering an antecedent law', so that, for example, 'the better mode would seem to be to create the coroner before laying down the law of the inquest'.[17] On the same basis, it was logical for the drafter of the Prison Act 1865 to establish prison authorities before stating the law governing the conduct of prisons.

Secondly, subordinate provisions containing a great deal of detail (such as definition sections) should be placed at the end of an Act. Furthermore, this should be taken to its logical conclusion in the cases of detailed administrative and procedural matters, which should either be placed in schedules or removed from the Act altogether and dealt with by subordinate legislation.

Thirdly, and more controversially, where a number of provisions deal with separate but related matters of substance, the simpler (or lesser) should precede the more complex (or greater). By way of example, Thring says that 'in an Act relating to offences against property, theft should precede theft with

[13] *Ibid*, 41.
[14] *Ibid*, 42.
[15] *Ibid*, 43.
[16] *Ibid*, 44.
[17] *Ibid*, 39.

violence, or robbery and so forth'.[18] Similarly, statutes dealing with schemes which are administered by both local and national authorities should place the local ones before the national ones. Among many modern examples of the application of this rule is the relationship between sections 9 and 10 of the Theft Act 1968. Section 9 defines the offence of burglary (which is punishable with imprisonment for up to ten years), while section 10 of the Act defines the offence of aggravated burglary (which is punishable with up to life imprisonment) as being burglary committed while the defendant has with him a firearm, an imitation forearm, any weapon or any explosive. (Even if the aggravated offence did not require proof of additional facts, Thring's rule might still suggest that the difference in the maximum penalties indicate that it should be placed after the simple offence.)

Thring's own recognition that his rules 'admit of considerable variation'[19] may be illustrated by sections 1–5 of the Public Order Act 1986, which contain a hierarchy constructed in the opposite direction. Section 1 of the Act defines the offence of riot, which it defines in terms of at least 12 people, acting together for a common purpose, to use (or threaten to use) unlawful violence such as would cause a person of reasonableness firmness present at the scene to fear for his or her personal safety. The maximum penalty is ten years' imprisonment. The Act then proceeds through a number of intermediate offences, before coming (in section 5) to certain specified kinds of conduct which are likely to cause harassment, alarm or distress to people who see or hear them. The maximum penalty is a fine not exceeding level 3 on the standard scale. (See page 156 for the standard scale of fines.)

The Placing of Subordinate Provisions in Practice

Historically, there has been no standard order for the subordinate components of Westminster statutes, but the Drafting Technique Group of the Office of the Parliamentary Counsel suggests the following running order for the appearance of subordinate provisions:[20]

- General provisions about offences (bodies corporate, unincorporated associations)
- Orders and regulations (including parliamentary procedure)
- Notices/service of documents
- Interpretation
- Amendments, transitional provisions and savings, repeals
- Financial provisions
- Crown application
- Extent
- Commencement

[18] *Ibid*, 41.
[19] See the text to n 9, above.
[20] www.parliamentary-counsel.gov.uk/, *drafting techniques* tab, p11.

- [Index]
- Short title

However, without wishing to detract from the basic point about the importance of uniformity, it must be conceded that the specific requirements of uniformity in the context of any particular type of instrument are largely arbitrary. For example, in some jurisdictions definition sections are placed at the beginning of Bills, while the usual Westminster convention is to place them towards the end. However, some Westminster statutes are drafted with the definitions of key terms in close proximity to the relevant principal provisions, while some others, which are substantial enough to be divided into Parts or Chapters, contain mini-definition sections in each Part or Chapter.

The Explanatory Notes to the Financial Services and Markets Act 2000 explain one way in which definitions can be handled in a long and complicated Act:

> Interpretation
>
> 22. There are many defined words and expressions in the Act.
>
> 23. Most of the definitions are for the purpose only of the section or Schedule in which they are used. So, for example, the three words defined in subsections (13), (14) and (15) of section 21 are defined only for the purposes of that section.
>
> 24. Where there is no indication that a definition is intended to apply to a group of provisions, a Part of the Act or the Act as a whole, it applies only for the purposes of the section or Schedule in which it appears.
>
> 25. Many of these single-provision definitions are just drafting devices to avoid clumsy repetition which would make an already long Act even longer. For example, in section 38 the word 'specified' is used on its own on five occasions. The definition in subsection (4) is there to save repeating the words 'in an exemption order' each time it is used.
>
> 26. Some of the words and expressions that are defined just for the purposes of the particular provision in which the definition occurs are used (and defined separately) in other provisions—where they may have a different meaning. For example 'consumers' is defined separately for the purposes of sections 5(3), 10(7), 14(5) and 138(7) (the definition in section 10(7) differing from the others).
>
> 27. The Act consists of a large number of separate Parts. Where a particular Part deals with a self-contained subject there may be a separate interpretation section within the Part (for example section 193, which deals with the interpretation of Part XIII).
>
> 28. For the Act as a whole, Part XXIX contains a group of nine sections which deal with expressions used in a number of provisions and other matters which bear on the interpretation of provisions of the Act.
>
> 29. The purpose of this glossary is to provide the reader with a guide to words or expressions which are defined generally and so liable to be met in provisions which do not themselves contain the definition.

The Explanatory Notes to this Act also contain a grid showing where particular terms are defined within the Act. Similar techniques could obviously be useful in explanatory guidance to other long and complicated instruments, whether legislative or regulatory in character.

The practice of putting the majority of definitions in a single definition section towards the end of an Act presents an interesting example of a possible conflict between the interests of users of Bills as political documents and the interests of users of Acts as legal instruments.

From the point of view of parliamentarians wishing to identify what a Bill is truly about, there is much to be said for beginning with the main substantive provisions, rather than beginning with a list of definitions which do not advance the reader's understanding of the Bill until the substantive provisions to which they relate have also been read. And when the Bill becomes an Act, lawyers and other skilled readers may safely be assumed to know where to look for definitions. On the other hand, in the case of a statute such as the Animal Boarding Establishments Act 1963, it is not until the definition section is reached that the reader discovers that 'animals' has the very limited meaning of 'any dog or cat'. In cases such as this, knowledge of the definition is necessary before anyone (including both parliamentarians and lawyers) can discover what the Bill or Act is truly about. (The question of whether many parliamentarians actually read Bills—rather than relying on the Explanatory Notes and briefings from their parties' business managers and interest groups—is beyond the scope of this book.)

The fact that the positioning of definitions can cause the interests of a Bill to conflict with the interests of the users of an Act, is the sort of thing that prompted the Renton Committee to recommend that

> in principle the interests of the ultimate users should always have priority over those of legislators: a Bill, which serves a merely temporary purpose, should always be regarded primarily as a future Act, and should be drafted and arranged in this way.[21]

The interests of uniformity do not end with structural matters, but include using words consistently. (See page 73.)

Layout

Introduction

Having discussed the structure of an instrument as a whole, the next stage is to consider its visual structure on the printed page (or the computer screen),

[21] 'The Preparation of Legislation: Report of a Committee Appointed by the Lord President of the Council' (Cmnd 6053, 1975) para 10.3.

since laying out the text in a way which improves its readability is an important aspect of effective communication.

Sentence Length

Most readers, including those with high levels of literacy, find it easier to assimilate several short sentences rather than one long one. In ordinary writing, the conventional wisdom is that something in the region of twenty words is the normally desirable maximum number of words in a single sentence. However, matters are a little more complicated in the context of drafting, where there is the possibility of breaking up the text of a substantial section into subsections, paragraphs and subparagraphs. The evidence of Sir John Fiennes (a former First Parliamentary Counsel) to the Renton Committee provides a useful overview:

> Shorter sentences are easier in themselves, and it would probably help overall to have them shorter, but of course you are then faced with having to find the relationship between that sentence and another sentence two sentences away, which, if you have it all in one sentence, is really done for you by the draftsman.[22]

Over a long period of time, there has been a very noticeable trend for Westminster legislation to be written in the form of shorter slabs of text and in many modern Acts there are few units of text exceeding four lines. Butt and Castle[23] refer to slabs of unbroken text which appear at each numbered or lettered point as 'sense-bites':

> Modern drafters are often exhorted to write short sentences. But a better exhortation would be: write short sense-bites. Blind adherence to a policy of short sentences is not always appropriate. For example, sentences that list a series of obligations or events are inevitably long.

Some people feel uneasy about using the phrase sense-bites because of its pejorative associations with sound-bites and political spin, but others accept it as a convenient label for a sensible idea. What matters more than labels, however, is that drafters should never lose sight of effective communication as their objective. In the words of the Renton Report:

> We think it would be unwise to lay down any general rule about drafting in short sentences, or to suggest that draftsmen should impose limits of length on themselves. We would, however, emphasise the desirability of reducing to a minimum the number of subordinate phrases having to be read before the grammatical subject of a sentence is reached or intervening between the subject and its attendant verb, at any rate where the sentence is not 'paragraphed' [*sc.* broken up into sub-units].[24]

[22] *Ibid*, para 11.9.

[23] P Butt and R Castle, *Modern Legal Drafting* 2nd edn (Cambridge, Cambridge University Press, 2006) 181.

[24] 'The Preparation of Legislation', above n 21 at para 11.10.

In other words, 'what counts is not the number of words in a sentence, but how easily we get from beginning to end while understanding everything in between'.[25]

Matters Requiring Particular Care and Attention

Using Words Consistently

Drafters should be careful to choose their words in the light of the presumption of interpretation that the same word is intended to have the same meaning throughout an instrument[26] and its corollary that different words are presumed to have different meanings.

Using the Active rather than the Passive

The active voice has the double advantage of being both shorter and, generally speaking, more direct in its meaning, than the passive:

- The form must be signed by the applicant personally.
- The applicant must sign the form personally.

While a saving of two words may seem trivial, in this sentence it is more than a fifth.

However, there are contexts in which the passive is more direct than the active and the increase in length is a price worth paying, as the following examples show:

- The application may be made by the Home Secretary, the Chief Constable, the Chief Crown Prosecutor, or the chief executive of the local authority.
- The Home Secretary, the Chief Constable, the Chief Crown Prosecutor, or the chief executive of the local authority may make the application.

In the first example, the passive verb comes towards the beginning of the sentence and, therefore, tells the reader what is happening (*an application is being made*) at an early stage. In the second example, the appearance of the active verb towards the end of the sentence delays the point at which the reader discovers what is actually happening.

In some cases the differential use of the active and the passive within a single instrument may serve to emphasise contrasting meanings. For example, in *Ghaidon v Godin-Mendoza*,[27] Lord Rodger discussed the use of the active and

[25] JM Williams, *Style: Toward Clarity and Grace* (Chicago, Chicago University Press, 1990) 25.
[26] *Courtauld v Legh* (1869) LR 4 Exch 126.
[27] *Ghaidon v Godin-Mendoza* [2004] UKHL 30, [2004] 2 AC 557.

passive in sections 3, 4 and 6 of the Human Rights Act 1998, which (so far as is relevant) are in the following terms:

> 3 Interpretation of legislation
>
> (1) So far as it is possible to do so, primary legislation and subordinate legislation must be read and given effect in a way which is compatible with the Convention rights.
>
> 4 Declaration of incompatibility
>
> (1) Subsection (2) applies in any proceedings in which a court determines whether a provision of primary legislation is compatible with a Convention right.
> (2) If the court is satisfied that the provision is incompatible with a Convention right, it may make a declaration of that incompatibility.
>
> 6 Acts of public authorities
>
> (1) It is unlawful for a public authority to act in a way which is incompatible with a Convention right.

Lord Rodger said:

> [106] Inevitably, when s 3 comes to be considered by a court, the focus is on the approach which s 3(1) requires the court to adopt when reading a statutory provision that, on a conventional interpretation, would be incompatible with a convention right. Nevertheless, the section is not aimed exclusively, or indeed mainly, at the courts. In contrast to s 4—which applies in terms only to 'a court' of the level of the High Court or above—and in contrast also to s 6—which applies only to public authorities—s 3 is carefully drafted in the passive voice to avoid specifying, and so limiting, the class of persons who are to read and give effect to the legislation in accordance with it. Parliament thereby indicates that the section is of general application. It applies, of course, to the courts, but it applies also to everyone else who may have to interpret and give effect to legislation. The most obvious examples are public authorities such as organs of central and local government, but the section is not confined to them.

A formula which illustrates one of the most obvious—and common—examples of a provision in which the identity of the subject of the action is irrelevant and in which, therefore, the passive is entirely appropriate, is: This Act may be cited as the Legislative Drafting Act 20XX.

Drafting Positively

As a general proposition, provisions which are drafted positively are more immediately understandable (because they are more direct) than provisions which are drafted negatively. For example:

> a man who [satisfies certain stated conditions] is entitled to [a particular welfare benefit]

is more direct than

> a man is not entitled to [a particular welfare benefit] unless he [satisfies certain stated conditions].

By way of an exception to the general desirability of drafting positively, prohibitions are often more naturally (and therefore better) expressed negatively:

> a member of a local authority cannot be employed by that local authority.

Constructing Legislative Sentences

Introduction

Although legislative sentences vary in grammatical structure according to their subject-matter, one very common form specifies a consequence which flows from a specified circumstance. The range of possible circumstances is too extensive for any useful comment to be made about it, but typical consequences include imposing a penalty, conferring a power and imposing a duty.

Coode asserted that any legislative sentence consists of a case (or cases); a condition (or conditions); a legal subject; and a legal action. He also asserted that this is the appropriate order in which they should appear within a sentence.[28] Applying this in a modern and hypothetical example produces:

- (case) where a taxpayer is in arrears with council tax;
- (condition) and the local authority brings proceedings against him;
- (legal subject) a magistrates' court;
- (legal action) may commit the taxpayer to prison.

Although legislative sentences constructed according to this formula are not uncommon they do depart from one of the basic tenets of plain language drafting, namely that ordinary sentence structures should normally be used. Coode's prescription should, therefore, be followed with caution (if at all).

Following Conventional Sentence Structure

Since the natural word order in English is subject-verb-object, sentences that follow this pattern are more readily understandable than those that do not do so. For example, both the following provisions mean exactly the same thing, but the second is plainly more easily understandable than the first:

- When a local planning authority has received an application for planning permission, it must determine that application within eight weeks of the date on which the application as received.
- A local planning authority must determine applications for planning permission within eight weeks of receiving them.

[28] G Coode, *On Legislative Expression or the Language of the Written Law* (London, William Benning & Co, 1845).

Gender-neutral Drafting

Introduction

Since grammatical gender has no place in the English language, it is often possible to write in an entirely gender-neutral way. However, any communication dealing with people is likely to be expressed in gender-specific terms. This led to the introduction of a presumption that words importing the masculine include the feminine,[29] which, in its current form, has been extended so that words importing the feminine are presumed to include the masculine.[30] However, substance and style may be two very different things; and, as a matter of style, modern sensibilities in relation to sexual equality are not easily satisfied by reliance on a presumption of interpretation. Thus, many jurisdictions (including the United Kingdom since the beginning of the parliamentary year 2007–08) practise explicitly gender-neutral expression.

Some Drafting Techniques

In many situations, gender-specific expression can be avoided by minor redrafting, in the form of omitting pronouns, using the plural, or combining masculine and feminine forms. Beginning with a provision in the traditional form of:

> The minister may exercise his powers if [so-and-so],

it is a simple matter to avoid a gender-specific pronoun by repeating a noun:

> The minister may exercise the minister's powers if [so-and-so].

Although the redraft is gender-neutral, it is open to the objection of inelegance and (since nobody normally speaks or writes in this way) it also fails to conform to the ideals of plain language drafting. In some simple sentences, the force of these objections can be reduced, with minimal inelegance and deviation from ordinary English usage, by omitting the pronoun without substituting anything. This technique turns

> The chief executive may resign his office,

into:

> The chief executive may resign office.

In more complicated sentences, pronouns may be omitted if letters are used to represent people:

[29] Interpretation Act 1850, s 4.

[30] *Ibid*, s 6(a) and (b).

> Conduct by a person (A) which would otherwise be an offence under this section against another person (B) is not an offence if A gave B advance warning of A's intentions and B did not object to A's proposed conduct.

Turning to the use of plurals, the standard practice is to draft in the singular and rely on the presumption that the singular includes the plural.[31] However, using the plural does provide a possible alternative technique for avoiding gender-specific expression. For example:

> Students will receive their results within three weeks after the end of the examination period.

Another alternative technique would produce, for example:

> A student will receive their results within three weeks after the end of the examination period.

Many readers consider this combination of a singular noun and a plural pronoun to be unacceptably ungrammatical (although very few people would object to the equally ungrammatical combination of singular pronoun and a plural verb which produces something like the second part of *I am writing this book, aren't I?*). Many drafters, therefore, prefer to avoid it. However, Burchfield describes the issue as being 'unresolved', before saying that the usage 'is now passing unnoticed by standard speakers (except those trained in traditional grammar) and is being left unaltered by copy editors.[32]

Finally, one of the obvious ways to avoid gender-specific drafting is to combine masculine and feminine forms, thus producing *he or she* (or *she or he*), coupled with *his or her* (or *her or his*) as appropriate. However, many people consider this solution to be unduly cumbersome, as well as being not entirely gender-neutral, since one of the pronouns must come first. (Alternating *he or she* and *she or he* is a possibility, but maintaining this alternation as new provisions are inserted into, or existing provisions are deleted from, a draft may be an unattractive addition to the drafter's burdens, as well as creating the problem of which form should come first.)

A final possibility is drafting in terms of *s/he*, but this formulation has at least three disadvantages compared with *he or she* and *she or he*.

First, it is unpronounceable, other than in the intrinsically meaningless form of *ess stroke he* (which itself leaves the masculine form as the only one which is recognisable, thus revealing the whole expression as being not quite gender-neutral).

Secondly, it leaves no choice as to whether the masculine or the feminine is placed first.

[31] *Ibid*, s 6(c)

[32] RW Burchfield, *Fowler's Modern English Usage* 3rd edn revised (Oxford, Oxford University Press, 2004) being a re-issue of *The New Fowler's Modern English Usage* 3rd edn with a title change (1998) 776.

Thirdly, it has no associated forms corresponding to *his or her* (or *her or his*).

A possible fourth objection that it is grossly inelegant is, of course, no more than a matter of taste.

Any technique which combines masculine and feminine terminology must deal with the difficulty of non-human actors, such as companies and local authorities, which are naturally neither male not female. Where *he or she* (or *she or he*) is the preferred technique (together with the appropriate possessives), it is possible to amend the formula to *he, she or it* (or *she, he or it*) (together with the appropriate possessives). Similarly, *s/he* can be extended to *s/he or it*. If this solution is thought to be unacceptably inelegant, a more traditional drafting technique would require any Bill in which this problem arises to include a provision along the lines of:

> In this Act *he or she* and *his or her* [or, as the case may be, *she or he* and *her or his*, or *s/he*] apply to unincorporated associations and offices, and bodies corporate, as they apply to natural persons.

Any jurisdiction adopting this kind of solution could usefully consider an appropriate amendment to its Interpretation Act, to remove the need for endless re-enactment of the standard formula.

Of course, provisions relating to only non-human actors (such as companies) cause no problems and *it* is the obvious pronoun.

Being Careful with Modifiers

Modifiers are words, phrases or clauses which modify the meanings of other words, phrases or clauses. They are a potent source of difficulty. Beginning with a non-legal example, where the author of a book is described as *formerly a Professor of Law at the University of Christminster and a Circuit Judge*, does this mean that the author is no longer either a professor or a judge, or that, having been a professor he or she is now a judge?

Turning to a phrase more likely to be found in legislative drafting, consider a provision which applies to *buildings of architectural and historic importance*. In a specific case, does this apply only to a building which possesses both kinds of importance, or does it also apply to a building of architectural (but not historic) importance and to a building of historic (but not architectural) importance? Clarification in favour of the first meaning could be achieved by re-drafting as *buildings which are both architecturally and historically important*, while clarification in favour of the second meaning could be achieved by re-drafting as *buildings which are either architecturally or historically important*. An inexperienced drafter may be tempted to add *or both* at the end of the second piece of re-drafting. However, this would be superfluous because it would be absurd to conclude that the presence of either one of two qualifications is enough but the presence of both is not.

Using Past, Present and Future Tenses

The presumption that statutes are 'always speaking' (see page 30) makes it natural to draft in the present tense unless the context otherwise requires. The following examples illustrate both the general proposition and two situations where the context does require a past or future tense:

- The powers of a local authority include [so-and-so].
- As soon as a local authority becomes aware that it has exceeded its budget for the current year [it must do so-and-so].
- As soon as a local authority becomes aware that it will exceed its budget for the current year [it must do so-and-so].

(The meaning of *shall* to create powers and duties, when it is used in a non-temporal sense, is discussed in chapter six.)

Using *And*, *Or* and *And/Or*

As a matter of semantics, *and* is usually said to be *conjunctive* (or *additive*, *cumulative* or *inclusive*) while *or* is usually said to be disjunctive (or *alternative* or *exclusive*). So a child who is told that he or she can have X *and* Y for Christmas can reasonably expect to receive both, but a child who is told that he or she can have X *or* Y can reasonably expect to receive only one. However, ordinary usage can be more fluid that this distinction suggests.

For example, a sign on a bus stating that certain seats are *reserved for elderly and disabled passengers* would normally be taken to mean that passengers who are either elderly *or* disabled, as well as those who are both elderly *and* disabled, may use those seats. (A drafter who feels uneasy about relying on this commonsense approach could easily if unnecessarily re-draft in terms of *passengers who are either elderly or disabled or both*.)

On the other hand, a poster in the window of a café saying *Fish and Chips £5* would normally be taken to mean that £5 buys a meal consisting of both fish *and* chips. (It is, of course, true that the first example could also—or alternatively?—have been included under the heading of 'Being Careful with Modifiers' (see page 78); but this merely illustrates the danger of thinking about drafting technique in a strictly compartmentalised way.)

The Drafting Technique Group of the Office of the Parliamentary Counsel[33] recommends that, when drafting a list, members of the Office should start from the assumption that *or* is inclusive, so that (to take the Group's example) 'a power to impose conditions relating to cats, dogs or rabbits would normally allow conditions relating to one or more of these'.

[33] www.parliamentary-counsel.gov.uk/, *drafting techniques* tab, 7.

The use of *and/or* in legislative drafting has few supporters, although in *Federal Steam Navigation Co Ltd v Department of Trade and Industry*,[34] Lord Diplock did speak of the need to be careful 'in the use of *or* and *and* or even if I dare to say so *and/or*'. More typically disapproving, however, was Lord Simon LC's reference to 'the bastard conjunction *and/or*'.[35]

Is a Body Corporate Singular or Plural?

The idea that a body corporate takes a verb in the singular fits perfectly well with the doctrine in *Salomon v Salomon*[36] that a body corporate has a separate identity which is distinct from the individual identities of its members. It is not surprising, therefore, that using singular verbs when drafting provisions relating to bodies corporate is very common indeed. However, Westminster legislation is less than consistent in this respect, with some local government Acts using a plural verb where the subject of the sentence is a local authority. The Drafting Technique Group of the Office of the Parliamentary Counsel recommends[37] the use of a singular verb in all cases, except where a textual amendment requires the use of the plural in order to maintain the internal consistency of an instrument. (An old proposition that a body with a common seal is singular while one without a common seal is plural has nothing to commend it, since parish councils divide between those which have commons seals and those which execute documents through two of their members or officers.)

Avoiding Nominalisations

Nominalisations are abstract nouns formed from verbs. They are best avoided wherever possible because their status as nouns, combined with their abstract nature, means that they describe undynamic unreality, which (even if only subconsciously) engages its readers less than a sentence which describes real people and bodies doing things. For example, the first of the following examples includes a nominalisation, while the second does not (and also has the benefit of brevity):

- The board had a meeting on Friday.
- The board met on Friday.

[34] *Federal Steam Navigation Co Ltd v Department of Trade and Industry* [1974] 1 WLR 505, 523.

[35] *Bonitto v Fuerst Brothers & Co Ltd* [1944] AC 75, 82.

[36] *Salomon v Salomon* [1897] AC 22.

[37] www.parliamentary-counsel.gov.uk/, *drafting techniques* tab, 2.

Using Ordinary Words

Introduction

Some drafters are trained to believe in something they like to call 'drafting language'. The practical consequence of this belief is that they are reluctant to use ordinary words where their predecessors (and perhaps their current senior colleagues) have established a practice of using conventional alternatives. However, the reality is that drafting seldom, if ever, requires the use of anything other than ordinary language, except where technically complex subject-matter requires the use of its own vocabulary.

The following list headed *Avoid* contains many words and phrases which have traditionally been used by drafters who seem to imagine that they contain some quasi-magical power, while the list headed *Use* suggests some alternatives.[38]

Avoid:	**Use:**
null and void	void
accorded	given
adequate number of	enough
admit of	allow
afforded (*for example, an opportunity*)	given
aggregate	total (except in the context of gravel)
among and between	among (*if more than two*); between (*if two*)
approximately	about
at the place where	where
attempt (*as a verb*)	try
by means of	by
category	kind, class *or* group
cease	stop
conceal	hide
consequence	result
deem	consider *or* decide (depending on the context)
donate	give
during such time as	while
during the course of	during
endeavour (*as a verb*)	try

[38] These lists owe much to the 'Legislative Drafting Manuals' of Maryland and Massachusetts.

enter into a contract with	contract with
evince	show
except that	but
excessive number of	too many
expiration	end
feasible	possible
for the duration of	during (*or* while)
for the reason that	because
forthwith	immediately
frequently	often
herein	in this Act (or section, or paragraph, etc)
in accordance with	under
in the event that	if
initiate	begin *or* start
institute (*as a verb*)	begin *or* start
is able to	can
is applicable	applies
is binding upon	binds
is entitled (*in the sense of* has the name)	is called
is unable to	cannot
it is the duty of X	X must
manner	way
modify	change
obtain	get
occasion (*as a verb*)	cause
or, in the alternative	or
per annum	per year
per centum	per cent
portion	part (except in the context of an interest under a strict settlement of land)
preserve	keep
prior *or* prior to	before *or* earlier (according to the sense)
procure	obtain (*or* get)
purchase (*as a verb*)	buy (except in the context of land law where the technical meaning is required)
pursuant to (for example, *a statute*)	under (for example, a statute)

remainder	rest (except in the context of land law where the technical meaning is required)
render (*in the sense of* give)	give
use one's best endeavours	do one's best
without prejudice to the generality of	but

Using Plain Language Guides

Opponents of plain language drafting sometimes argue that the interests of public accessibility can be served by providing plain language guides alongside instruments which are drafted in the traditional style. In relation to Acts of Parliament, the accompanying explanatory notes already serve this purpose to a significant extent. However, they have the inescapable—and serious—limitation that, while the texts of Bills evolve as they are amended during their passage through Parliament, they cannot continue to evolve after they have been enacted. It follows that they can become seriously misleading in the light of subsequent judicial interpretation or amending legislation.

Guidance issued by the appropriate government department in order to explain the effect of legislation is commonplace and does have the advantage that it can evolve over time. The Department for Business, Enterprise and Regulatory Reform's 'Code of Practice on Guidance on Regulation' sets out what it calls 'the golden rules which the government will follow when providing guidance on legislation having a significant impact on business and third sector [sc. charitable and not-for-profit] organisations'. However, the authors of similar guidance on either legislation relating to any field of activity or regulations made by regulation-making bodies, will find that many of the ideas embodied in the Code are transferable. (See appendix three for the text of the Code.)

Provisos

In everyday usage, *provided* (or *provided that* or *providing*) generally means *if*: I shall go to the theatre tonight *provided that/provided/providing/if* I finish writing this chapter in time.

Legal usage, on the other hand, differs in two respects. First, only the *provided that* form is normally encountered. Secondly, it is used with a far wider range of meanings, including, according to Driedger,[39] *and, or, but, except that, nevertheless, moreover* and *furthermore*. Driedger also describes it as 'an all-purpose conjunction, invented by lawyers but not known to or understood by grammarians'.[40] Perhaps fortunately, provisos are very much out of

[39] EA Driedger, *The Composition of Legislation* 2nd edn revised (Ottawa, Department of Justice, 1976) 96.

[40] *Ibid.*

fashion and the general hope of commentators on drafting is that they should remain so.

Nothing can be achieved by a proviso that cannot be achieved more directly by changing either the wording or the structure, or both. The following example may be instructive:

> A former employee's pension is calculated by multiplying one eightieth of his or her final annual salary by his or her number of years of service; provided that no employee's pension can exceed half his or her final annual salary.

In this context, *provided that* simply means *but* or *except that* and there is no reason why the provision should not be drafted in that way. Alternatively, the provision could be re-structured as:

> (1) Subject to subsection (2), a former employee's pension is calculated by
>
> multiplying one eightieth of his or her final annual salary by his or her number of years of service.
>
> (2) But no employee's pension can exceed half his or her final annual salary.

Some drafters might argue that the relationship between these two subsections is made clear by using only *subject to subsection (2)* or *but*, and that using both is an example of the kind of repetition which modern drafters shun. On the other hand, some drafters might feel that *subject to subsection (2)* signals the existence of an exception or qualification, which may be particularly useful where either or both provisions are longer or more complicated than those in this example.

Finally, drafters who prefer traditional forms of words may derive reassurance from the fact there is nothing distinctively modern about introducing an exception with *but*, rather than using a proviso. Section 1 of the Partnership Act 1890 states:

> (1) Partnership is the relation which subsists between persons carrying on a business in common with a view of profit.
>
> (2) But the relation between members of any company or association which is
>
> (a) . . .; or
>
> (b) . . .;
>
> is not a partnership within the meaning of this Act.

Ranges of Items

When drafting a provision which contains a range of items, such as ages, dates and distances, it is important to leave no doubt as to the starting and finishing point of the range. The specific examples taken here all relate to ages, but essentially the same principles apply to any other ranges.

Many people would read the phrase *between December and March* as indicating a period which begins with 1 December and ends with 31 March.

However, anyone who combines attention to detail with a more literal turn of mind, could argue that the months which come between December and March are January and February; and that, therefore, the drafter must have meant this two month period. The same point of language arises where a provision says *between 1 December and 31 March*, on the basis that this could exclude both 1 December and 31 March. (And, of course, reading *between 30 November and 1 December* in this way produces nonsense.)

The obvious plain language solution to the problem represented by *between 1 December and 31 March* is simply to add the word *inclusive* after the word *March*. However, drafters who are resistant to the charms of plain language may prefer the approach which Reed Dickerson advocated before the plain language movement had become established.[41] Dickerson's approach to the example of *December to March* would define the period as being 'after 30 November and before 1 April'. Another example of the need to give very careful attention to precisely what is intended arises where drafting instructions require a provision to apply to anyone who is (say) 'more than 17 years old'. As Dickerson puts it, this phrase 'is ambiguous because it is not clear whether a person becomes more than 17 on the day after his 17th birthday or on his 18th birthday', but drafting in terms of anyone 'who has passed his 17th birthday' or 'who has reached his 18th birthday' improves the clarity of the provision.[42]

When stating ages, dates or measurements which adjoin each other in order to create two categories, care should be taken to ensure that everything falls within one of the categories, with no possibility of anything falling into the *undistributed middle*. For example, if a welfare benefit is payable to 'a person born *before* 1 January 1950' but not to 'a person born *after* 1 January 1950', what is the position of people born *on* 1 January 1950? If the intention is that these people should be excluded, the simplest solution is to draft the second category as 'a person born on or after 1 January 1950.'

Punctuation

Introduction

There are many classic illustrations of the power of punctuation to affect the meaning of a text. One frequently quoted example of the extent to which punctuation can create different meanings from the same words begins with an unpunctuated statement:

> woman without her man is nothing

[41] R Dickerson, *Fundamentals of Legal Drafting* (Boston and Toronto, Little, Brown & Co, 1965) 93–95.
[42] *Ibid*, 95.

before proceeding to the following variations:

> woman, without her man, is nothing

and

> woman: without her, man is nothing.

For further classic illustrations of punctuation as the linguistic equivalent of the philosopher's stone, consider the following examples:

> The condemned man walked round the yard three minutes after he was hanged.

What this means is, of course:

> The condemned man walked round the yard: three minutes after, he was hanged.

And the truly mind boggling:

> Janet where John had had had had had had had had had had had the examiners approval.

Once this is understood to be a comment on an English language exercise, it becomes relatively easy to punctuate:

> Janet, where John had had 'had had', had had 'had'; 'had had' had had the examiner's approval.

The semicolon in the middle of this sentence could, without error, be replaced with a colon, while moving the apostrophe in *examiner's* one place to the right would, of course, be correct if there was more than one examiner. Nevertheless, the essential point of the example remains.

The following rhyme provides another classic example which, though non-legal, has been cited judicially.[43] When punctuated badly, it reads as follows:

> Every lady in this land
> Hath twenty nails upon each hand:
> Five and twenty on hands and feet;
> And this is true without deceit.

But re-punctuation can conjure sense out of nonsense thus:

> Every lady in this land
> Hath twenty nails; upon each hand
> Five, and twenty on hands on feet;
> And this is true without deceit.

Turning to specifically legislative texts, in *Inland Revenue Commissioners v Hinchy*,[44] Lord Reid said that before 1850 the manuscript copy of a Bill, in the form in which it received the Royal Assent, did not contain any punctuation and the punctuation which subsequently appeared in the Queen's

[43] Megarry V-C in *Marshall v Cottingham* [1982] 2 Ch 82.
[44] *Inland Revenue Commissioners v Hinchy* [1960] AC 748.

Printer's copy was inserted by the printer without authority. However, this is plainly wrong,[45] and even if it were an accurate statement of historical fact, there can be no doubt that punctuation is now a fact of legislative drafting and is used by the courts when interpreting statutes. Lord Lowry succinctly expressed the modern judicial approach to the status of punctuation in legislation thus:

> I consider that not to take account of punctuation disregards the reality that literate people, such as parliamentary draftsmen, punctuate what they write, if not identically, at least in accordance with grammatical principles. Why should not other literate people, such as judges, look at the punctuation in order to interpret the meaning of the legislation as accepted by Parliament?[46]

Clearly, therefore, drafters must understand the principles of punctuation, but they should not lose sight of the fact that meaning depends primarily on the choice and arrangement of words. As Jonathan Swift has it,

> when a man's thoughts are clear, the properest words will generally offer themselves first, and his own judgment will direct him in what order to place them so as they may be best understood.[47]

Or, as Bennion puts it, 'punctuation is a device not for making meaning, but for making meaning plain'.[48]

Despite the fact that, historically, Bills were read aloud three times as they progressed through Parliament (a long-dead practice whose ghost still walks in the phrases *first reading*, *second reading* and *third reading*), drafters should punctuate for meaning rather than as a substitute for stage directions as to how a text should read aloud: 'punctuation is an aid to understanding, not to respiration'.[49]

Round Brackets (or Parentheses) and Square Brackets (or Brackets Properly So-called)

Words within round brackets (parentheses) are an aside or explanation that can be omitted without affecting the meaning of what is being said. So, taking a legislative example in addition to that contained in both the previous sentence itself and the heading to this section of text, the drafter might say:

> The local authorities specified in section 2 (all of which are the proprietors of airports) must [do so-and-so].

The statement that the specified local authorities are all the proprietors of airports adds nothing to the legal effect of the text; but readers who are unaware

[45] See, eg, *R v Casement* [1917] 1 KB 98, decided on the Treason Act 1351.

[46] *Hanlon v Law Society* [1981] AC 124, 198.

[47] J Swift, *Letter to a Young Gentleman Lately Entered into Holy Orders* (1721).

[48] F Bennion, *Bennion on Statutory Interpretation* 5th edn (London, LexisNexis Butterworths, 2008) 751.

[49] Trask, *Penguin Guide to Punctuation* (London, Penguin Books, 1997) 45.

of this aspect of the specified local authorities' activities may find the statement speeds their understanding of the provision's purpose, especially if the cross-reference is to a provision which is some distance away.

Square brackets (or brackets properly so-called) contain insertions and are seldom used in legislative and regulatory drafting except where new sections are being inserted into existing instruments. On the other hand, in unofficial publications (such as *Halsbury's Statutes of England*) where legislation is printed as subsequently amended, square brackets are often used to differentiate between amendments and the original text.

Apostrophes

Apostrophes are used either to indicate a possessive or a contraction. Since conventional wisdom dictates that contractions such as *isn't*, *can't* and *won't* are too casual to be used in so formal a context as legislation, it follows that drafters should use apostrophes only to denote possessives (as, for example, in *the Crown Court's jurisdiction*).

Commas

Commas are used to separate items in lists and to separate modifying phrases and clauses from main clauses. They may be used, together with conjunctions, to separate co-ordinate clauses.

The use of commas to separate items in lists may be illustrated by:

> building, mining, engineering or other operations, in, on, over or under land.

Since the comma after each item is itself a substitute for the word *or*, there is no need for one before the *or* which precedes the final item in a list (or, in the example given above, the final item in each sub-list). The same logic applies to lists of items which are to be read cumulatively, so that the comma after each item is a substitute for *and*, which avoids the need for one before the final *and*.

The generally accepted principles of punctuation allow for a little more variation when commas are used to separate modifying phrases and clauses from main clauses. Where a sentence consists of an introductory modifying phrase or clause followed by a main clause, separating the two with a comma will never be wrong but may be superfluous. A sentence containing a long introductory phrase or clause will often yield its meaning more easily with a comma:

> For the purpose of providing applicants with an understanding of the legal basis on which the decisions in their cases have been reached, the Council must give reasons for its decisions.

But where the modifying phrase or clause is short, the comma may reasonably be omitted:

For the purposes of this Act 'dwelling' does not include a tent.

Unfortunately, it is difficult to maintain consistency in the distinction between long and short modifying phrases and clauses, because it makes the insertion or omission of a comma depend on the drafter's judgment as to how long is long and how short is short. There is, therefore, something to be said for using a comma in all cases.

A comma on its own is never sufficient to separate co-ordinate clauses, although a comma followed by *and*, *or*, *but*, *yet* or *while* may be used. However, even where there is no need for a comma, using one does no harm. For example, in the following sentence the comma is unnecessary because the two clauses are obviously separate, but its inclusion neither obscures or confuses the meaning:

This Act may be cited as the Legislative Drafting Act 20XX, and comes into force on 1 January 20XX.

However, in the following sentence, there is a greater degree of similarity between the content of both co-ordinate clauses, which means that the insertion of a comma makes for easier—and, therefore, speedier—understanding, even though it is not essential in terms of meaning:

The chief executive is responsible to the Council for the implementation of the Council's policy, and the chief officers of each department are responsible to the chief executive.

Finally, the question of when commas should be used to enclose modifying phrases and clauses is best discussed in the context of that topic, rather than in the context of commas generally.

Restrictive and Non-restrictive Phrases and Clauses

Whether a phrase or clause is restrictive or non-restrictive depends on whether it restricts the meaning of another element of the sentence. For example, the italicised phrase in the following sentence is restrictive because it restricts the meaning of the rest of the sentence:

A local authority which may, *with the consent of the Secretary of State*, make an order.

On the other hand, the italicised words in the following sentence do not restrict the meaning of the rest of the sentence, and therefore they are non-restrictive:

The Local Government Act 20XX *which is referred to in this Act as the principal Act* applies to joint boards as it applies to local authorities.

Although the meaning of each of these examples happens to be clear without any punctuation, enclosing the italicised words in the second example within a pair of commas would serve the same purpose as putting them in parenthesis (by taking them out of the mainstream of the sentence):

> The Local Government Act 20XX, which is referred to in this Act as 'the principal Act', applies to joint boards as it applies to local authorities.

Some writers insist on beginning restrictive clauses with the word *that* and non-restrictive clauses with the word *which*, but whether they deserve to be described as *careful users of language*, or *traditionalists* or *pedants* is a matter for debate. However, two things are clear.

First, the maintenance of a rigorous distinction between *that* and *which* in this context is by no means universal in spoken, or even in educated written, English.

Secondly, there used to be a convention that where a natural person was the subject of the reference, the appropriate relative pronoun was *who*, whether the context was restrictive or non-restrictive. However, certain spell-check programs have seriously undermined this convention in recent years by mechanistically suggesting the substitution of *that* for *who*. As a result of this development, the use of *who* as a relative pronoun may well come to be seen as self-conscious traditionalism bordering on idiosyncrasy.

Enacting Formulas, Titles and Preambles

Introduction

Every statute contains an enacting formula and has both a short title and a long title. The short title is *created* towards the end of the statute, although it *appears* as the first line of the statute as printed, where it is followed by the long title, together with the date of the Royal Assent (in square brackets), and the enacting formula. The following example is typical.

> Human Rights Act 1998
>
> An Act to give further effect to rights and freedoms guaranteed under the European Convention on Human Rights; to make provision with respect to holders of certain judicial offices who become judges of the European Court of Human Rights; and for connected purposes.
>
> [9th November 1998]
>
> Be it enacted by the Queen's most Excellent Majesty, by and with the advice and consent of the Lords Spiritual and Temporal, and Commons, in this present Parliament assembled, and by the authority of the same, as follows:
>
> Although a short title always contains a year, it cannot be treated as a reliable indication of when an Act comes into force. (See page 94 for the commencement of statutes.)

Enacting Formulas

In many jurisdictions, very little attention need be given to the enacting formula, since it will be absolutely standard in all cases. However, some jurisdictions may use different formulas for different types of legislation. The Westminster practice is to use a standard formula (as shown above) in practically all cases, but with variations being used for Bills certified by the Speaker of the House of Commons as being Money Bills and Bills passed under the provisions of the Parliament Acts 1911 and 1949 (which ensure the primacy of the Commons over the Lords).

Historically, enacting words preceded every section of every Act, but the modern practice is for the formula to appear only once. (See section 1, Interpretation Act 1978, deriving from section 8, Interpretation Act 1889, which provides: 'Every section of an Act takes effect as a substantive enactment without introductory words'.)

Titles and Preambles

Essentially, a short title (for example, the Human Rights Act 1998) is a label which exists in order to provide a convenient way of identifying a statute; or, in Lord Moulton's phrase, it is 'a statutory nickname . . . [the object of which] . . . is identification and not description'.[50]

The long title, which was 'formerly and more correctly called the title'[51] simply appears on the face of the statute, without being created by any words of enactment. It is intended, within the space of a few lines at most, to provide a general indication of the scope of the statute. It commonly ends with a form of words to cover provisions which are incidental to those which are specified, with the words 'and for connected purposes' (which conclude the long title of the Human Rights Act 1998) being typical.

The main reason for including the final four words (or some other formula to the same effect) derives from the principle of parliamentary procedure which requires that everything in a Bill must be covered by the long title. Quite apart from its effect on the Bill as originally drafted, this principle affects the scope of possible amendments to the Bill as it progresses through Parliament.

A long title is not the same as a preamble. Where the function of a long title is descriptive, the function of a preamble is explanatory and justificatory. Preambles are very seldom used in modern statutes, except for private ones (where it is necessary to justify parliamentary intervention in what is, by definition, an essentially private matter) and public ones which implement treaty obligations (where the purpose of the treaty will be recited). In other words, preambles to statutes are very closely related to recitals in deeds.

[50] *Vacher & Sons v London Society of Compositors* [1913] AC 107, 128–29.
[51] *Bennion on Statutory Interpretation*, above n 48 at 727.

The use of titles and preambles as aids to interpretation is discussed in chapter two.

Amending Provisions

Introduction

Provisions which amend provisions in earlier instruments may do so either textually or non-textually.

Textual Amendment

Textual amendment either inserts words into, or deletes words from, or both inserts words into and deletes words from, an original provision. For example, if section 1 of the Knives (Control of Sale) Act 20XX provides:

> The sale of flick-knives and lock-knives is prohibited.

all the following would be textual amendments:

> In s 1 of the Knives (Control of Sale) Act 20XX, the words 'and lock-knives' are repealed.
>
> In s 1 of the Knives (Control of Sale) Act 20XX, ', stilettos' is inserted after 'flick-knives'.
>
> In s 1 of the Knives (Control of Sale) Act 20XX, the word 'and' is repealed and replaced by a comma, and 'and such other knives as the Secretary of State may by order prescribe' is inserted after 'lock-knives'.

Non-textual Amendment

Non-textual amendments producing the same effects would read:

> Section 1 of the Knives (Control of Sale) Act 20XX applies only to flick-knives.
>
> Section 1 of the Knives (Control of Sale) Act 20XX also applies to stilettos.
>
> Section 1 of the Knives (Control of Sale) Act 20XX also applies to such other knives as the Secretary of State may by order prescribe.

The Drafting Technique Group of the Office of the Parliamentary Counsel recommends[52] non-textual techniques. The Group illustrates this by contrasting the following (non-preferred) textual example:

> (1) Section 3 applies to fine defaulters as to offenders but with the following modifications—
>
> (a) in subsection (1) for 'offence' substitute 'default'; and
> (b) in subsection (2) for '6 months' substitute '3 months',

[52] www.parliamentary-counsel.gov.uk/, *drafting techniques* tab, 6.

with the following (preferred) non-textual example:

(1) Section 3 applies to fine defaulters as to offenders but as if

(a) in subsection (1) the reference to an offence were to a default; and
(b) in subsection (2) the reference to 6 months were to 3 months'.

Amending by Repeal and Re-enactment

All these amendments discussed above are examples of *legislation by reference*, because none of them can be understood without referring to the provision which is being amended and they all leave the reader with the task of reconstructing the provision in its amended form. The alternative technique of repealing the original provision and re-enacting it in its amended form makes the law significantly more accessible. One hybrid technique, known in the context of Westminster legislation as a *Keeling schedule* (after EH Keeling, the Member of Parliament who suggested it), is to enact the amendments at the appropriate places in the body of the Act and then reproduce the provisions in their amended forms in a schedule. This technique is seldom used because it causes confusion if the earlier Act is subsequently amended, leaving the Keeling schedule included in the later Act as an inaccurate version of the law. However, using explanatory notes to set out the changes in a form akin to a Keeling schedule can be very useful to anyone who has to grasp their effect.

The technique of repeal and re-enactment, whether or not in the form of a Keeling schedule, may be unduly cumbersome if it is adopted for consequential amendments and repeals, which, as the Renton Report noted, 'are generally taken pretty well on trust'.[53]

When only part of a provision is amended or repealed textually, some care is required if the resulting provision is to be totally coherent. For example, in the second example of textual amendment given above in relation to the Knives (Control of Sale) Act 20XX, the need to insert a comma before *stilettos* could easily be overlooked.

Where the whole of a subsection is repealed, in addition to care being needed with respect to punctuation, a question may arise as to the status of a conjunction linking the repealed text with the remaining text. Suppose section 1(1) of the Knives (Control of Sale) Act 20XX had originally been drafted as:

The sale of

(a) flick-knives;
(b) lock-knives; and
(c) such other knives as the Secretary of State may by order prescribe

is prohibited.

[53] Cmnd 6053, para. 13.22.

Also suppose that lock-knives are to be removed from the prohibition. Would repealing para (b) also repeal the semi-colon and the *and*? If they are both regarded as being part of the paragraph (in the sense of being essential to the meaning which the paragraph conveys), it follows that they are part of the paragraph. However, it is much easier to argue that both the semicolon and the *and* are not part of the paragraph, with the semicolon merely indicating that the paragraph has done its work and come to an end, and the *and* showing the relation of that paragraph to the next one. So, if the *and* is inadvertently repealed, the remaining text consists of two subsections with no verbal link. (In passing it may be noted that although in a case such as this it might be logical to renumber para (c) as subs (b), it would be bad practice to do so, because it could upset both internal cross-references in that Act and external cross-references in others.)

Amending Provisions and Gender-neutral Drafting

Where gender-neutral drafting is a recent development, amendments to older instruments need to be drafted with particular care. More particularly, it may be preferable to continue to use the old style, rather than importing the new one which could bring with it the risk of inadvertently creating scope for argument arising from internal consistency.

Numbering Newly-inserted Provisions

The Drafting Technique Group of the Office of the Parliamentary Counsel recommends the following:[54]

- Provisions inserted between 1 and 2 should be designated 1A, 1B, 1C, etc.
- Provisions inserted between 1A and 1B should be designated 1AA, 1AB, 1AC, etc.
- Provisions inserted between 1 and 1A should be designated 1ZA, 1ZB, 1ZC, etc.
- Provisions inserted between 1A and 1AA should be designated 1AZA, 1AZB, 1AZC, etc.

In the rare cases where more than 26 new sections are inserted, Z1, Z2, Z3, etc should be inserted after Z, so that, for example, in the Capital Allowances Act 2001, section 360Z is followed by sectionss 360Z1–360Z4.

The same principles should be applied where the insertions are into levels of text which are designated as (a), (b), (c), etc, or (i), (ii), (iii), etc.

Commencement (*or* Coming into Force)

There is no requirement that the whole of an Act must come into force on a single occasion and it is commonplace for different provisions within a single

[54] www.parliamentary-counsel.gov.uk/, *drafting techniques* tab, 10–11.

Act to come into force on different days. Moreover, it is not unknown for an Act, or a provision of an Act, to be repealed without having come into force. There are three ways of identifying the date on which an Act, or part of an Act, comes into force.

Section 4(b) of the Interpretation Act 1978 provides that an Act which makes no provision for its own coming into force will come into force at the beginning of the day on which it receives the Royal Assent. However, following a recommendation of the Drafting Technique Group of the Office of the Parliamentary Counsel,[55] the current practice is to include a provision bringing an Act into force when it receives the Royal Assent, if that is the desired date. (This practice has the advantage of making the matter plain even to readers who know nothing of the 1978 Act).

Where an Act comes into force after the date of the Royal Assent, there are three possibilities.

First, the Act may itself specify a date on which it will come into force.

Secondly, the Act may specify a period of time (say two months) after the Royal Assent on which it will come into force. The advantage of this technique, as compared with the first one, is that any unforeseen delays in the legislative progress of the Bill through Parliament will not affect the length of the period during which people can prepare for the coming into force of the Act.

Thirdly, the Act may authorise a named person (typically a Secretary of State) to specify the date on which the Act will come into force. The standard drafting technique to implement this alternative is for the Act itself to authorise the making of a statutory instrument in the form of either an *appointed day order* or a *commencement order*. (The Drafting Technique Group of the Office of the Parliamentary Counsel recommends[56] the use of appointed day provisions and orders.) This technique of bringing Acts into force by order is particularly useful where it is clear that some time must be allowed before the Act comes into force, but the precise length of time cannot be predicted with precision. For example, official forms to be used for procedural matters arising under the Act may need to be designed, subordinate legislation may need to be made, existing civil servants and local government employees may need to be trained, new staff may need to be recruited and office accommodation may need to be provided.

Where the scheme of an Act as a whole is to be brought into force by order or orders, it is essential to make an exception for the provision which contains this order-making power. Unless that provision comes into force in one of the first two ways mentioned above, additional legislation will be required to bring the Act into force.

In practice, the commencement of statutes very seldom causes any difficulty but two notable exceptions have arisen, namely the Easter Act 1928 and

[55] *Ibid*, 2.
[56] *Ibid*, 3.

the situation which gave rise to the case of *R v Secretary of State for the Home Department ex parte Fire Brigades Union*.[57]

Dealing with these exceptions in turn; in 1926, the League of Nations proposed that the date of Easter should be fixed as the first Sunday after the second Saturday of April. With reasonable promptness, Parliament passed the Easter Act 1928 in order to achieve this objective within the United Kingdom. The problem is that section 2(2) of the Act contains an extremely unusual piece of drafting, as a result of which no commencement order can be made unless a draft has been approved by both Houses of Parliament, and 'before making such draft order, regard shall be had to any opinion officially expressed by any Church or other Christian body'. Unfortunately, no relevant opinion has been officially expressed and successive governments have persisted in misinterpreting the subsection as meaning that no commencement order can be made in the absence of such an opinion. Accordingly, the Act has not come into force.

The decision of the House of Lords in *R v Secretary of State for the Home Department ex parte Fire Brigades Union*,[58] arose from a situation in which a statute had created a new scheme under which victims of crime who sustained injuries could claim compensation from the state. This scheme was a replacement for an existing, non-statutory one. The statute authorised the Home Secretary to bring the new scheme into force on a date of his choosing. In fact, however, the Home Secretary devised a third (and non-statutory) scheme, as a result of which the statutory scheme became effectively a dead-letter and would never be brought into force.

The applicant for judicial review was a trade union, which wished to see the statutory scheme brought into force because it was the most favourable of the three schemes from the point of view of its members who were injured as a result of criminal conduct. The House of Lords held (by 3:2) that the Court could not compel the Home Secretary to bring the statutory scheme into force, but could prevent him making another decision which would have the consequence that he would never be able to bring it into force. In other words, only another statute could consign the statutory scheme to the dustbin of legal history.

The Easter Act problem is continuing but is unlikely to arise again. On the other hand, a governmental decision to do something which means that a particular provision or Act will never be brought into effect could easily arise again.

Application and Extent

Although the terms *application* and *extent* sound as if they should be more or less interchangeable, in the context of legislation they are clearly distinguishable.

[57] *R v Secretary of State for the Home Department ex parte Fire Brigades Union.* [1995] 2 AC 513.
[58] *Ibid.*

The *application* of a statute refers to the people to whom the statute applies. The most obvious question which arises in the case of many statutes is whether a statute binds the Crown (or whatever term the jurisdiction in question uses to convey the same idea).

The *extent* of a statute refers to its geographical or temporal effect, or both. Taking geographical extent first, in many jurisdictions there will seldom, if ever, be any issue. However, taking the case of the United Kingdom as an example, in the absence of any provision to the contrary a statute applies to the whole kingdom, but in practice the territorial scope of statutes is often limited to one or two of England and Wales, Scotland and Northern Ireland.

If Parliament wishes to legislate with extra-territorial affect, it has at least two techniques at its disposal.

The first technique is simply to include a provision to the effect that the United Kingdom's courts have jurisdiction irrespective of the place where the relevant conduct occurs. A provision of this sort may or may not be limited to British citizens. Section 9 of the Offences Against the Person Act 1861 asserts extra-territorial jurisdiction in respect of murder and manslaughter, but limits this assertion to British subjects:

> Murder or manslaughter abroad
>
> Where any murder or manslaughter shall be committed on land out of the United Kingdom, whether within the Queen's dominions or without, and whether the person killed were a subject of Her Majesty or not, every offence committed by any subject of Her Majesty in respect of any such case, whether the same shall amount to the offence of murder or of manslaughter, . . . may be dealt with, inquired of, tried, determined, and punished . . . in England . . .

On the other hand, section 1(1) of the Aviation Security Act 1982 asserts jurisdiction both extra-territorially and over foreign nationals:

> (1) A person on board an aircraft in flight who unlawfully, by the use of force or by threats of any kind, seizes the aircraft or exercises control of it commits the offence of hijacking, whatever his nationality, whatever the State in which the aircraft is registered and whether the aircraft is in the United Kingdom or elsewhere . . .

Section 1(3) provides that the offence is punishable, on conviction on indictment, by life imprisonment. (The fact that subsection (2) goes on to specify exceptional cases in which the United Kingdom's jurisdiction is not asserted does not detract from the basically extra-territorial thrust of the section.)

The second technique is to provide that conduct occurring outside the United Kingdom is deemed to have occurred within the United Kingdom, thus automatically giving jurisdiction to the United Kingdom's courts. However, relying as it does on the fiction of deeming when there is a more straightforward alternative available leaves this technique as an unnecessarily crude and, therefore, rather unsatisfactory, option.

Turning to temporal extent, two topics arise, namely when does an Act come into force and when (if at all) does an Act cease to have effect. Coming into force is discussed at page 94. It is rare for an Act to provide for its own demise, but temporary provisions may sometimes be appropriate and an express provision for an Act to lapse (known as a *sunset clause*) avoids the need for express repeal later. There is also the possibility of a conditional sunset clause where an Act, or part of an Act, lapses on a fixed or determinable future date, unless its period of operation is extended while it is still in force. The Act containing this provision should also specify the procedure for effecting an extension.

Although, in conceptual terms, a sunset clause amounts to lapse rather than repeal, viewing it in practical terms as a kind of advance notice of repeal provides a useful prompt that there may be a need for savings and transitional provisions (both of which are discussed in the immediately following section of this chapter). Theoretically, these provisions could be contained in the Act containing the sunset clause but, in practice, this would involve difficult matters of prediction. It is, therefore, better to create a power for savings and transitional provisions to be dealt with in due course by way of subordinate legislation, so that the relevant provisions can take into account the precise circumstances which are prevailing when they are made.

Savings and Transitional Provisions

Introduction

Savings and transitional provisions are intended to smooth the operation of the law when an Act is repealed, whether or not it is replaced by another one. As Thornton comments, 'both terms are loosely used with overlapping meanings; there is little or no advantage in seeking to pursue a watertight distinction between them'.[59]

In the context of savings and transitional provisions, it is particularly important that drafters are able to identify the gaps in their instructions which the instructing department would have plugged if it had appreciated the need to do so and then ask appropriate questions. In Thornton's view, the problem stems essentially from the fact that the instructing department is often too absorbed in the new project to be able to spare the time and energy to think about savings and transitional arrangements.[60]

Some Examples of Savings and Transitional Provisions

The potential range of savings and transitional provisions is too great for any exhaustive list to be attempted, but two examples may be useful.

[59] GC Thornton, *Legislative Drafting* 4th edn (London, Butterworths, 1996 (subsequently transferred to Tottel) 383.
[60] *Ibid.*

First, where an existing statutory corporation is being replaced by a new one, transitional provisions are necessary to deal with a range of purely practical matters. For example, rights of action vested in the old corporation must be transferred to the new one, along with the power to take over litigation which was being carried on by or against the old one at the time of its demise. Similarly, provision must be made for the transfer of ownership of property and for continuity of employment for staff who transfer from the old corporation to the new one, and so on.

Secondly, where an Act is repealed and replaced by a new Act, it is obviously sensible to avoid the need to re-make all the subordinate legislation made under the old Act. In the English legal system, section 17 of the Interpretation Act 1978 addresses this problem by providing:

> (1) Where an Act repeals and re-enacts, with or without modification, a previous enactment then, unless the contrary intention appears,—
>
> . . .
>
> (b) in so far as any subordinate legislation made or other thing done under the enactment so repealed, or having effect as if so made or done, could have been made or done under the provision re-enacted, it shall have effect as if made or done under that provision.[61]

A cautionary tale about the importance of transitional provisions arose from the Sexual Offences Act 2003. The Act, which came into effect on 1 May 2004, repealed the Sexual Offences Act 1956, which contained most sexual offences, including rape. Offences committed under the 1956 Act and before 1 May 2004 continued to be prosecutable (as of course were those committed under the 2003 Act and after that date). However, there were no transitional provisions to cover the situation where an offence was alleged to have been committed round about 1 May 2004 but it was impossible to prove the precise date. As a result, some alleged rapists were acquitted solely on the basis that it was impossible to prove which Act they had contravened.

Transitional provisions were subsequently made by the Violent Crime Reduction Act 2006. The effect of these provisions is that a defendant who is alleged to have committed an offence under the 2003 Act *which would also have been an offence under the 1956 Act* can be convicted under the 2003 Act. The liberty of the subject is safeguarded by a provision that where the penalty under the 1956 Act was lighter than it would be under the 2003 Act, the penalty is limited to the 1956 Act level.

Consequential Amendments and Repeals

Although many amendments and repeals appear within the bodies of the provisions which enact them, many other amendments and repeals become

[61] For the full text of the section, see app 1.

necessary simply as consequences of a new statute. Those in the latter category are effected by a short section referring to a schedule which contains the details.

Definition Sections

Introduction

Where an instrument contains a single definition section, it will usually be placed towards the end of an Act but towards the beginning of a statutory instrument. (For an example of an Act in which the definitions are spread throughout the text, see page 70.)

Matters of Fact and Matters of Law

One of the most basic principles of interpretation is that the meaning of an ordinary word of the English language is a question of fact. (See *Brutus v Cozens*,[62] which is discussed at page 12.) It is implicit in this statement that no binding precedent can arise from a decision as to the meaning of an ordinary word because the doctrine of binding precedent applies only to matters of law. The substantial discretion which this leaves in the hands of magistrates, judges, juries and other adjudicating tribunals, may be a good thing in terms of enhancing their ability to work justice in individual cases. On the other hand, in some contexts the interests of consistency and certainty may usefully be served if instruments define some of their key terms

In practice, drafters use various forms of words when formulating definitions, each of which needs to be considered.

'Means' *and* 'Includes'

English legislative drafting embraces two types of definition, one using the word *means* and the other using the word *includes*.

A definition in terms of *means* is a true (or exclusive), definition, because it limits the meaning of the word of phrase which is being defined. For example:

> *Motor vehicle* means a wheeled vehicle powered by an internal combustion engine.

On the other hand, a definition in terms of *includes* is, as the word *includes* suggests, inclusive and is not, therefore, truly a definition at all. However, inclusive definitions are useful where the drafter wishes to clarify some particular aspects of the outer limits of the category which is being defined. For example:

> *Aircraft* includes hot-air balloons.

[62] *Brutus v Cozens* [1973] AC 854.

It follows that words which are the subject of inclusive definitions have both the meaning specifically ascribed to them and their 'ordinary, popular and natural sense whenever that would be applicable'.[63]

It is obvious that the exclusivity of a true definition means that courts and tribunals cannot venture beyond the terms used. Similarly, though less obviously, inclusive definitions may give rise to the same difficulty by opening the way to the argument that where Parliament has listed A, B, C, and D as being included, perhaps it intended to exclude E and F. (This principle, which is known variously as *unius inclusio, alterius exclusio* and *expressio unius, exclusio alterius*, is illustrated at page 22.)

At the risk of doing violence to language, it may be said that inclusive definitions can be drafted negatively in order to exclude specified things. For example:

> *Aircraft* does not include tethered balloons.

Although it is bad drafting practice to provide that a word 'means and includes [so-and-so]', this form is sometimes found in practice. It follows that even drafters who are sufficiently alert to avoid using this form themselves may encounter it when ensuring they understand the existing law relating to a new proposal. A purposive interpretation is likely to produce the best results when faced with this kind of definition.

On the other hand, there is nothing objectionable in the following form of definition, where the words after *includes* clarify those before it:

> *Motor vehicle* means cars, cycles and goods vehicles powered by internal combustion engines and includes road-making equipment.

Typography

Although it is not the English practice to do so, some drafters advocate using typographical devices to indicate which words within an instrument bear a specific definition for the purposes of that instrument. Obvious possibilities include underlining, the adoption of a different font, **bold type**, *italics*, or CAPITAL LETTERS. However, the use of Initial Capital Letters is bad practice because it can cause confusion with words and expressions which would ordinarily take initial capital letters anyway, but which do not bear any specific definition. Many drafters feel that the use of typographical devices simply gives the printed page an unnecessarily cluttered appearance.

Even where it is technically possible to do so, the use of different colours is bad practice for various reasons, including the fact that it discriminates against readers who are colour blind and the fact that all photocopiers and facsimile machines do not reproduce all colours equally well.

[63] Lord Selbourne LC, in *Robinson v Barton-Eccles Local Board* (1883) App Cas 798.

Disapplying Definitions

It is standard practice to introduce definition sections with some form of words to indicate that the specific definitions (whether true or inclusive) either apply unless a contrary intention appears or do not apply where the context otherwise requires. The courts seldom need to rely on this kind of exception, whichever way it is expressed, but the most likely ground on which they will do so is that, in all the circumstances of the case, the statutory definition would produce a result which would be contrary to the legislative purpose.

Interpretation Acts

Interpretation Acts may follow one of three main models. The first model deals with the general methodological principles of interpretation (for example, the relevance of the purpose of an Act and the admissibility of reports of proceedings in the legislature). The second model deals with a variety of matters which would otherwise have to be included in a very large proportion of Acts (for example, the meaning of common words such as *month*, and whether subordinate legislation survives the repeal of the statute under which it was made). The third model combines the other two.

Since the first Interpretation Act in 1850, the Westminster practice has been to adopt only the second of these possibilities, leaving the methodology of legislative interpretation entirely within the remit of the common law. (For extracts from the Interpretation Act 1978, see appendix one.)

In common with interpretation sections, it is standard form for Interpretation Acts to contain provisions to the effect that they either apply unless a contrary intention appears or do not apply where the context otherwise requires.

6

Powers and Duties

Introduction

Although it is commonplace for statutory provisions to confer powers and impose duties, such provisions can give rise to two difficulties. First, there is the question of whether a particular provision creates a duty or only a power. Secondly, there is the question of the enforceability of duties, whether by way of judicial review or otherwise. The rest of this chapter discusses both these difficulties, before concluding with sections 12 and 13 of the Interpretation Act 1978, which deal with *continuity of powers and duties* and *anticipatory exercise of powers* respectively.

The Distinction Between Powers and Duties

Introduction

Drafters in many common law jurisdictions have tended to use the word *may* to confer a power and the word *shall* to impose a duty; and the Interpretation Acts of some jurisdictions have turned these usages into principles of interpretation. However, in those jurisdictions whose Interpretation Acts offer no assistance, matters are much less certain than the commonplace usage suggests, while the existence of some statutory endorsements are also less helpful than they might appear to be. For example, in the context of the British Columbia Interpretation Act 1996, which provides that *may* is *permissive and empowering*, while *shall* is *imperative*, Sullivan says:

> The assistance offered by these provisions is limited in that they do not address the two issues that repeatedly arise concerning the use of 'may' and 'shall'. In fact, they make it harder to deal with those issues in so far as they imply that 'may' and 'shall' are opposites and create mutually exclusive categories. Both conceptually and in practice, permission and obligation are overlapping categories. An official who is

> obliged to do a thing is implicitly permitted to do it; an official who is permitted to do a thing may, in addition, be obliged to do it.[1]

Clearly, the best approach in many, if not all, common law jurisdictions is to go back to first principles as developed by the common law. Curiously, this leads to the counter-intuitive conclusion that *shall* can, in some contexts, confer a power or discretion (rather than imposing a duty), while *may* can, in some contexts, lead to the imposition of a duty.

May and *Shall* in the context of Powers and Duties

Introduction

In ordinary usage both *may* and *shall* often signify future possibilities and events. (See page 79 for drafting in the past, present and future tenses.) However, both *may* and *shall* are far more troublesome when used to create powers and duties.

At the outset it is worth remembering that a judicial decision as to whether a function is a power or a duty is almost always only an intermediate step between findings of fact and a final decision as to the legal consequences of those findings. Accordingly, much litigation would be avoided if drafters were in the habit of stating the consequences of non-compliance with all statutory provisions which either confer powers or impose duties.

The conventional starting point for discussing judicial attitudes to the effect of the word *may* in relation to powers and duties is *Julius v Lord Bishop of Oxford*,[2] in which the House of Lords reviewed authorities extending back for 200 years and Lord Cairns said that the words *shall be lawful*

> confer a faculty or a power, and they do not of themselves do more than confer a faculty or power. But there may be something in the nature of the thing empowered to be done, something in the object for which it is to be done, something in the conditions under which it is to be done, something in the title of the person or persons for whose benefit the power is to be exercised, which may couple the power with a duty, and make it the duty of the person in whom the power is reposed, to exercise that power when called upon to do so.

But this comment must be read carefully. In particular, it is important to avoid the trap for the unwary which Cotton LJ identified a few years later, in *Re Baker*:[3]

> I think that great misconception is caused by saying that in some cases 'may' means 'must'. It never can mean 'must', so long as the English language retains its meaning; but it gives a power, and then it may be a question in what cases, where a Judge has a power given him by the word 'may', it becomes his duty to exercise it.

[1] R Sullivan, *Sullivan and Driedger on the Construction of Statutes* 4th edn (Vancouver, Butterworths Canada, 2002) 56.

[2] *Julius v Lord Bishop of Oxford* (1880) 5 App Cas 214, 222–23

[3] *Re Baker* (1890) 44 ChD 262, 270.

The question, therefore, is not 'when does *may* create a duty, but when is there a duty to exercise a power? Coleridge J provided a succinct answer to this question in *R v Tithe Commissioners*:[4]

> The words undoubtedly are only empowering; but it has been so often decided as to become an axiom that in public statutes words only directory, permissory [*sic*] or enabling, may have compulsory force where the thing to be done is *for the public benefit or in advancement of public justice*. (emphasis added)

A moment's thought enables the modern common lawyer to recognise this comment as being, in effect, an application of the *Padfield* principle, according to which a statutory discretion cannot lawfully be exercised in such a way as to frustrate the purpose of the statute which confers it.[5] It is also clear that any decision-maker (and not only a judge) who has to decide whether there is a duty to exercise a power, must do so in the light of all the relevant considerations in each case, rather than making a blanket decision as to whether such a duty arises in every case which is governed by a specific provision.[6] Against this background, it is now appropriate to consider some of the leading cases.

R v Tower Hamlets London Borough Council ex parte Chetnik Developments Ltd,[7] provides a late twentieth century example of the problem. Section 9(1) of the General Rate Act 1967 provided that rating authorities *may* refund overpayments of rates which had been made in error. (Rates are a form of local taxation chargeable on the occupiers of land. The House of Lords held that whenever a local authority declined to use this power, it *must* justify its decision by identifying a relevant and sufficient reason (such as unmeritorious conduct on the part of the ratepayer). Lord Bridge explained the reasoning thus:

> If the rating authority, or the Crown Court on appeal, are not to be guided by the justice of making a refund, having regard to the circumstances in which the overpayment was made, I find it impossible to articulate any sensible alternative principle to which the exercise of the discretion can sensibly be related. If there is no guiding principle, the practical consequence must be that the decision whether or not to make a refund in any particular case may be purely arbitrary. I cannot believe that this is what Parliament intended.[8]

Turning to prohibitions, it is clear that the distinction between *may not* and *shall not* is much less likely to give rise to difficulty than *may* and *shall* when used without accompanying negatives. Both phrases generally convey straightforward prohibitions, although occasionally *may not* is used

[4] *R v Tithe Commissioners* (1849) 14 QBD 459, 474.
[5] *Padfield v Minister of Agriculture, Fisheries and Food* [1968] AC 997.
[6] This is simply an example of the *Wednesbury* principle in operation (see p 167).
[7] *R v Tower Hamlets London Borough Council ex parte Chetnik Developments Ltd* [1988] AC 858.
[8] *Ibid*, 881.

to indicate simply that there is a possibility of something not happening, rather than a prohibition. In practice, the context usually avoids any doubt whether a provision is of this kind. For example, the statement that 'a person named in a will as the sole executor may not apply for a grant of probate, in which case someone else will obtain a grant of letters of administration with the will annexed' cannot reasonably be interpreted as a prohibition on the person named as sole executor applying for probate.

However, even where the statute genuinely does create a prohibition, it is important to be alert to the possibility that the prohibition may not be as absolute as it appears to be. For example, a statutory scheme dealing with the possibility of a tenant making an application to the court for an order requiring a landlord to grant a new tenancy contained a provision that 'no application shall be entertained unless' it was made within a specified period.[9] The House of Lords[10] construed this restriction as providing protection for the landlord, from which it followed that the section did not necessarily prevent the court from hearing an application made outside the specified period. The basis of this decision was that there was nothing to stop a landlord waiving the protection which the provision gave him; and, if he chose to do so, it would be unfair to allow him to renege on that waiver. Therefore, whenever an application is made outside the specified period, the court's first question must be *has there been a waiver?* and it is only where there has been no waiver that the court is truly prohibited from allowing the application to proceed.

Similarly, section 285(3) of the Insolvency Act 1986 seems to be plain enough:

> After the making of a bankruptcy order no person who is a creditor of the bankrupt in respect of a debt provable in the bankruptcy shall . . . (b) before the discharge of the bankrupt, commence any action or other legal proceedings against the bankrupt except with the leave of the court.

Nevertheless, in a case where plaintiffs began actions without seeking the leave of the court because they did not know that the debtors had become bankrupt, the court held that the interests of justice required that it should have the discretion to grant retrospective leave to continue the actions.[11]

And again, in *Secretary of State for Trade and Industry v Langridge*,[12] the Court of Appeal held that failure to comply strictly with section 16(1) of the Company Directors Disqualification Act 1986, under which the Secretary of State 'shall give not less than ten days notice' before applying to the court for an order of disqualification, did not necessarily invalidate the notice. More particularly, what was required was a balancing exercise, having regard to protection of the competing interests of the public on the one hand, and individuals on the other.

[9] See s 29(3) Landlord and Tenant Act 1954.
[10] *Kammins Ballrooms Co Ltd v Zenith Investments (Torquay) Ltd* [1971] AC 850.
[11] *Re Saunders* [1997] Ch 60.
[12] *Secretary of State for Trade and Industry v Langridge* [1991] Ch 402.

By way of a final example, in *Attorney-General v Antigua Times*,[13] the Newspaper Surety Ordinance (Amendment) Act 1971 sought to ensure that newspapers would have the means to meet awards of damages made against them in libel actions. The basic scheme was that newspapers should lodge deposits of $10,000 but a proviso to section 3(2) of the Act stated that

> the Minister responsible for newspapers on being satisfied with the sufficiency of the security in the form of a policy of insurance or on a guarantee of a bank may waive the requirement of the said deposit.

The Privy Council held that the minister's discretion was limited to determining the sufficiency of the alternative security, and that once he was satisfied as to that matter, he was under a duty to waive the requirement of a deposit.

Finally, it is interesting to notice that the Drafting Technique Group of the Office of the Parliamentary Counsel has adopted a policy of minimising the use of *shall* in legislative drafting, preferring to use *must* in most cases where a duty is being imposed.[14] However, this usage does not address the problem of interpretation which arose in *Langridge*.[15]

Enforcing Duties by Judicial Review

Introduction

If all the other requirements for judicial review are met (essentially, that the subject-matter arises under public law, that the applicant has standing and that the time limit has not expired) many statutory duties are enforceable by way of claims for judicial review. However, it is important to note that some statutory obligations are expressed in such general terms that the courts regard them as providing targets that public authorities must aim to achieve, rather than establishing benchmarks they must actually achieve. For example, in *R v Inner London Education Authority ex parte Ali and Another*,[16] the High Court held that duties 'to promote the education of the people of England and Wales' and 'to secure that there shall be available . . . sufficient schools' (under sections 1(1) and 8(1) of the Education Act 1944) had 'a degree of elasticity'[17] which precluded the court from saying that individuals acquired rights which they could enforce by way of judicial review.

Whether a Secretary of State, acting on behalf of the public at large, could obtain a mandatory order to enforce the performance of similarly elastic duties would have to be decided on a case-by-case basis. However, the

[13] *Attorney-General v Antigua Times* [1976] AC 16.
[14] www.parliamentary-counsel.gov.uk/, *drafting techniques* tab, 8.
[15] See n 12.
[16] *R v Inner London Education Authority ex parte Ali and Another* (1990) 2 Admin LR 822.
[17] *Ibid*, 828.

chances of success would be greatly increased if the case could be put on the basis of a breach of the doctrine of ultra vires (such as failure to have regard to the right considerations, or acting totally unreasonably) rather than simply on the basis of failure to perform the duty as such. (See pages 162–171.) In all cases, the question is the familiar one of identifying the appropriate place to draw the line. The decision of the House of Lords in *R(G) v Barnet London Borough Council and Other Cases*[18] provides some valuable judicial insights. The case turned on the effect of section 17(1) of the Children Act 1989:

> It shall be the general duty of every local authority (in addition to the other duties imposed on them by this Part) (a) to safeguard and promote the welfare of children within their area who are in need; and (b) so far as is consistent with that duty, to promote the upbringing of such children by their families, by providing a range and level of services appropriate to those children's needs.

Section 17(2) provided:

> For the purpose principally of facilitating the discharge of their general duty under this section, every local authority shall have the specific duties and powers set out in Part 1 of Schedule 2.

Part 1 of schedule 2 sets out a range of further duties in relation to local authoritiy support for children and families.

Lord Millett saw the matter thus:

> [106] . . . In my opinion [s 17(1)] imposes a general and overriding duty to maintain a level and range of services sufficient to enable the authority to discharge its functions under Part III of the Act.
>
> [107] Section 17(1) contains three indications of the nature of the duty which it imposes. The first is that it is described as a general duty. I agree that this is not decisive by itself. It may be contrasted with the specific duties and powers mentioned in section 17(2). But it does suggest that what is to follow is a general and comprehensive duty owed to all persons within the authority's area rather than a duty which is owed to particular individuals.
>
> [108] The second indication is that it is a duty to safeguard and promote the welfare of 'children within their area who are in need' and to promote the upbringing of such children by their families. This is couched in terms which suggest that it is a broad and general duty to cater for the needs of all the children concerned, rather than a duty to meet the needs of any particular child. This feature, too, cannot be decisive, for the words can be read as involving a duty in respect of the welfare and upbringing of each child. But it cannot be assumed that they do involve such a duty, for this is the very question to be decided.
>
> [109] In my opinion, however, the third indication is decisive. The duty is not a duty to safeguard and promote the welfare of the children concerned simpliciter, but to do so 'by providing a range and level of services appropriate to those children's

[18] *R(G) v Barnet London Borough Council and Other Cases* [2003] UKHL 57, [2004] 2 AC 208.

> needs'. A social services authority which provides a range and level of services appropriate to meet the various needs of children in its area has discharged its duty under section 17(1). This cannot be read as a duty to meet the needs of any particular child. It is sufficient that the authority maintains services for which his particular needs make him eligible.

Lord Scott stated his view thus:

> [113] The language of this provision seems to me to provide very infertile soil for the extraction of a targeted, specific duty owed to an individual child.
>
> [114] First, the adjective 'general', qualifying the 'duty', is indicative of an overarching duty applying to a class rather than to individuals and of a 'framework' duty under the umbrella of which specific duties imposed by other statutory provisions may from time to time come into existence in relation to specific children. The point is underlined by subsection (2) which says that: 'For the purpose principally of facilitating the discharge of their general duty under this section, every local authority shall have the specific duties and powers set out in Part I of Schedule 2.' The contrast in subsection (2) between the 'general duty' imposed by subsection (1) and the 'specific duties' to be found elsewhere is explicit.
>
> [115] Second, the context of the subsection (1) 'general duty' is expressed in broad aspirational terms that would not easily lend themselves to mandatory enforcement. The local authority must 'safeguard and promote the welfare' of the children. It must 'promote the upbringing of such children by their families'. Nothing could be less specific.
>
> [116] Third, subsection (1) specifies, again in very broad terms, the manner in which the 'general duty' is to be discharged, namely, 'by providing a range and level of services appropriate to those children's needs'. This language is contemplating the children, the objects of the general duty, as a class.
>
> [117] Part I of Schedule 2 to the Act, as section 17(2) has led one to expect, imposes specific duties and confers specific powers on local authorities. Paragraph 1(1) says that: 'Every local authority shall take reasonable steps to identify the extent to which there are children in need within their area'. This obligation is not expressed in absolute terms. The local authority will have discharged its mandatory duty if it has taken 'reasonable steps'. Having identified a child 'in need' it will often be necessary for the local authority to assess the actual needs of the child. Somewhat surprisingly the requirement for the local authority to do so is nowhere expressly spelt out. Paragraph 3 of the Schedule says that:
>
>> 'Where it appears to a local authority that a child within their area is in need, the authority may assess his needs for the purposes of this Act at the same time as any assessment of his needs is made under—(a) the Chronically Sick and Disabled Persons Act 1970; (b) Part IV of the Education Act 1996; (c) the Disabled Persons (Services, Consultation and Representation) Act 1986; or (d) any other enactment.'
>
> It is, I think, implicit in this provision that the local authority will assess the actual needs of a child in need whenever it appears necessary to do so.

[118] Most of the specific duties imposed on local authorities under Part I of Schedule 2 are expressed in proportionate rather than absolute terms. Thus, paragraph 4(1) requires every local authority to 'take *reasonable* steps . . . to prevent children within their area suffering ill-treatment or neglect'. Paragraph 7 requires every local authority to 'take *reasonable* steps designed' to benefit the children in various specified ways (emphasis in each case added). Paragraph 8 requires every local authority to 'make such provision as they consider appropriate' for specified types of services to be made available to children in need who are living with their families. Paragraph 10 requires every local authority to 'take *such steps as are reasonably practicable*' to enable a child in need living apart from his family to live with his family (emphasis again added). It is plain, in my opinion, that in relation to each of these specific duties the local authority can take into account among other things, its overall financial resources and, in particular, the cost of taking a specific step that, if taken, would benefit the child and meet some need. Whether the taking of a particular step is 'reasonable' or 'reasonably practicable' cannot be divorced from the financial implications of taking the step.

[119] Viewed in the context of these specific duties imposed on local authorities under Part I of Schedule 2 to the Act it would be odd to find that the section 17(1) general duty had imposed on a local authority a mandatory obligation to take some specific step in relation to the child irrespective of the local authority's financial resources and of the cost of the step in question. But that is the result for which counsel for the claimants in these three appeals contend.

When creating public law duties, therefore, drafters should ensure that they communicate as clearly as possible their intention, whether it is to create merely target duties, or confer correlative rights which are enforceable by individuals in claims for judicial review. As a third possibility, of course, they may be thinking outwith the field of judicial review altogether and be intending the creation of a duty to give rise to a right of action in damages for the tort of breach of statutory duty. It is to this aspect of enforceability that we now turn.

Damages for Breach of Statutory Duty

Introduction

Although there are very many cases on the point, the common law has been less than entirely successful in developing a set of principles which can be relied on to provide a predictable answer to the question of whether the breach of a statutory duty will give rise to an right of action in damages.

The classic case is *Cutler v Wandsworth Stadium*[19] where the House of Lords held that a statutory requirement that the proprietors of a dog-racing

[19] *Cutler v Wandsworth Stadium* [1949] AC 398.

track must make provision for bookmakers was intended to benefit the public rather than individual bookmakers. It followed that a bookmaker who was excluded from the track had no claim in damages for breach of statutory duty. Unfortunately, however, the line between public and private interests has proved very difficult to draw with any degree of predictability.

In *Atkinson v Newcastle and Gateshead Waterworks Co*,[20] the Waterworks Clauses Act 1847 imposed a statutory duty to provide and maintain fire plugs and to maintain a specified level of water pressure for fire-fighting purposes. The statute provided for penalties for breach of this duty in the form of £10 (plus an additional £2 for each day on which the breach of duty continued after it had been brought to the water company's attention) to be recoverable summarily. The magistrates had power to award not more than half the penalty to the person who suffered loss, with the rest going to the overseers of the parish. (The overseers of the parish were responsible for the administration of the Poor Law.) The court held that there was no cause of action in damages when a house burned down as result of the water pressure at a fire plug being insufficient to enable the fire to be extinguished.

In *Read v Croydon Corporation*,[21] on the other hand, breach of a statutory duty to provide wholesome water did confer a right of action in damages on a person who became ill as a result of drinking contaminated water.

It is not surprising, therefore, that Lord Denning felt moved to say that 'the dividing line between the pro-cases and the contra-cases is so blurred and ill-defined that you may as well toss a coin to decide it'.[22]

As a matter of pure drafting, the solution to this problem is perfectly straightforward, with the question *damages or no?* being dealt with explicitly and unambiguously. As Lord du Parq said, in *Cutler v Wandsworth Stadium Ltd*:[23]

> To a person unversed in the science or art of legislation it may well seem strange that Parliament has not by now made it a rule to state explicitly what its intention is in a matter which is often of no little importance . . . I trust, however, that it will not be thought impertinent . . . to suggest respectfully that those responsible for framing legislation might consider whether the traditional practice, which obscures, if it does not conceal, the intention which Parliament has, or must be presumed to have, might not be safely abandoned.

The Law Commissions' approach to the problem was to suggest the enactment of the following as a principle of general application:

> Where any Act passed after this Act imposes or authorises the imposition of a duty, whether positive or negative and whether with or without a special remedy for its enforcement, it shall be presumed, unless express provision to the contrary is made,

[20] *Atkinson v Newcastle and Gateshead Waterworks Co* (1877) 2 ExD 441.
[21] *Read v Croydon Corporation* [1938] 4 All ER 631.
[22] *Ex parte Island Records Ltd* [1978] Ch 122, 135.
[23] [1949] AC 398, 410.

> that a breach of the duty is intended to be actionable (subject to the defences and other incidents applying to actions for breach of statutory duty) at the suit of any person who sustains damage in consequence of the breach.

Neither Lord du Parq's suggestion, nor that of the Law Commissions, has had any significant impact on drafting practice. Of course, the reason for this failure may not lie with the drafters. In *M v Newham London Borough Council*,[24] Staughton LJ suggested that the cause of legislative inaction may lie in the political difficulty that a government would face in creating a right while refusing to give any right of action to those who suffer loss caused by its breach. All that can be said here is that a drafter who is instructed to create a duty without also being instructed as to the desired consequences of a breach of that duty, has a professional responsibility to press for further instructions. (As in other matters, of course, the drafter must ultimately proceed on whatever instructions are given, even if they are less than satisfactory.)

Two other specific problems, relating to duties and rights in certain contexts, can also arise with sufficient frequency to be worth consideration.

Two Specific Problems

Introduction

Drafters should be aware of the danger of creating situations which leave the following questions unanswered.

First, does a statute which imposes a duty and specifies a penalty for breach of that duty, impliedly exclude all other remedies?

Secondly, does a statute which creates a right and specifies a remedy to enforce that right, impliedly exclude all other remedies?

Does a Statute which imposes a Duty and also specifies a Penalty for Breach of that Duty, impliedly exclude all other Remedies?

Where a statute imposes a duty and specifies a penalty for breach of that duty, there is a presumption that the penalty is the only remedy for breach, from which it follows that an individual who is injured as a result of the breach cannot have damages. But this presumption may be rebutted where the interests of justice so require. For example, in *Groves v Lord Wimborne*,[25] an employer was in breach of a statutory duty to fence dangerous machinery. The Act provided not only that breach of the duty was an offence punishable by a fine, but that the Secretary State had power to direct that some of the money paid by way of a fine was to be used for the benefit of the injured person, or his family, or in some other way. The court held that a workman who was injured by the unfenced machinery was entitled to damages, despite the fact that the

[24] *M v Newham London Borough Council* [1995] 2 AC 633.
[25] *Groves v Lord Wimborne* [1898] 2 QB 402.

Act made it possible for him to benefit directly from the fine. The court was particularly influenced by the fact that the fine would be quantified according to the gravity of the offence, rather than the seriousness of its financial consequences for the workman.

Does a Statute which creates a Right and specifies a Remedy to enforce that Right, impliedly exclude all other Remedies?

A statute which creates a right and specifies a remedy to enforce that right, provides a variation on the previous situation which is worthy of consideration. In *Barraclough v Brown*,[26] the undertakers who were responsible for a waterway had a statutory right to remove and sell any boat that sank within their jurisdiction. Furthermore, if the costs of removal exceeded the proceeds of sale, the statute gave them an express right to recover the shortfall in the magistrates' court. In the present case, the sum involved was £3000 (which was greatly in excess of the normal jurisdiction of the magistrates) so the undertakers tried to recover the money in the High Court. Their claim failed, on the basis that where both the right and the remedy are given at the same time, no other remedy is available. (If the legislative background had included a provision along the lines of that suggested by the Law Commissions—see page 111—the outcome could well have been different.)

The Drafting Solution to Both Problems

The drafting solution to both these problems is simply to state the intended position, unless there is an insuperable practical difficulty in obtaining appropriate instructions.

Where Breach of Statutory Duty gives rise to a Claim in Damages, do the Normal Principles of Vicarious Liability apply?

In *Majrwoski v Guy's & St Thomas's NHS Trust*,[27] the House of Lords held that where the statute in question contains no indication (either expressly or impliedly) to the contrary, the normal principles of vicarious liability will apply where an employee commits a breach of statutory duty while acting within the scope of his employment.

Continuity of Powers and Duties

Under the heading *continuity of powers and duties*, section 12(1) of the Interpretation Act 1978 provides that unless the contrary intention appears,

[26] *Barraclough v Brown* [1897] AC 615.
[27] *Majrwoski v Guy's & St Thomas's NHS Trust* [2007] 1 AC 224.

powers may be exercised and duties are to be performed, from time to time and as occasion requires. (See appendix one for the full text of the section.) However, the case of *Nottingham City District Council v Newton*[28] shows that reliance on section 12(1) is not always effective to achieve a sensible result.

The facts of the case were that the magistrates found that a house within a slum clearance area declared by the council under Part III of the Housing Act 1957 was also a statutory nuisance under section 92(1) of the Public Health Act 1936. As a result of that finding, the magistrates came under a duty to make an order requiring the nuisance to be abated and accordingly they made such an order. The problem was that although the house was likely to be demolished within about 12 months, the magistrates' order allowed less than three months for the necessary work to be done.

The High Court accepted that the magistrates had had no alternative to making an order but said that they had had a discretion as to the time allowed for compliance. More particularly, Lord Widgery CJ said that it was the duty of the justices 'to look at the whole circumstances of the case and try to make an order which [was] in its terms sensible and just having regard to the entire prevailing situation'.[29] Having already pointed out that, in a case where there was 'a real danger to the health of the occupier',[30] the magistrates had a specific power to make an order prohibiting the continued use of the premises for human habitation until remedial work had been done, he went on to say that allowing a longer period for compliance with the magistrates' order could have been a useful way of avoiding abortive expenditure on a house which was due to be demolished. When drafting a provision such as section 92(1), therefore, there is much to be said for including a provision based on Lord Widgery's comments.

Anticipatory Exercise of Powers

Under the heading *anticipatory exercise of powers*, section 13 of the Interpretation Act 1978 confers a variety of powers to do things in order to facilitate 'bringing an Act or any provision of an Act into force', or 'giving full effect to the Act or any such provision at or after the time when it comes into force'. (See appendix one for the full text of the section.)

There will seldom be any need to draft specific provisions to negative section 13, but there may sometimes be a need to extend it by means of paving legislation (see page 58).

[28] *Nottingham City District Council v Newton* [1974] 1 WLR 923.
[29] *Ibid*, 930.
[30] *Ibid*, 929.

7

Licensing and Registration

Introduction

It seems to be an inescapable aspect of modern life that an ever-increasing range of activities is subjected to control through schemes of licensing and registration. Although the activities concerned are too diverse to be identified with any degree of confidence, and although the creation of each scheme must be approached in the light of the specific purposes which it is designed to serve, such schemes often have a great deal in common with each other. It is, therefore, possible to identify a range of problems which often occupy the drafter's attention. However, before identifying these problems it must be said that the extent to which there are common issues is not always reflected in common terminology. Thus, for example, the key concept may be expressed as being a *certificate*, a *concession*, a *consent*, a *licence*, a *permission* or a *permit* (and a comprehensive trawl of all legislation would no doubt reveal other possibilities). For the sake of clarity, the word *licence* will be used in this chapter to represent all possibilities, except where reference to an actual scheme requires the use of another term for the sake of accuracy.

Designing the Legislative Scheme

The structure of legislation creating licensing schemes will, in common with the structure of any other legislation, depend on the detail of the material with which it is dealing. However, the following topics arise either universally, or at least with sufficient frequency, to justify consideration here: application procedures; first-time applications, renewals and revocations; the criteria for granting or withholding licences; conditional licences; the duration of licences; enforcement; transitional provisions (including grand-parenting); and the status of qualifications from other jurisdictions.

Application Procedures

Introduction

All licensing schemes contain procedural requirements. These often contain relatively standard provisions, as a result of which busy drafters may be tempted to regard them as routine. However, procedural provisions can be a particularly fertile source of litigation. Therefore, even when adopting an established verbal formula, drafters need to pay particular attention to whether any adjustments to that formula are necessary in all the circumstances of the particular case, as well as being alert to the fact that even an established formula may be open to improvement. In this context, it is worth noting that the introduction of explicitly plain language drafting requires many established formulas to be revised.

The range of possible express procedural requirements is so wide that it is difficult to say very much of truly general application, but requirements to give notice of applications and to implement consultation processes are both sufficiently common to merit consideration. Before doing so, however, there is one truly general point which can usefully be identified, namely that breach of a procedural requirement will not necessarily be fatal in all cases. In the words of Lord Hailsham, there is a

> spectrum [at one end of which] there may be cases in which a fundamental obligation may have been . . . outrageously and flagrantly ignored or defied . . . At the other end . . . the defect . . . may be . . . nugatory or trivial.[1]

Much litigation can be avoided if drafters are able and willing to specify the consequences of failure to comply with each individual requirement. In practical terms, of course, there may be real difficulty in obtaining appropriate instructions; but it is not unknown for drafters to be able to influence this kind of micro-policy question.

Standard Application Forms

The assessment of applications is usually greatly facilitated by the use of standard application forms, so there is much to be said for prescribing forms and making copies of them freely available. The Internet is obviously a useful means of communication in this context, but other means should also be available. If applications are to be accepted electronically, the provisions of section 7 of the Electronic Communications Act 2000, relating to electronic signatures, should be borne in mind, in case the application should ever be required to be produced in evidence before a court. The section provides as follows:

[1] *London & Clydeside Estates Ltd v Aberdeen District Council* [1980] 1 WLR 182, 189.

7.

Electronic signatures and related certificates.

(1) In any legal proceedings—

(a) an electronic signature incorporated into or logically associated with a particular electronic communication or particular electronic data, and
(b) the certification by any person of such a signature,

shall each be admissible in evidence in relation to any question as to the authenticity of the communication or data or as to the integrity of the communication or data.

(2) For the purposes of this section an electronic signature is so much of anything in electronic form as—

(a) is incorporated into or otherwise logically associated with any electronic communication or electronic data; and
(b) purports to be so incorporated or associated for the purpose of being used in establishing the authenticity of the communication or data, the integrity of the communication or data, or both.

(3) For the purposes of this section an electronic signature incorporated into or associated with a particular electronic communication or particular electronic data is certified by any person if that person (whether before or after the making of the communication) has made a statement confirming that—

(a) the signature,
(b) a means of producing, communicating or verifying the signature, or
(c) a procedure applied to the signature,

is (either alone or in combination with other factors) a valid means of establishing the authenticity of the communication or data, the integrity of the communication or data, or both.

Fees

If fees are payable in respect of an application, provision must be made for their initial quantification and periodical amendment. This will usually be done by creating a power to make subordinate legislation, which will, in due course, contain the detailed figures.

Provision should be made to the effect that an application will be returned to the applicant unprocessed (on the ground that it is incomplete) unless it is accompanied by the appropriate fee.

Requirements as to Giving Notice of Applications

Applicants for licences are often required to give notice of their applications and licensing authorities may be required to give notice that they have received applications. In either case, notice may be targeted at either specific categories of people (for example, owners and occupiers of nearby premises) or the general public. Detailed provisions, which are often contained in subordinate legislation, then specify how notice is to be given, with the most obvious means being either service in person or by post (including email), displaying a notice on or near the premises to which the application relates, or placing an advertisement in a local newspaper. The use of at least two methods is usual. Where service by post is envisaged, regard should be had to section 7 of the Interpretation Act 1978 (see appendix one), while if email is included the provisions of section 7 of the Electronic Communications Act 2000, relating to electronic signatures, should again be borne in mind. Both the direct cost and the administrative cost of giving notice should be built in to the application fee.

Notices displayed on or near premises are notoriously prone to being destroyed by the weather or removed or defaced by unauthorised people, which makes it a sensible precaution to provide that displaying the notice is conclusive evidence that that part of the notice-giving process has been effective, without the need to show that the notice has continued to be displayed.

Irrespective of the way in which notice is given, the notice itself must state how, to whom and by what date objections or other representations must be made. Where the law restricts the grounds on which objections can be based or representations can be made, identifying these restrictions in the notice itself can be useful. However, a legislative scheme which specifies such matters with great particularity may be offering a hostage to fortune by increasing the possibility of oversights on the part of the licensing authority resulting in the validity of notices being challenged in the courts.

If applicants themselves have to give notice, the statute should contain (or specify that subordinate legislation must contain) a form of certificate for them to complete and lodge with the licensing authority, as well as creating an offence of giving a false certificate. The certificate should state the details of the application to which it refers and specify the notice that has been given. It should also acknowledge that the applicant understands that giving a false certificate is a criminal offence. The certificate must be signed by (or, in the case of a body corporate or an unincorporated association, on behalf of) the applicant. (Whenever the opportunity to communicate electronically is available, the provisions of section 7 of the Electronic Communications Act 2000, relating to electronic signatures, should be borne in mind yet again.)

While requirements to give notice of applications are very common, in some situations it may be considered desirable to make licensing authorities go one stage further and undertake consultation processes.

Requirements as to Consultation

In *R v Secretary of State for Social Services ex parte Association of Metropolitan Authorities*,[2] Webster J provided a particularly succinct account of what the common law requires of any consultation process:

[2] *R v Secretary of State for Social Services ex parte Association of Metropolitan Authorities* [1986] 1 WLR 1, 4.

> The essence of consultation is the communication of a genuine invitation to give advice and a genuine consideration of that advice . . . it must go without saying that to achieve consultation sufficient information must be supplied by the consulting to the consulted party to enable it to tender helpful advice . . . Sufficient time must be given by the consulting to the consulted party to enable it to do that, and sufficient time must be available for such advice to be considered by the consulting party. *Sufficient* . . . does not mean ample but at least enough to enable the relevant purpose to be fulfilled. By *helpful advice*, in this context, I mean sufficiently informed and considered information or advice about aspects of the form or substance of the proposals, or their implications for the consulted party, being aspects material to the implementation of the proposal as to which [the consulting party] might not be fully informed or advised and as to which the party consulted might have relevant information or advice to offer. (emphases added)

One of the most persistently troublesome of the common law's requirements is the amount of time allowed for respondents to make their views known, which explains why drafters often make express provisions to cover this matter. On the assumption that this kind of detail is most likely to be contained in subordinate legislation (which does not enjoy the protection of the legislative supremacy of Parliament—see page 45) it is imprudent for the drafter to create schemes which are likely to be quashed simply because they impose unrealistically tight timetables.

When deciding how much time should be allowed, regard should be had to the nature of the respondent in question. More particularly, organisations which function through committee structures and professional bodies and trade associations which may have to consult their members before formulating their responses, are both examples of respondents who are likely to need more time to formulate effective responses than organisations with more streamlined internal decision-making processes, or fewer members, would need. However, prudent drafters will remain aware of the need for caution even after they have taken into account the nature of the likely respondents.

One useful approach is to decide what would be a realistic period and then (bearing in mind the fact that the court may not agree) double it. If the subject-matter of the decision-making process is such that there is likely to be some degree of urgency in individual cases, reducing the safety margin by adding only 50 per cent to the original figure may be justifiable. If there is likely to be a significant degree of urgency, using the original figure may remain the only solution.

Another problem can arise where only some of the people who are entitled to be consulted actually are consulted. In *Agricultural, Horticultural and Forestry Industry Training Board v Aylesbury Mushrooms Ltd*,[3] the Minister of Labour failed to consult the Mushroom Growers Association before setting up a training board which had power to raise a levy on employers in

[3] *Agricultural, Horticultural and Forestry Industry Training Board v Aylesbury Mushrooms Ltd* [1971] 1 WLR 190.

order to pay for training schemes. The court held that this failure did not invalidate the decision to create the board, nor did it affect the exercise of the power to raise the levy generally, but it did mean that mushroom growers were not liable to pay the levy. However, drafters of provisions which make the exercise of powers subject to consultation processes can avoid the application of this common law principle. All that is necessary is to provide that decisions will be binding on all those who ought to have been, but were not, consulted, provided that the consultation process as a whole was conducted with due diligence and in good faith and that no substantial injustice will result if those who were not consulted are bound. Although allocating the burdens of proof could be left to the courts to work out, litigation could be avoided by including specific provisions. It would seem reasonable to require the decision-maker to establish that the consultation process was conducted with due diligence and in good faith, after which the onus would shift to anyone who had not been consulted to prove both the fact of non-consultation and that substantial hardship had resulted, or would result.

First-Time Applications, Renewals, Revocations and Appeals

In *McInnes v Onslow-Fane*,[4] Sir Robert Megarry V-C divided the spectrum of possible applicants into three broad categories. At one end of the spectrum lies the first time applicant, who has neither the right to be granted a licence nor a legitimate expectation that a licence will be granted. An applicant in this category is entitled to be treated honestly and with a lack of caprice, but no more. At the other extreme lies the licence-holder who is facing revocation of his or her licence. Since the licence confers on the licence-holder the *right* to engage in the licensed activity, a very high degree of fairness is required. Finally, there is the intermediate case of a licence-holder who is applying for renewal of an expiring licence. An applicant in this category has more than a hope of, but less than a right to, renewal. Accordingly, the applicant may be said to have a *legitimate expectation of renewal* (provided, of course, that the terms of the licence have been observed and there have been no relevant changes in extraneous circumstances since the licence was originally granted or last renewed).

Having established this background, the following propositions may be distilled, with reasonable confidence, from a mass of case law which is by no means always entirely consistent.

First, a hearing (in the technical sense of an opportunity to present a case) is appropriate in all cases involving rights and most (and it might be safer to assume all) cases involving legitimate expectations.

[4] *McInnes v Onslow-Fane* [1978] 1 WLR 1520.

Secondly, the opportunity to make written representations will often satisfy the requirement of a hearing, although a hearing should be oral in situations where matters of fact are in dispute, because the alternative of written representations does not readily enable the credibility of witnesses to be evaluated. There is, therefore, something distinctly odd about an oral hearing where cross-examination is not allowed, because cross-examination is almost always the best way of testing a witness's credibility. (On the criteria for oral hearings generally see, *R v Army Board of the Defence Council ex parte Anderson.*[5])

Thirdly, there is no general right to legal representation, although it should be allowed where the interests of justice so require.

All these principles may be excluded, varied or reinforced by express statutory provisions, although if this is done by way of subordinate legislation there is always the possibility of challenge on the usual grounds of ultra vires—see page 167. Regulation-making bodies who seek to limit the right to a hearing may also get short shrift from the courts, especially where the outcome of the hearing affects the individual's ability to earn a living.

Whether or not a hearing is oral, attention must be given to the question of what immunity (if any) is to be given to the witnesses (including the people submitting written representations).

In addition to the points outlined above, the decision-maker must be unbiased. The nature of bias in this context has come before the court on many occasions, with many subtle differences of language emerging from the judgments. However, the current approach is to ask 'whether the fair-minded and informed observer, having considered the facts, would conclude that there was a real possibility that the [decision-maker] was biased'.[6] In passing, it is worth noticing that the fact that elected politicians pursue policies to which they are committed goes to the essence of democracy and cannot, therefore, be classified as bias for the present purposes.[7]

Criteria for Granting or Withholding Licences

The first question that arises in many contexts is whether the suitability of the applicant is relevant when deciding whether to grant a licence. Where a licensing scheme is designed simply to raise revenue (for example, television licences) a negative answer may easily be given to this question. However, where a licensing scheme is designed to control a particular activity, the

[5] *R v Army Board of the Defence Council ex parte Anderson.* [1992] QB 169.

[6] *Porter v Magill* [2002] UKHL 67, [2002] AC 357 at para. [103]. The House of Lords has endorsed this test in *Lawal v Northern Spirits Ltd* [2003] UKHL 35, [2003] ICR 856 and *Davidson v Scottish Ministers* [2004] UKHL 34, [2004] UKHRR 1079.

[7] *R v Reading Borough Council ex parte Quietlynn* (1987) 85 LGR 387.

question is likely to resolve itself into a number of sub-questions, the precise content of which will vary from scheme to scheme. Sometimes, the applicant's age may be relevant (with either a minimum or a maximum age, or both, being important) while in others his or her financial standing (including, perhaps, insurance cover), previous experience or moral probity may be material considerations. *Chief Constable of Essex v Germain*[8] illustrates one particular type of difficulty. The question was whether a chief constable who had revoked a shotgun certificate had been entitled to take into account the fact that the holder of the certificate had been convicted of driving with excess alcohol in his blood. On appeal, the Crown Court, considering itself bound by authority,[9] held that only conduct in relation to the shotgun had been relevant. On the chief constable's appeal, the High Court held that the Crown Court had misunderstood the earlier authority and that the chief constable had been entitled to conclude that 'the appellant was . . . prone to act in an intemperate and irresponsible manner when . . . frustrated'.[10] (Although this case involved a revocation, the same principle would also apply to an application.) In the case of applications for renewal, the applicant will usually have a legitimate expectation of success, unless there has been a material change of relevant circumstances.[11]

Conditional Licences

It is commonplace for licences to be granted subject to conditions. In practice, two issues tend to arise. First, what is the lawful scope of conditions? Secondly, what effect does the imposition of an unlawful condition have on the licence itself? If left to its own devices, the common law can answer both these questions.

First, the common law will identify the lawful scope of conditions, according to either the *Wednesbury* principles of *relevance* and *reasonableness*, or the *GCHQ* criteria of *illegality* and *irrationality*. (See pages 167–170 for these concepts.) However, it is always open to drafters to make express provision in order to clarify, reinforce, extend, restrict or negative the common law approach. For example, under section 70(2) of the Town and Country Planning Act 1990, a local planning authority which is determining an application for planning permission must have regard to certain specified policy statements and 'to any other material considerations'. Section 72 gives the authority express power to make the planning permission subject to conditions 'so far as it appears . . . to be expedient for the purposes of, or in

8 *Chief Constable of Essex v Germain* (1991) 156 JP 109.
9 *Ackers v Taylor* [1974] 1 All ER 771.
10 (1991) 156 JP 109, 112.
11 *Ibid.*

connection with' the authorised development. The common law, in the form of the *Wednesbury* principle (see page 167) would have supplied the requirement to have regard to material considerations. It would also have supplied the requirement for conditions to relate to, or be connected with, the authorised development. However, there is room for doubt as to whether the common law would have been able to imply a power to attach conditions in the first place. In other words, the drafter of these provisions effectively re-stated the common law in two respects, while supplementing it (or at least avoiding a doubt) in a third.

The extent to which it is desirable to undertake this kind of re-statement must always be a matter of judgment. On the one hand, simply re-stating common law principles which are (or should be) obvious to any lawyer can be argued to be a recipe for needlessly lengthening statutes. On the other hand, it can be argued that such re-statement does at least emphasise the fact that the licensing authority's powers are not entirely unfettered, which may be useful to those readers of the text who are not lawyers.

The possibility of a licence being granted subject to conditions inevitably raises another question: if a condition is held to be void, does this result in the whole licence being void, or can the condition be severed, leaving the licence to operate validly but free from the constraint of the condition? Conceptually, this is the same problem as that which is discussed in chapter ten in relation to subordinate legislation which is void as to part and good as to the remainder, namely whether the bad part can be severed, leaving the good part to operate on its own. In that context (as the discussion at page 164 shows) both textual and substantial severability may be important; but, in the context of conditional licences, it is difficult to imagine a condition that is not textually severable. However, at a purely terminological level, the waters become slightly muddied by the fact that although substantial severability appears to offer the only scope for argument, this phrase is seldom used in the context of severing conditions. Instead, the same idea is conveyed by asking: is the condition *fundamental* to the grant of the licence?

Fundamentality, in this context, can be approached either conceptually or practically. The conceptual approach involves asking whether the licence subject to the condition is of the same character as the licence without the condition, while the practical approach involves asking whether the licensing authority would still have granted the licence even if it had understood that the condition was unlawful. Essentially, of course, both approaches are simply different ways of asking what is, in substance, the same question. The case of *R v Hillingdon London Borough Council ex parte Royco Homes Ltd*[12] is instructive.

A conditional planning permission for residential development required the developer to use the properties to rehouse people who were on the local planning authority's waiting list for council accommodation and to give them

12 *R v Hillingdon London Borough Council ex parte Royco Homes Ltd* [1974] QB 720.

security of tenure for ten years. The court held the condition to be void since its purpose was to reduce the burden on the local planning authority in its capacity as a local housing authority, rather than having anything to do with land use as such. Furthermore, the court quashed the whole planning permission, on the basis that it would not have been granted if the planning authority had realised that the condition was unlawful.

The problem for drafters is predicting which unlawful conditions will be severed from the licences to which they are attached and which will not. While leaving it to the courts to decide the issue on a case-by-case basis can easily be defended on the basis that this is very much the kind of thing which the courts do, under the constitutional doctrine of the separation of powers, there are two other possibilities. The drafter may provide either that any illegality as to the condition will always render the whole licence void, or that it will never do so. Both these possibilities have the obvious attraction of promoting certainty in respect of the consequences of illegality, but neither would offer any assistance on the logically antecedent question of whether illegality exists. But both share the disadvantage, which always flows from removing discretion from the court, that preventing regard being had to all the circumstances of each case may sometimes preclude the court from doing justice.

Three final points in relation to drafting provisions which authorise the granting of conditional licences may usefully be made.

First, a court which is sensitive to the requirements of the doctrine of the separation of powers may be reluctant to sever and quash an offending condition, because the effect of doing so is that the court is making the final decision on the content of the licence. (If the court pursues the alternative of quashing the whole licence, the original licensing authority will have to consider the matter again and will, therefore, be performing the function which Parliament allocated to it in the first place. A drafter who wishes to reinforce the likelihood of this outcome may, therefore, wish to create a presumption that the court will quash the licence as a whole, unless it can identify some good reason for not doing so. A drafter who feels that the court may benefit from further encouragement could also provide that any court which concludes that the circumstances of a particular case are such that this presumption is rebutted, must record, in a publicly accessible way, the grounds on which it has based this conclusion.

Secondly, the drafter may opt for either one of two more straightforward techniques. The first technique is to provide that conditions will never be severable (and, therefore, a court which quashes any condition must always quash the licence as a whole). The second technique is to provide that conditions will always be severable (and, therefore, a court which quashes a condition cannot quash the licence as a whole). Both these alternatives would be equally easily drafted, but the second is likely to be less attractive for two reasons. First, by removing the possibility of reconsideration by the licensing authority, it ensures that there will be a breach of the doctrine of the separation of powers. Secondly, it may trigger the operation of the law of unintended consequences by increasing the number of applications which are refused, since licensing authorities may take the view that this is safer than trying to find a middle way in the form of a conditional grant.

Thirdly, it may be worth following the precedent of section 73 of the Town and Country Planning Act 1990, which provides that an applicant who wishes to challenge a condition attached to a planning permission may apply to the planning authority for the question of the condition to be reconsidered. When dealing with such an application, the authority is limited to reconsidering the condition (without having the power to revisit the decision to grant the permission itself) and may only confirm, vary or remove the condition.

Duration of Licences

One common question is whether licences are to be valid indefinitely or only for a fixed term. In the absence of an express statutory provision, there is a presumption of indefinite validity. It follows from this that if a licensing authority which is administering such a regime seeks to impose a time limit, the court will have to determine its validity by reference to first principles of administrative law. The inherent uncertainty flowing from this state of affairs means that there is much to be said for making express provision within the statutory scheme itself. However, the drafter who decides to follow this advice must bear in mind that there are two possible types of provision. One possibility is that a licence lapses if it is not implemented within a specified period, while the other possibility is that, even if implemented promptly, a licence expires after a fixed or determinable period of time has elapsed. It is convenient to discuss these possibilities in turn.

Imposing a requirement of prompt implementation is appropriate in cases where the licensed activity or state of affairs is beneficial (or, at least, is not intrinsically detrimental) to the community, provided that too many examples of it do not occur at the same time. In this situation, it is obviously desirable for the licensing authority to be able to keep track of how many instances are authorised (and may therefore, come into being) at any given time.

One useful technique when drafting provisions requiring prompt implementation of licences is to make every decision to grant a licence subject to an implied condition that it will lapse unless it is implemented within a specified period, while at the same time giving the licensing authority power to specify whatever other period it may consider to be appropriate in all the circumstances. This is the technique adopted in the Town and Country Planning Act 1990 and in practice it has resulted in the default period (which in the case of the 1990 Act is five years) being almost always imposed by way of an express condition.

It may be appropriate to impose a condition requiring a licensed activity or state of affairs to terminate after a specified period or on a specific date when it is parasitic on another activity or state of affairs. For example, when an attempt on the world water speed record is being made in a national park such as the Lake District, the planning authority may well be willing to grant permission for the change of use of specified buildings from use for agricultural purposes to use as engineering workshops. However, the permission would almost certainly be granted on the basis of the wholly exceptional nature of the main activity and the authority would, therefore, be amply justified in requiring the engineering use to cease on the conclusion of the attempt on the record. In order to avoid any suggestion that the time restriction is void for uncertainty, it would be prudent to express it as a fixed period of sufficient duration to enable the record attempt to be concluded.

From a purely technical point of view, there is no difficulty in drafting provisions authorising either or both kinds of time restriction. However, if a licence is not implemented within the prescribed period there may well be an application for a new licence. Similarly, if a licence has been implemented, there may be an application for renewal while the original licence is still current. In either case, the question which then arises is the extent (if any) to which the original grant is relevant to the decision-making process in relation to the further application. Again, there is no technical difficulty in drafting an appropriate provision to deal with whatever approach the policy-makers may adopt. However, it is worth noting that in the case of an application for renewal, the default position at common law is that, all other things being equal, an applicant is likely to have a legitimate expectation of renewal.[13]

Where licences are granted to individuals in their personal capacity, the position which arises on the death of the licensee must be considered. Clearly, much will depend on the nature of the licensed activity and the extent to which the personal skill and knowledge of the licensee is crucial to the propriety of the grant of a licence. However, where such skill and knowledge are not crucial, section 43(2) of the Food Safety Act 1990 provides a useful precedent which can easily be adapted:

(2) The registration or licence shall subsist for the benefit of the deceased's personal representative, or his widow or any other member of his family, until the end of—

(a) the period of three months beginning with his death; or
(b) such longer period as the enforcement authority may allow.

[13] *McInnes v Onslow-Fane* [1978] 1 WLR 1520, and see the text to n 4 above.

Enforcement

One of the first decisions to be made when designing any enforcement regime is whether a specialised inspectorate is required or whether the detection of breaches of the regime can be realistically left to the police or local authorities or some other existing agencies.

However, in many cases and in particular those where the licensed activity has a substantial technical content, some kind of specialist inspectorate is required.

Assuming a specialist inspectorate is required (for example because of the scale of the task or because inspectors require technical expertise), the next decision is whether it should be established as a separate body or whether it should simply be left as a function of the licensing authority. In many cases this choice will be dealt with as a purely political decision, which will be made in the light of the extent to which (if at all) there is a real or perceived need for the enforcement function to be independent of the licensing function.

Finally, whether inspectors belong to a specialist inspectorate or are employees of a pre-existing body such as a local authority, consideration must be given to what (if any) powers of entry, search and seizure they should have. It is also necessary to create offences consisting of conduct such as impersonating inspectors and obstructing or assaulting them in the execution of their duty. (The offence of obstruction can be drafted in terms of the form of words used in the Emergency Workers (Obstruction) Act 2006, namely *obstructing or hindering*.) It will also be necessary to consider a provision giving inspectors immunity from personal liability for things done by them while acting in good faith in their official capacity.

Section 44 of the Food Safety Act 1990 provides a useful precedent which can easily be adapted to fit other statutory schemes (with the extension of immunity to part-time consultants by subs (4) being particularly worthy of notice). The section provides:

> 44 Protection of officers acting in good faith.
>
> (1) An officer of a food authority is not personally liable in respect of any act done by him—
>
> (a) in the execution or purported execution of this Act; and
> (b) within the scope of his employment,
>
> if he did that act in the honest belief that his duty under this Act required or entitled him to do it.
>
> (2) Nothing in subsection (1) above shall be construed as relieving any food authority from any liability in respect of the acts of their officers.
>
> (3) Where an action has been brought against an officer of a food authority in respect of an act done by him—

(a) in the execution or purported execution of this Act; but
(b) outside the scope of his employment,

the authority may indemnify him against the whole or a part of any damages which he has been ordered to pay or any costs which he may have incurred if they are satisfied that he honestly believed that the act complained of was within the scope of his employment.

(4) A public analyst appointed by a food authority shall be treated for the purposes of this section as being an officer of the authority, whether or not his appointment is a whole-time appointment.

The most obvious basis for any scheme of enforcement is that enforcement action such as a prosecution may be triggered by non-compliance with the licensing scheme. However, while enforcement on this basis presents no particular challenge in some contexts, it may be fraught with practical difficulties in others.

For example, a magistrates' court should have no difficulty in deciding whether, on the evidence put before it, premises had been used for the purposes of entertainment without a licence. However, the position might be very different if the issue is whether development has taken place without planning permission. Here, the magistrates are very unlikely to be equipped (even with the assistance of their legal adviser) to decide what falls within the statutory definition of 'development'. (Section 55(1) of the Town and Country Planning Act 1990, defines development as 'the carrying out of building, engineering, mining or other operations in, on, over or under land' or 'the making of any material change in the use of any buildings or other land'. Not surprisingly, there is a substantial body of case law on the meaning of the key terms.)

Even where development has plainly occurred, there remains the question of whether planning permission has been granted for it. In many cases the answer will be obvious, but in others it will be necessary to interpret and apply a range of provisions, contained in both statute and subordinate legislation, which grant *deemed* planning permission in certain circumstances. In still other cases, it may be necessary to interpret an express grant of planning permission in order to decide whether something which is plainly development falls within its terms.

Of course, cases involving complex and technical matters such as the meaning of 'development' and the need for planning permission, may be assigned to specialist tribunals rather than to ordinary courts. However, where there are sound policy reasons for keeping an enforcement regime within the jurisdiction of the ordinary courts, it will be useful to adopt a technique which makes recourse to prosecution or other legal proceedings into a two-stage process. This involves creating a scheme under which the enforcement authority (which may or may not be the same as the licensing authority) requires whoever is responsible for the breach of the terms of the licensing scheme to put matters right (either by putting an end to the activity or state of affairs which constitutes the breach, or by obtaining a licence). This requirement will usually take the form of a document which may be called an enforcement notice. (As a matter of convenience, this terminology is used in this chapter, although in practice there is no universal terminology.) It is failure to comply with an enforcement notice which then gives rise to the possibility of prosecution or other judicial proceedings. However, even this solution requires some careful drafting.

The problem arises from the fact that there may be more than one recipient of an enforcement notice (either because more than one person is responsible for the breach of the licensing regime, or because other people, such as freeholders, leaseholders and mortgagees, may have legitimate interests in the land and its uses). In this sort of situation, there is clearly the possibility that one or more of the recipients of an enforcement notice may not receive it. Alternatively, they may all receive it but may not all do so on the same date, which creates an obvious difficulty where the enforcement notice requires the breach to be terminated 'not later than x days after receipt of this notice'. In either of these situations, there will be non-compliance with a statutory provision which is expressed in terms of '*serving* an enforcement notice' on all the relevant people. The reason is that in the first case this will plainly not have happened as a matter of fact, while in the second case it will not have happened, as a matter of law (because the various notices will effectively contain different dates for compliance and, therefore, there will not be *an* enforcement notice). In either case, therefore, the purported enforcement notice will be void.

The drafting solution is to authorise the *issue* of an enforcement notice, accompanied by the *service of copies of the notice* on various people. It follows that a notice comes into legal existence once the licensing authority has completed its procedures for issuing it. Crucially, therefore, failure to serve copies on some intended recipients will not affect the liability of those on whom it has been served, while the problem of multiple dates for compliance simply cannot arise.

Apart from prosecution, whether as a first level means of enforcement or as a second level means following on from failure to comply with an enforcement notice, a useful means of enforcement in some cases (especially those involving some uses of land) is to give the inspectorate power to enter on land in question and undertake remedial action. If this expedient is adopted, it is also necessary to make provision for the cost of the remedial action to be recoverable from whoever is responsible for the breach of the licensing regime.

Transitional Provisions (Including Grandparenting)

The introduction of new licensing schemes is likely to cause particular problems in terms of transitional provisions.

For example, where a particular use of land exists when a licensing scheme is introduced in order to regulate the bringing about of future examples of that use of land, the question arises as to how the existing examples should be treated. The most straightforward and equitable way of dealing with existing instances is for the new scheme to grant them deemed consent, which will have the same legal status as express consent granted under the new regime. Almost as straightforward in principle, although in practice more burdensome for the people whom it affects, is for the deemed consent to lapse after a specified period unless an application for an express consent has been made. The lawfulness or otherwise of the continued use in the longer term will then, of course, depend on the outcome of the application for express consent.

Another example arises where an activity becomes licensed for the first time, on terms that only licence-holders will be allowed to practise that activity in the future. In this situation, a decision has to be made as to what is to be done with existing practitioners. One possibility (and probably the most common one) is to adopt a process (usually known as *grandparenting*) under which existing practitioners of a certain level of experience (or a certain level of qualification, or both) are allowed a specified period of time in which to apply for licences, which will be granted automatically. Variations are, of course, possible. For example, submission of a portfolio of work, or of a professional diary accompanied by an evaluative commentary, may be required. However, specific possibilities such as these are likely to create a great deal of work, which will have to be done in a relatively short period of time by whoever is responsible for evaluating the submissions. Furthermore, some process of appeal must be created, bearing in mind that people's livelihoods are probably at risk. Overall, therefore, very good reason will be required for adopting either of these variations.

The Status of Qualifications From Other Jurisdictions

This paragraph assumes that there are no relevant provisions of European Community law. In practice, of course, there may well be such provisions.

The fact that the ability lawfully to practise some trades and professions depends on holding certain qualifications means that, in those cases, some method must be established for evaluating qualifications gained in other jurisdictions, in order to decide whether automatic licensing will be appropriate.

As an alternative to automatic licensing, there may be cases where some kind of fast-track procedure (possibly involving a conversion qualification) will be appropriate. In either case it will be necessary to create some method of establishing whether applicants actually have the qualifications which they claim to have. A system of appeals will be necessary.

8

Statutory Corporations

Introduction

Corporations may be created in a variety of ways. Some are created by Royal Charter, although this is relatively rare in modern times; some, such as companies, are created by agreement but in accordance with statute; and some, such as local authorities and a very wide range of other public bodies, are created directly by statute. This chapter is concerned with the last of these categories.

The Nature of Statutory Corporations

Corporations, including statutory corporations, may be either sole or aggregate. Both have members, but in the case of corporations sole (of which the Crown and individual secretaries of state are the most obvious examples) there will be a succession of individual members, only one of whom will be a member at any given time. In the case of corporations aggregate (of which companies and local authorities are the most obvious examples) there will be a multiplicity of members at any given time (and in the case of companies, where every shareholder is a member, there may be many thousands of members). Whether a corporation is sole or aggregate, its most important characteristic is that it has a separate legal existence from the existence (or existences) of its member (or members) for the time being.[1]

[1] *Salomon v Salomon* [1897] AC 22.

Creating Statutory Corporations

Introduction

Although much of the detail involved in the creation of a statutory corporation must inevitably depend on the character and objects of the corporation concerned, some points of general application may be made. However, independently of any instructions, an initial point arises as to the verbal formula which is most appropriate to the creation of a corporation.

For many years, the standard usage in Westminster legislation was to say (for example):

> There shall be an Environmental Protection Agency

but as part of a policy of minimising the use of *shall* in legislative drafting, the Drafting Technique Group of the Office of the Parliamentary Counsel now recommends:

> There is to be an Environmental Protection Agency.[2]

Common Provisions

Introduction

Drafters of legislation establishing new corporations will need to ensure that they have instructions on a number of matters. In practice, more matters will arise in the case of corporations aggregate than in the case of corporations sole, simply because the former are organisationally more complex than the latter.

The Name

Every corporation must have a name because a corporation without a name would encounter great difficulty with many routine matters such as making contracts and holding property. When creating a name, care should be taken to avoid forms of words which might themselves (or when reduced to acronyms) reasonably cause confusion with any existing institution or organisation. Difficulties with acronyms are not limited to potential confusion. They are also a potentially fertile source of embarrassment, which means that drafters with a good knowledge of informal usages of language have a distinct advantage over their colleagues whose vocabularies are more exclusively genteel.

[2] www.parliamentary-counsel.gov.uk/, *drafting techniques* tab, 8.

The Objects

The objects (or purposes) of the corporation must be specified, because many corporations (with companies being the principal exception) are subject to the doctrine of ultra vires, under which a corporation acts unlawfully if it purports to do anything which it has no power to do. (The doctrine of ultra vires is discussed more fully in chapter ten.)

In practice, the rigour of the ultra vires doctrine is moderated by the common law principle that a corporation has power to do anything which is reasonably incidental to its express powers.[3] (For a more detailed discussion of the reasonably incidental principle and a well-known statutory re-statement of it, see page 163.)

Members

The fact that corporations sole have a succession of individual members, while corporations aggregate have a multiplicity of members at any given time, will inevitably give rise to some variations of detail between the two in terms of the provisions relating to members.

Beginning with corporations sole, good drafting will provide for appointment (by whom and according to what criteria), removal (by whom and on what grounds) and resignation, as well as providing for the making of arrangements (perhaps by the exercise of the royal prerogative or by subordinate legislation depending on the importance of the appointment) for lapses in membership (arising, for example, from cases of sudden incapacity or death).

Consideration must also be given to arrangements for remuneration (including reimbursement of expenses and, where appropriate, payment of fees or salaries and pensions).

In the case of corporations aggregate, when dealing with the appointment of members, once again consideration must be given to the criteria for appointment (including qualifications and experience) as well as whether provisions are required to deal with matters such as the geographical spread of members and balanced representation between various interest groups. Similarly, it must be decided what payments (if any) members are to receive by way of remuneration and attendance and expense allowances, although the detailed amounts should be left for subordinate legislation, because they are likely to change relatively frequently.

Additionally, provision needs to be made for members' periods of tenure of office. Where members are either elected or appointed by bodies which are elected, retirement by rotation is not uncommon. Under this system, a proportion of the membership retires each year, thus achieving some degree of balance between the competing interests of continuity and electoral

[3] *Attorney-General v Great Eastern Railway* (1880) 5 App Cas 473.

accountability. Clearly, if this approach is adopted, provision must be made for the initial membership to take office simultaneously when the corporation begins to function, together with some means of identifying the tranches of the membership whose retirements will make up the first cycle of rotation. Drawing lots has the advantage of being transparently fair but where party-political considerations are important, the adoption of a system which preserves the original political balance of the body throughout the first cycle of rotation may be preferred. No matter how the process of retirement is managed, consideration must be given to whether it is appropriate to restrict the number of each member's possible terms of office.

Meetings

Corporations sole, consisting of a number of members who hold office sequentially, do not discharge their functions through the medium of meetings. However, all the business of a corporation aggregate (apart from anything which has been lawfully delegated to its officers, agents or individual members) must inevitably be transacted through meetings consisting of some or all of its members. Accordingly, the drafter must ensure that provision is made for a variety of matters, including the frequency of meetings, the rules of conduct governing meetings and (in the case of some public sector corporations) establishing and maintaining political balance. Questions as to the availability of information about the affairs of a corporation and public access to its meetings, are typically covered by general legislation. Where this is the case, therefore, there is no need to deal with these matters on a case-by-case basis unless there is a need to add to, or subtract from, the general law. However, where there is no relevant general legislation there is much to be said for making specific provision whenever a corporation is created, rather than relying on the common law.

The statute which creates the corporation will either prescribe the frequency of ordinary meetings or require the corporation itself to do so, although a drafter who pursues the latter option may still consider it wise to specify a minimum frequency. In relation to special meetings, there is no reason in principle why a single specified minimum number of members should not have the power to requisition a special meeting to deal with such business as the requisition specifies. However, a common variant in practice is to provide for two specified minimum numbers of members. The first additional provision states that where the smaller minimum number of members requisition a special meeting, either the chair or some other specified person has a power to call the meeting if, in his or her opinion, the specified business is too urgent to be held over until the next scheduled meeting. The second additional provision states that if the larger minimum number of members requisitions a meeting, the chair (or other specified person) has a duty to call a special meeting.

Many of the provisions outlined above are likely to be very detailed, and so may be conveniently placed in a schedule or schedules.

Employees

Almost all corporations need powers to employ staff. This may require detailed provisions to be made, probably by subordinate legislation (see chapter ten), in respect of matters such as salaries, pensions and conditions of service generally. The traditional term for employees of corporations is *officers and servants*. However, this is best avoided because as well as being simply archaic it has the potential for giving rise to problems such as that which arose in *Moberly v Allsop*.[4] The point at issue was whether a ticket inspector on the railways was an *officer* or a *servant* (and therefore did or did not have the power to detain passengers who refused to produce their tickets). When creating a statutory corporation there can be few, if any, contexts in which either *employee* or *member of staff* would be inappropriate, although the word *officer* still comes more naturally to mind in respect of some job titles (such as *chief financial officer*). Additionally, the expression *proper officer* can be a substantial convenience where the drafter wishes to ensure that someone is responsible for a specific function but recognises that it is appropriate to leave the designation of the post occupied by that person to be determined in the light of the detailed operational structure of the corporation. In other words, a statute which imposes a duty on the proper officer must also contain a provision requiring the corporation to designate the proper officer (or proper officers where there are several duties which are likely to be performed by people from widely differing backgrounds).

Dissolution

Although the dissolution of a corporation is unlikely to be at the forefront of the minds of those who are involved in its creation, experience shows that even the most fashionable or necessary corporations may outlive their usefulness or their political attractiveness. Where it is politically possible to do so, therefore, a statute which creates a corporation can usefully also make provision for its dissolution, thus avoiding the need for further primary legislation. Typical matters requiring attention are likely to include the question of compensation (if any) for the corporation's employees, together with the disposal of its surplus assets (if any) and the satisfaction of its liabilities (if any). Liability must also be allocated elsewhere for the continuing conduct of any litigation to which the corporation is a party, as well as the conduct of any new litigation which begins after the dissolution of the corporation but in respect of earlier events or transactions and to which the corporation would have been a party if it had continued in existence.

4 *Moberly v Allsop* (1996) 156 JP 514.

When a corporation is created, there is no way of knowing the circumstances which will prevail at the time of its dissolution; and, as a matter of practical politics, it may well be that even the possibility of dissolution cannot be mentioned. However, in an ideal world, there would be much to be said for the statute which creates a corporation to create a power to make subordinate legislation dealing with matters arising in the event of dissolution. The identity of the recipient of this power would vary according to all the circumstances of each corporation but would often be the relevant Secretary of State.

Miscellaneous Matters

At a purely practical level, corporations need powers to acquire and dispose of property and to bring and defend legal proceedings. Additionally, the proper functioning of a corporation requires appropriate and robust systems of financial management to be put in place.

Paving Legislation

Although the possible need for paving legislation is not restricted to the creation of statutory corporations, in practice it may well need to be considered more frequently in this context than in most others. (See page 58 for the nature of paving legislation.)

9

Penal Provisions

Introduction

While the issues arising from the creation of penal provisions in the form of criminal offences is clearly of interest to many legislative drafters, many of the same issues are equally relevant to regulatory drafters who draft disciplinary provisions. However, the overlap between the interests of legislative and regulatory drafters gives rise to two significant difficulties in terms of presentation. First, the overlap is not generally reflected in shared terminology. Secondly, there are significant differences in the functioning of the different tribunals which determine whether there have been breaches of the law or regulations. For the sake of simplicity, however, this chapter is written principally in terms of the criminal law and the courts, with only a few express references to regulatory drafting. Nevertheless, the extent to which the underlying principles in both fields are based on common considerations is such that regulatory drafters will have no difficulty in adapting the explicitly legal terminology to fit their own situations.

The Nature of Criminal Liability

Introduction

The classification of a matter as being criminal rather than civil may have various consequences, including the capacity to bring proceedings, the identity of the court which has jurisdiction, the relevant rules of evidence, the standard of proof, the extent of the disposal powers of the court (together with ancillary orders, including those relating to costs), the avenues of appeal and the relevance of article 6 of the European Convention on Human Rights (and, therefore, the relevance of the Human Rights Act 1998). (The relationship between the Convention and the Act is discussed generally in chapter four, and the text of article 6 of the Convention is reproduced in appendix two.)

Once a decision as to classification has been made, identifying the consequences of the classification will seldom, if ever, be problematic. Furthermore, the drafter can always include provisions deviating from the general principles, unless there is some constitutional inhibition against doing so. However, these propositions do not address the most important and logically antecedent matter of the conceptual distinction between criminal or civil matters; neither does the fact that the answer to this question is almost always so obvious that no argument is possible detract from its importance in those marginal cases in which it does arise. Perhaps, fortunately, the conceptual distinction between civil and criminal liability can be dealt with quite shortly in a book on drafting, where it is more appropriate to focus on essentially practical questions surrounding drafting techniques for the creation of criminal liability, together with issues of proof and interpretation.

Penalties and their Enforcement

It is tempting to say that the essential distinction between criminal and civil law is that the former involves punishing offenders, while the latter involves compensating victims. However, the truth is rather more complicated.

A useful starting point is that many criminal cases produce non-punitive outcomes, with community orders requiring offenders to undertake treatment for alcohol and drug dependency being obvious examples.[1] On the other hand, some civil cases produce punitive outcomes in the form of damages which not only compensate the victims, but also punish the defendants.[2] An award of punitive damages (or exemplary damages as they are also known) does not prevent those cases in which they are awarded being classified as civil.

The following two cases illustrate the difficulty of distinguishing between civil and criminal liability when the relevant provisions are less than explicit. Progressing one stage further, a number of specific statutory provisions have troubled the courts, all of which could have been put beyond doubt if the drafters (and those who instructed them) had foreseen the difficulties

The legal background to the case of *Northern Ireland Trailers Ltd v County Borough of Preston*,[3] has two elements. First, in the context of a magistrates' court, *making a complaint* was the standard way of beginning civil proceedings, while *laying an information* was the standard way of beginning criminal proceedings. Secondly, the Public Health Act 1936 contained the procedure for controlling that category of environmental hazards known as statutory nuisances. More particularly, section 94(1) provided for a local authority to 'cause a complaint to be made to a justice of the peace', while section 94(2)

[1] For community orders generally, see s 177 of the Criminal Justice Act 2003.

[2] See, generally, *Cassell & Co Ltd v Broome* [1972] AC 1027.

[3] *Northern Ireland Trailers Ltd v County Borough of Preston* [1972] 1 All ER 260.

provided for the court to make a nuisance abatement order 'on the hearing of the complaint' where the facts on which the complaint was based were proved. A nuisance abatement order could require the abatement of a nuisance and prohibit its recurrence. Crucially, it could also impose a fine. In the present case, the local authority began the proceedings by laying an information and the court proceeded to make a nuisance abatement order (although, in all the circumstances of the case, this did not include the imposition of a fine).

The appeal was based on the proposition that where the statute expressly required the making of a complaint, the fact that the case had proceeded on the basis of an information was fatal to the court's jurisdiction. More particularly, the appellant argued that the court's acceptance of an information amounted to an implied acceptance that the proceedings were criminal in nature, while Parliament's use of the word *complaint* indicated that they were civil. The issue on appeal was, therefore, the nature of the proceedings. The High Court held that the magistrates' court had had jurisdiction, because 'the word "fine" is a characteristic of a penalty for a criminal act'[4] and that, therefore, laying an information had been appropriate. (It was the *possibility* of a fine which made the matter criminal: the fact that no fine was imposed in this case was irrelevant.) The statutory nuisance provisions have been revised since this case to eliminate the doubt which arose in it, but experienced drafters are aware that old pitfalls can suddenly reappear in new contexts as traps for the unwary.

The court contrasted its decision with that in *Brown v Allweather Mechanical Grouting Co Ltd*,[5] where the relevant statute imposed a penalty for displaying an inappropriate excise licence on a motor vehicle and referred to a breach of the requirement as an 'offence'. The High Court held that this wording merely imposed a penalty which was then recoverable by way of civil proceedings, rather than creating a criminal offence. The Court was influenced by the fact that the word *fine* (rather than *penalty*) is generally used in a criminal context, as indeed it was in the statute under consideration when criminal liability flowed from its use in conjunction with the word *offence*. (In passing, it is worth noting that the crucial consequence of the Court's view of the law in this case was that nobody could be convicted of aiding and abetting the use of the inappropriate licence.)

The contrast between these two decisions illustrates the importance of drafters being absolutely clear in their own minds whether they are creating criminal offences or imposing penalties which are recoverable by civil proceedings; and then ensuring that they express their intentions clearly. The most straightforward way of creating the former is to use the words *offence*, *conviction* and *fine* (and possibly, *guilty*) where criminal proceedings are

[4] *Ibid*, 263.
[5] *Brown v Allweather Mechanical Grouting Co Ltd* [1954] 2 QB 443.

intended, while avoiding the use of the word *fine* but stating explicitly that a *penalty* is *recoverable as a civil debt* in other cases.

Three final points may usefully be made in relation to the distinction between criminal and civil liability.

First, the distinction between criminal liability and liability to a penalty recoverable by civil proceedings must itself be carefully distinguished from the distinction which is sometimes drawn between *truly criminal* offences and *regulatory* offences. (See page 150.)

Secondly, the imposition of a penalty which is recoverable by way of civil proceedings is an established feature of some administrative schemes. For example, it is commonplace for taxing statutes to specify deadlines for the submission of appropriate returns, with penalties being recoverable in respect of late delivery.

Thirdly, and most importantly from the point of view of drafters and those who instruct them, there is a clear conceptual distinction between the two kinds of liability. Furthermore, when properly understood, this distinction provides clear guidance as to how to think about which kind of liability should be created in individual cases, by taking the mind back to the purposes of criminal and civil law respectively. Both kinds of law protect potential victims of unlawful conduct but the protection offered by the criminal law is generalised, being intended to benefit society as a whole, while the protection offered by the civil law is targeted much more precisely, being intended to protect individuals.

Crucially, the generalised nature of the protection provided by the criminal law is reflected in the fact that the decision to start criminal proceedings is almost always made by an official, such as a member of the Crown Prosecution Service or a member of the staff of some other enforcement agency such as a local authority. (The anomalous exception in the case of private prosecutions is less important than it appears to be because of the Director of Public Prosecutions' powers to take over, and discontinue, prosecutions).[6] The role of the state in relation to criminal law continues after conviction, so that, for example, orders on conviction are automatically enforced by the state. The most obvious example is that offenders who are sentenced to immediate imprisonment will be simply taken to prison without more ado.[7]

By way of contrast, a person who claims to have suffered a civil wrong is entirely free to pursue, or not to pursue, a legal remedy. Similarly, a person who obtains a civil remedy is entirely free to decide whether to enforce that remedy. For example, a major distributor of pre-recorded compact discs may wish to obtain a substantial award of damages against those who make illicit copies on any significant scale, because the mere fact of the judgment will serve as a public warning to others that legal action can and will be taken. The

[6] Prosecution of Offenders Act 1985, s 6(2) and s 23, respectively.

[7] S Pollock, 'The Distinguishing Mark of Crime' (1959) 22 *Modern Law Review* 495.

question of whether a particular defendant has sufficient means to make it worthwhile to seek to enforce the award may be quite another thing.

Drafting Techniques for Creating Criminal Offences

Introduction

Drafters usually create criminal offences by adopting one of three standard techniques, although, as the *Northern Ireland Trailers* case shows,[8] it is also possible to create criminal offences by implication. The structure of this section of this chapter reflects the three standard techniques, before concluding with a discussion of continuing offences.

Techniques for Creating Criminal Offences

The most straightforward way of creating a criminal offence is to say, for example:

> A person who [*does so-and-so*] is guilty of (*or* commits) an offence and is liable on conviction to [*the penalty*].

Where the offence has a name, this will be expanded by inserting the name:

> A person who [*does so-and-so*] is guilty (*or* commits the offence) of [*name of the offence*] and is liable on conviction to [*the penalty*].

Since most jurisdictions have a two-tier system of criminal courts, whichever form is used is, in practice, likely to be extended in such a way as to read either *is liable on summary conviction to* [the penalty] or *is liable on conviction on indictment to* [the penalty]. (This duality of form applies equally to all the techniques for creating criminal offences which are discussed below.) Thornton recommends formulations to this effect as being the most straightforward of the available variants.[9] However, Crabbe recommends the version which provides that someone 'commits an offence', but objects to the version which states that people are 'guilty of an offence'.[10] His objection is based partly on the ground that guilt comes from the decision of the court rather than from the wording of the statute and partly on the fact that constitutions and Bills of Rights commonly contain a presumption of innocence. Unfortunately, both points are fundamentally misconceived.

Crabbe's first point ignores the fact that innocence and guilt are factual situations which exist before (and independently of) criminal proceedings and their outcome. Assuming criminal proceedings are brought, the question for the court (at least in an adversarial system) is whether the evidence establishes

[8] Above, n 3.

[9] GC Thornton, *Legislative Drafting* 4th edn (London, Butterworths, 1996) (subsequently transferred to Tottel) 356.

[10] VCRAC Crabbe, *Legislative Drafting* (London, Cavendish Publishing, 1993) 172.

guilt beyond reasonable doubt, rather than whether the defendant is, as a matter of objective fact, guilty. If the prosecution does not prove its case to the required standard, a defendant is entitled to be acquitted. However, it is contrary to both common sense and experience to say that all defendants who are acquitted are not guilty, just as it cannot credibly be said that all defendants who are convicted are guilty. Therefore, there is no reason why a statute should not define the factual elements of guiltiness, while making the imposition of a conviction (together with a penalty and any other legal consequences such as disqualification) dependent on an appropriate finding of guilt in each case.

Turning to Crabbe's second point, the presumption of innocence simply puts the burden of proof on the prosecution. Legal systems commonly treat people who are merely suspected of having committed offences, or who have been charged with offences, in ways which would be totally unacceptable in the absence of suspicion or charge. Obvious examples include loss of liberty on arrest, remand in custody or remand on bail subject to conditions pending trial and surrender of passports. The fact that some of these practices may require judicial authorisation does not detract from the fact that they all contravene a presumption of innocence, provided that they are all authorised by law.

A second way of creating a criminal offence, consisting of a slight variation on the first one, is to say, for example:

> A person commits an offence if that person [*does so and so*] and is liable on conviction to [*the penalty*].

Where the offence has a name, this is adapted in the same way as the previous form and becomes:

> If a person [*does so-and-so*] that person is guilty of the offence of [*name of offence*] and is liable on conviction to [*the penalty*].

This possibility has nothing to commend it, being slightly more complicated than the previous one without delivering any advantage in return.

Finally, the most complicated way of creating a criminal offence is by way of two provisions. For example:

> A local authority must maintain a register of accidents causing injury to members of the public who are on its premises.

The disadvantage of this form is that, as it stands, it creates only a requirement, which means that a further provision is necessary in order to complete the creation of the offence where that requirement is breached. Thus, if the provision quoted above is presented as subsection (a), it is necessary to add either:

> (b) a local authority contravening subsection (a) is guilty of (*or* commits) an offence and is liable on summary conviction [*or* conviction on indictment] to [*the penalty*]

or

> (b) a local authority contravening subsection (a) is guilty of (*or* commits) the offence of [*name of the offence*] and is liable on summary conviction [*or* on conviction on indictment] to [*the penalty*].

Where this technique is used to create an isolated offence, it has no advantages but does have the disadvantage of being longer than either of the other techniques. On the other hand, where several offences are being created, this technique may seem to be attractive as a way of saving words. More particularly, the drafter can set out the provisions containing the relevant requirements, followed by a single omnibus provision imposing criminal liability in respect of breaches of any or all of those requirements. However, a drafter who adopts this technique must be very careful to ensure not only that the provisions specifying the requirements specify absolutely nothing beyond the elements of the offences, but that the provisions creating the offences relate only to the provisions imposing the requirements. The consequences of being less than scrupulously careful can be illustrated by a provision, coming at the end of a Part of an Act, which provides:

> A person who fails to comply with any of the requirements of this Part of this Act commits an offence and is liable on conviction to [*the penalty*].

Since it will usually be the case that a Part of an Act will contain other requirements in addition to those containing the elements of offences, the effect will be to create offences where the drafter did not intend to do so. For example, if that Part of that Act contains a requirement that a certain kind of application must be made in a prescribed form, it will become an offence to make an application in a non-prescribed form. This contrasts strongly with the normal 'penalty' for submitting an application in a non-prescribed form, namely that the application is rejected. (Admittedly, if all drafters were infallible such errors would not occur; but in the real world where drafters have their fair share of human fallibility, it is prudent to adopt techniques that reduce the scope for error.)

Continuing Offences

Introduction

Most offences are committed on a once-and-for-all basis but the commission of some offences extends over a period of time. Closer analysis of offences which extend over a period of time shows that this category can itself be broken down into two sub-categories, which it is convenient to label as *continuous* and *continuing* offences. Unfortunately, this terminology is not always used consistently but (as always) consistency is an indispensable tool in avoiding confusion.

It is in the nature of some offences that they are committed over a period of time. Conspiracy is the classic example, where the offence begins with the making of an agreement and continues as long as the agreement is in force. Offences of this type are continuous and may exist at common law or under statute, but the essential point is that on each occasion there is only one offence and therefore only one sentence can be imposed.

However, where statutory offences are concerned there is also the possibility of creating *continuing offences* in the sense that a separate offence is committed on each day of the period during which the wrongdoing continues. Closer consideration shows that continuing offences fall into two categories, namely those which continue *before* conviction and those which continue *after* conviction.

Offences which continue before Conviction

The following provision creates an offence that continues *before* conviction:

> A person who knowingly pollutes a river commits an offence and is liable on summary conviction to a fine not exceeding £1000 in respect of each day or part of a day on which the act or omission causing the pollution continues.

It may be objected that this kind of continuing offence is superfluous, because simply casting the offence in the form of causing or permitting the pollution would enable the prosecution to charge a separate offence in respect of each day. However, if the prosecution were to proceed on this basis, defendants who were pleading 'not guilty' would almost certainly apply for separate trials in respect of each offence and it is this possibility which is precluded by the creation of a continuing offence.

Offences which continue after Conviction

The following provision envisages unlawful conduct continuing *after* conviction:

> A person who knowingly pollutes a river commits an offence and is liable on summary conviction to
>
> (a) a fine not exceeding £1,000; and,
>
> if he knowingly permits the pollution to continue after he has been convicted of an offence under this section, on further conviction to
>
> (b) a further fine not exceeding £200 for each day or part of a day on which the Act or omission causing the pollution continues after conviction.

In *Hodgetts v Chiltern Rural District Council*,[11] the House of Lords held that this kind of provision creates two offences. The effect, therefore, is that the initial offence is subject to a maximum penalty, while the continuing offence is, in principle, subject to an open-ended penalty, with the actual maximum in

[11] *Hodgetts v Chiltern Rural District Council* [1983] 2 AC 120.

each case depending on the duration of the wrongdoing which is either proved or admitted.

Standards of Proof

It is usually said that in criminal cases the standard of proof is *beyond reasonable doubt*, while in civil cases the standard of proof is *on the balance of probabilities*. However, this broad statement conceals the fact that some cases which are undoubtedly civil will be tried according to the criminal standard of proof. For example, the criminal standard has been held to be appropriate in one case where an award of damages would amount to a finding that the defendant was guilty of murder[12] and in another which involved allegations of malpractice by a candidate during an election campaign.[13]

Legislative drafters who wish to deviate from the general principle may, of course, make express provision to relax or tighten the standard of proof in specific situations, unless they are functioning within a jurisdiction which contains some constitutional prohibition on doing so.

Similarly, regulatory drafters may make any provision which seems to them to be appropriate. The widespread practice of stating that the criminal standard must be applied in relation to alleged contraventions of disciplinary regulations does have the generally desirable effect of concentrating the minds of those who have to decide whether contraventions have been proved. However, in the interests of making regulatory provisions as easily understandable as possible to the people they affect, it is better to express the standard of proof in terms of *beyond reasonable doubt* rather than simply importing *the criminal standard*.

Interpretation

Introduction

There is often said to be a principle of interpretation that penal provisions will be construed strictly in favour of the person who is liable to be penalised. As Brett J said, *Dickenson v Fletcher*:[14]

> Those who contend that a penalty may be inflicted must show that the words of the Act distinctly enact that it shall be incurred under the present circumstances. They must fail if the words are merely equally capable of a construction that would, and one that would not, inflict the penalty.

[12] *Halford v Brookes* [1991] 3 All ER 559.
[13] *R v Local Government Election Commissioner ex parte Mainwaring* [1992] 1 WLR 1059.
[14] *Dickenson v Fletcher* (1873) LR 9 CP 1, 7.

The Presumption that *Mens Rea* is a Necessary Element of Statutory Offences

Introduction

The common law doctrine that criminal liability requires a combination of a guilty act (*actus reus*) and a guilty mind (*mens rea*) can often give rise to difficulty in relation to statutory offences. More particularly, does a statute which prescribes the *actus reus* of a new offence while remaining silent as to *mens rea* create an offence of strict liability?

One answer to this question is that the common law must be presumed to be coherent and (with the exception of specific statutory provisions, including, most notably, the details contained in Interpretation Acts), the principles of legislative interpretation are, of course, part of the common law. It follows from this that the requirement of *mens rea* is so obvious that it will be implied without needing to be expressed.

An alternative answer is also based on the fundamental importance of *mens rea* in common law offences. However, this answer proceeds to draw the diametrically opposite conclusion that, where Parliament creates an offence, it does so in order to fill a gap left by the common law. Since Parliament is, in this sense, overriding the common law, there is no reason why it should not also dispense with the common law's requirement of *mens rea*. In other words, the offence is intended to be one of strict liability. The conflict between these two answers is resolved by presuming that, in the words of Wright J in the High Court, '*mens rea*, or evil intention, or knowledge of the wrongfulness of the act, is an essential ingredient in every offence', while acknowledging that this presumption 'is liable to be displaced *either by the words of the statute* creating the offence *or by the subject-matter* with which it deals'.[15] (emphasis added) Or, in the somewhat more blunt words of the Judicial Committee of the Privy Council, 'it cannot be inferred that the legislature imposed strict liability merely in order to find a luckless victim'.[16]

Those who instruct drafters often take the view that the question of whether *mens rea* should be an element in specific offences (and if it is required, what it should be), are purely technical points of law. In fact, however, they are important issues of principle on which drafters are entitled to expect instructions, the content of which will depend on the policy objectives of each piece of legislation. If clear instructions are given, drafting the appropriate provision will seldom, if ever, be problematic; and they will often remove the need for clarificatory litigation. (Although it is not general practice to do so, it would also be helpful if provisions which are intended to create offences of strict liability could contain an express provision to this effect.)

[15] *Sherras v de Rutzen* [1895] 1 QB 918, 921.
[16] *Lim Chin Aik v R* [1963] AC 160, 174.

Expressions creating the Need for Mens Rea

The words which are most commonly used to express the requirement of *mens rea* include 'wilfully' and 'knowingly'. Both require comment.

Two cases suffice to illustrate the difficulty which can arise from using the word *wilfully*. In *Arrowsmith v Jenkins*,[17] a crowd gathered round a campaigner for nuclear disarmament while she (wilfully) held a public meeting on the highway. The crowd obstructed the highway. The question for the court was whether she had *wilfully* obstructed the highway. Upholding her conviction, Lord Parker CJ said:

> If a person, without lawful authority or excuse, intentionally as opposed to accidentally, that is, by an exercise of his or her free will, does something or omits to do something which will cause an obstruction or the continuance of an obstruction, he or she is guilty of an offence.[18]

In other words, the defendant had wilfully held the meeting, so it was irrelevant whether she also intended (or willed) the ensuing obstruction.

In *Cotterill v Penn*,[19] the defendant deliberately shot a bird which he believed to be a *wild* pigeon, but which was, in fact a *house* pigeon. (Shooting wild pigeons was not an offence but shooting house pigeons was.) He was convicted of *wilfully* killing a house pigeon, because his act of shooting was wilful (in the sense of not being accidental).

Decisions such as these are less than satisfactory, since the criminal law generally requires an act to be *wilful* in this sense before any conviction can be imposed. For example, a shooting is not wilful where the defendant trips while holding a gun which then goes off. In other words, even if all the other elements of a criminal offence are present, there will be no *mens rea* and, therefore, no liability.

However, these decisions are not the inevitable consequences of legal doctrine. All that is necessary is for the courts to give full weight to Lord Diplock's opinion that, in order to give the word 'wilfully' any effect beyond excluding mere accidents, it ought to be understood as implying a requirement of proof of knowledge of something beyond the mere doing of the act.[20] Unfortunately, drafters cannot be confident that all advocates and all courts will know, and rely upon, Lord Diplock's comment, so whenever *mens rea* is required, it is good drafting practice to specify its nature as clearly as possible. Returning to the two previous examples, this can easily be done by expressing the elements of the offence as

[17] *Arrowsmith v Jenkins* [1963] 2 QB 561.
[18] *Ibid*, 567.
[19] *Cotterill v Penn* [1936] 1 KB 53.
[20] *R v Sheppard* [1981] AC 394.

> knowingly doing an act either
>
> (i) with the intention of causing an obstruction of the highway; or
> (ii) as result of which an obstruction of the highway is likely to be caused;

or

> intentionally shooting a bird, knowing or believing it to be a house pigeon.

Expressing the *mens rea* of an offence as *knowingly* doing a specified act, can still leave a problem of interpretation as, for example, in relation to the statutory offence of

> knowingly using, causing or permitting the use of any premises as a sex establishment without a licence.

In *Westminster City Council v Croyalgrange Ltd*,[21] the House of Lords answered this question by holding that the prosecution must prove knowledge of both the use of the premises as a sex establishment and the absence of a licence.

Rebutting the Presumption of the Need for Mens Rea *by Express Language*

Much litigation could be avoided if provisions which are intended to create offences of strict liability were drafted on the express basis that this is the case.

Rebutting the Presumption of the Need for Mens Rea *by reference to the Subject Matter of the Offence*

The usual way of rebutting the presumption that *mens rea* is needed in order to establish the offence is by reference to the subject-matter of the offence. The leading case is *Gammon (Hong Kong) Ltd v Attorney-General for Hong Kong*.[22] Holding that it was an offence of strict liability to contravene the Hong Kong equivalent of the English Building Regulations (which prescribe standards aimed at ensuring the quality and safety of buildings), the Privy Council said:

> (1) There is a presumption of law that mens rea is required before a person can be guilty of a criminal offence; (2) the presumption is particularly strong where the offence is 'truly criminal' in character; (3) the presumption applies to statutory offences, and can be displaced only if this is clearly or by necessary implication the effect of the statute; (4) the only situation in which the presumption can be displaced is where the statute is concerned with an issue of social concern, and public safety is such an issue; (5) even where a statute is concerned with such an issue, the presumption of mens rea stands unless it can also be shown that the creation of strict liability will be effective to promote the objects of the statute by encouraging greater vigilance to prevent the commission of the prohibited act.[23]

[21] *Westminster City Council v Croyalgrange Ltd* [1986] 1 WLR 674.
[22] *Gammon (Hong Kong) Ltd v Attorney-General for Hong Kong* [1985] AC 1.
[23] *Ibid*, 14.

The reference in *Gammon* to offences which are 'truly criminal' in character is intended to distinguish between offences involving turpitude (conviction in respect of which, therefore, involves some moral stigma) and offences which are sometimes referred to as being merely 'regulatory' (conviction in respect of which is often said to carry no moral stigma). Offences which are merely regulatory are said to be those where a statutory prohibition is imposed in the public interest and is enforced by means of a penalty imposed on conviction. The House of Lords has held, for example, that publishing an inaccurate holiday brochure falls within this category. (See *Wings Ltd v Ellis*,[24] which was decided under the Trade Descriptions Act 1968.)

It is, of course, true that classifying an offence as regulatory rather than truly criminal involves downgrading its seriousness. However, a court may consider this to be a price worth paying in order to justify dispensing with the need for *mens rea* and thus promoting the statutory purpose of protecting the public by increasing the number of convictions. In practice, however, the distinction between offences which are truly criminal and those which are regulatory is seldom very satisfactory, because enforcement by means of a penalty imposed on conviction is usually a sign that the prohibition involves a matter of social concern. (In the absence of such concern, victims could simply be left to pursue the civil law remedies which often exist alongside regulatory offences.)

It can be argued, therefore, that the kind of selfishness that prioritises the interests of the wrongdoer over those of the public at large can legitimately be characterised as involving turpitude, and so can properly be stigmatised as being 'truly criminal'.

Nevertheless, it is clear that the courts are influenced by their perception of the seriousness of the conduct which constitutes the *actus reus*, even though the degree of seriousness may not always be immediately apparent to the untutored eye. For example, in *R v St Margaret's Trust Ltd*,[25] the defendant finance company unknowingly contravened delegated legislation which required substantial minimum deposits to be paid where goods were bought on hire purchase. Holding the offence to be one of strict liability, Donovan J, giving the judgment of the court, said:

> The object of the order was to help to defend the currency against the peril of inflation which, if unchecked, would bring disaster on the country. There is no need to elaborate this. The present generation has witnessed the collapse of the currency in other countries and the consequent chaos, misery and widespread ruin. It would not be at all surprising if Parliament, determined to prevent similar calamities here, enacted measures which it intended to be absolute prohibitions of acts which might increase the risk in however small a degree. Indeed, that would be the natural expectation. There would be little point in enacting that no one should breach the

[24] *Wings Ltd v Ellis* [1985] AC 272.
[25] *R v St Margaret's Trust Ltd* [1958] 1 WLR 522.

> defences against a flood, and at the same time excusing anyone who did it innocently.[26]

Similarly, in *R v Wells Street Magistrate ex parte Westminster City Council*,[27] the court held that protection of the national heritage is a serious matter; and, therefore, a defendant could be convicted of undertaking unauthorised works in respect of a building which was listed as being of special architectural or historic interest even though he did not know of the building's status.

On the other hand, in *Sweet v Parsley*,[28] the House of Lords held that the owner of a house could not be convicted of being concerned in the management of premises used for drug-taking when she did not know that her tenants were taking drugs. However, by way of further contrast, it is useful to consider *Pharmaceutical Society of Great Britain v Storkwain Ltd*,[29] which dealt with the offence of dispensing certain drugs on a forged prescription under the Medicines Act 1968.

The House of Lords held that a pharmacist committed the offence even without knowing, or having reason to believe, that the prescription was forged. Lord Goff, with whom the other four Law Lords agreed, laid heavy emphasis on the fact that various other provisions of the Act created offences which expressly required *mens rea* and therefore it was reasonable to suppose that the absence of any requirement of *mens rea* from the relevant section was intentional. The logical force of this is clear and thus *Storkwain* must be taken as having overruled Lord Reid's comment (in *Sweet v Parsley*) that

> it is . . . firmly established that the fact that other sections of the Act expressly require mens rea, for example because they contain the word 'knowingly', is not in itself sufficient to justify a decision that a section which is silent as to mens rea creates an absolute offence.[30]

Furthermore, Lord Reid's use of the expression 'absolute offence' must be treated with caution. The topic under discussion is *strict* liability, not *absolute* liability. The distinction is important because in all the cases we have considered the defendant intended to do something, even though in each case the intention was accompanied by a degree of ignorance as to at least some element of the surrounding circumstances. Absolute liability, on the other hand, could be interpreted as imposing liability on a defendant who has no knowledge of his or her actions (as, for example, when sleep-walking).

Another aspect of the difficulty of deciding whether an offence is one of strict liability is that there may be a need to balance a number of contentions which are individually convincing but collectively conflicting.

[26] *Ibid*, 527.
[27] *R v Wells Street Magistrate ex parte Westminster City Council* [1986] 1 WLR 1046.
[28] *Sweet v Parsley* [1970] AC 132.
[29] *Pharmaceutical Society of Great Britain v Storkwain Ltd* [1986] 1 WLR 903.
[30] [1970] AC 132, 149.

In *B (A Minor) v Director of Public Prosecutions*,[31] the issue was whether the offence of inciting a child under the age of fourteen to commit an act of gross indecency, contrary to section 1 of the Indecency with Children Act 1960, had been committed where the defendant honestly but mistakenly believed the child to be over the age of fourteen.

The House of Lords accepted that the purpose of the provision was the protection of young girls from sexual abuse, which Lord Steyn acknowledged was 'unquestionably a great social evil'.[32]

On the other side of the argument, however, the House accepted not only that conviction would seriously stigmatise the defendant, but that the provision penalised a very wide range of conduct, including (again in the words of Lord Steyn), 'any sexual overtures between teenagers if one of them is under 14'. Furthermore, the draft Criminal Code Bill, prepared by the Law Commission in 1989, had provided that a mistaken belief as to the age of the victim could be a defence in relation to certain sexual offences and therefore there was no general consensus that imposing strict liability was necessary in order to protect children in sexual matters.

Overall, having regard to these and other considerations, the House concluded that the balance of competing arguments justified the conclusion that the absence of an honest belief as to the victim's age was an essential element of the offence. In other words, the presumption that *mens rea* is an essential element in statutory offences had not been rebutted and therefore it was for the prosecution to prove that the defendant did not honestly believe that the victim was over fourteen.

The House of Lords returned to the presumption of *mens rea* in *R v K*,[33] where the offence was indecent assault on a girl under the age of sixteen, contrary to section 14 of the Sexual Offences Act 1956. The decision was to the same effect as that in *B (A Minor)*, but on this occasion the House emphasised that the honest and mistaken belief need not be reasonable (while acknowledging that the more unreasonable a belief is, the easier it will be to disprove that the defendant honestly held it). While this common law approach to the relevance of an honest (but mistaken) belief as to the age of a victim in the context of sexual offences may survive in some jurisdictions, as far as the English legal system is concerned the test under the Sexual Offences Act 2003 is whether the defendant had a reasonable belief that the child was of the specified age for the offence in question. However, there are other contexts in which knowledge of age is relevant and in which drafters must be clear in their own minds as to the requirements of the relevant legislative policy.

Finally, the courts may be less inclined to impose strict liability where members of the general public are liable to be convicted than in cases where it is

[31] *B (A Minor) v Director of Public Prosecutions* [2000] 2 AC 428.

[32] *Ibid*, 475.

[33] *R v K* [2002] 1 AC 462.

only members of some defined, and self-selected, group who are at risk. As Lord Diplock said, in *Sweet v Parsley*:[34]

> Where penal provisions are of general application to the conduct of ordinary citizens in the course of their everyday life, the presumption is that the standard of care required of them in informing themselves of facts which would make their conduct unlawful is that of the familiar common law duty of care. But where the subject-matter of a statute is the regulation of a particular activity involving potential danger to public health, safety or morals, in which citizens have a choice whether they participate or not, the court may feel driven to infer an intention of Parliament to impose, by penal actions, a higher duty of care on those who choose to participate and to place on them an obligation to take whatever measures may be necessary to prevent the prohibited act, without regard to those considerations of cost or business practicability which play a part in the determination of what would be required of them in order to fulfil the ordinary common law duty of care. But such an inference is not lightly to be drawn, nor is there any room for it unless there is something that the person on whom the obligation is imposed can do directly or indirectly, by supervision or inspection, by improvement of his business methods or by exhorting those whom he may be expected to influence or control, which will promote the observance of the obligation (see *Lim Chin Aik v R* [1963] AC 160, 174).

Mens Rea and Consent

The question of identifying the mens rea element of a statutory offence may overlap with the question of what is meant by *consent* and how the requisite states of mind (whatever they may be) can be proved. These questions may arise in a variety of different legislative and regulatory contexts, but a useful model is contained in the Sexual Offences Act 2003.

> Supplementary and general
>
> . . .
>
> 74 Consent
>
> For the purposes of this Part, a person consents if he agrees by choice, and has the freedom and capacity to make that choice.
>
> 75 Evidential presumptions about consent
>
> (1) If in proceedings for an offence to which this section applies it is proved—
>
> (a) that the defendant did the relevant act,
> (b) that any of the circumstances specified in subsection (2) existed, and
> (c) that the defendant knew that those circumstances existed,
>
> the complainant is to be taken not to have consented to the relevant act unless sufficient evidence is adduced to raise an issue as to whether he consented, and the defendant is to be taken not to have reasonably believed that the

[34] [1970] AC 132, 163.

complainant consented unless sufficient evidence is adduced to raise an issue as to whether he reasonably believed it.

(2) The circumstances are that—

(a) any person was, at the time of the relevant act or immediately before it began, using violence against the complainant or causing the complainant to fear that immediate violence would be used against him;
(b) any person was, at the time of the relevant act or immediately before it began, causing the complainant to fear that violence was being used, or that immediate violence would be used, against another person;
(c) the complainant was, and the defendant was not, unlawfully detained at the time of the relevant act;
(d) the complainant was asleep or otherwise unconscious at the time of the relevant act;
(e) because of the complainant's physical disability, the complainant would not have been able at the time of the relevant act to communicate to the defendant whether the complainant consented;
(f) any person had administered to or caused to be taken by the complainant, without the complainant's consent, a substance which, having regard to when it was administered or taken, was capable of causing or enabling the complainant to be stupefied or overpowered at the time of the relevant act.

(3) In subsection (2)(a) and (b), the reference to the time immediately before the relevant act began is, in the case of an act which is one of a continuous series of sexual activities, a reference to the time immediately before the first sexual activity began.

76 Conclusive presumptions about consent

(1) If in proceedings for an offence to which this section applies it is proved that the defendant did the relevant act and that any of the circumstances specified in subsection (2) existed, it is to be conclusively presumed—

(a) that the complainant did not consent to the relevant act, and
(b) that the defendant did not believe that the complainant consented to the relevant act.

(2) The circumstances are that—

(a) the defendant intentionally deceived the complainant as to the nature or purpose of the relevant act;
(b) the defendant intentionally induced the complainant to consent to the relevant act by impersonating a person known personally to the complainant.

Mens Rea and Offences Committed by Corporations

A recurrent problem arises where it is alleged that an offence requiring *mens rea* is committed by a corporation. The standard solution is found in the following provision.

Liability of company officers for offences by company

(1) Subsection (2) applies if an offence under this Act is committed by a body corporate.
(2) If the offence is proved to have been committed with the consent or connivance of—

(a) a director, manager, secretary or other similar officer of the body corporate, or
(b) a person who was purporting to act in any such capacity,

he (as well as the body corporate) is guilty of the offence and liable to be proceeded against and punished accordingly.
(3) If the affairs of a body corporate are managed by its members, subsection (2) applies in relation to the acts and defaults of a member in connection with his functions of management as if he were a director of the body corporate.

A non-standard solution is found in the Corporate Manslaughter and Corporate Homicide Act 2007. (The curious title is explained by the fact that the offence which the Act creates is known as corporate manslaughter in England, Wales and Northern Ireland, but as corporate homicide in Scotland.) This solution is based on the quality of the management and organisation of the potential defendant rather than on the state of mind of its senior employees. Section 1(1) of the Act provides:

1 The offence

(1) An organisation to which this section applies is guilty of an offence if the way in which its activities are managed or organised—
(a) causes a person's death, and
(b) amounts to a gross breach of a relevant duty of care owed by the organisation to the deceased.

Subsection 2 sets out the organisations to which s 1 applies (including a number of organisations which are not corporations, provided they are employers), while subsection (3) provides:

An organisation is guilty of an offence under this section only if the way in which its activities are managed or organised by its senior management is a substantial element in the breach referred to in subsection (1).

Subsection (4) defines a number of key terms, including 'relevant duty of care', 'gross' breach, and 'senior management'.

The Standard Scale of Fines

Given that inflation is almost always a fact of financial life, keeping the value of fines more or less up-to-date can be a perennial problem. The Westminster solution to this problem is to enact a standard scale of maximum fines. The standard scale consists of five levels, each indicating a maximum fine, as follows: Level 1 = £200; level 2 = £500; level 3 = £1000; level 4 = £2500; level 5 = £5000. (See section 37 of the Criminal Justice Act 1982, as substituted by section 17 of the Criminal Justice Act 1991.)

In the absence of any reason for keeping the level of fines for specific offences under individual control, each provision which makes a criminal offence punishable on summary conviction by a fine, specifies the appropriate level on the standard scale. (There is no general maximum level for fines imposed following conviction on indictment. In that context, therefore, the problem of keeping pace with inflation is simply a matter of sentencing policy rather than legal constraint.)

10

Subordinate Legislation

Introduction

The fact that Acts of Parliament, as primary legislation, frequently delegate to various people and bodies the power to make secondary legislation, is a purely practical consequence of the volume of detailed legislation which complex, modern states require, but which would overburden the standard parliamentary process. There is no limit to the people and bodies who can be given power to make secondary legislation but the most common examples are secretaries of state and local authorities. For the obvious reason, such legislation is often called 'delegated legislation' but the terms 'subordinate legislation' and 'secondary legislation' are both often used as alternatives, with all three terms carrying the essential point that any legislation which depends for its validity on some other legislation cannot be primary.

Nothing turns on which term is used but subordinate legislation is the preferred usage of parliamentary counsel and it is the only one which appears in the Interpretation Act 1978, section 21(1) of which provides:

> In this Act . . . 'subordinate legislation' means Orders in Council, orders, rules, regulations, schemes, warrants, byelaws and other instruments made or to be made under any Act.

Although academic commentators on public law tend to speak of delegated legislation, the specialised focus of this book makes it appropriate to follow the style of parliamentary counsel.

While any kind of statute can create a power to make subordinate legislation, those that are most likely to do so deal with broad areas of law within which significant amounts of detail are required in order to make relatively broad principles workable. Typical examples include topics such as development control and environmental protection, education, employment, financial services regulation and highways. Indeed, Greenberg goes so far as to describe some statutes as 'skeleton Acts' because they would be almost wholly lacking in substance without the addition of subordinate legislation.[1] On the

[1] D Greenberg (ed), *Craies on Legislation* 9th edn (London, Sweet & Maxwell, 2008) 109, para 3.1.1.

other hand, short, simple statutes are much less likely to require anything in the way of subordinate legislation, with the possible exception of commencement orders. (See page 95 for commencement orders.)

The relative speed with which subordinate legislation can be made means that it is eminently suitable as a vehicle for certain types of detailed provisions. Two examples will suffice. First, there are details which have not been fully worked out when the parent statute is passed. Secondly, there are details which are likely to change relatively frequently. Typical examples of this kind of detail include matters which, in their nature, require frequent attention (for example, the fees payable when applying for licences) and details which relate either to matters of social policy which are constantly being fine-tuned, or to areas in which technological development moves rapidly. (Details which are less likely to change find a more natural home in schedules to Acts.)

Subordinate legislation may take many forms, but in the English legal system statutory instruments (which are made in accordance with the Statutory Instruments Act 1946) are undoubtedly the most common. There is no definitive scheme for naming different types of statutory instruments but in 1932 the 'Report of the Committee on Ministers' Powers' (commonly known as the Donoughmore Report)[2] suggested that *regulations* should make substantive law, *rules* should prescribe procedural matters and *orders* should exercise executive power. Although the word *rules* is still generally used according to this scheme, the suggested distinction between *regulations* and *orders* has become blurred with the passage of time. However, in accordance with the general principle that consistency in drafting is a virtue, there is still something to be said for trying to maintain some distinction between different types of statutory instruments and this scheme is as good as any.

In addition to statutory instruments, both compulsory purchase orders and byelaws are sufficiently common to be worth identifying as forms of subordinate legislation. There is no standard spelling of this word, with byelaws, bylaws, bye-laws and by-laws all being encountered, but parliamentary counsel favour byelaws, which is, therefore, the spelling used in this book. (The etymological root of the first element of the word *byelaw* is the Old Norse word for a settlement, which is still quite common as the final syllable of English place names such as Oadby, Scotby and Whitby. This explains why byelaws are sometimes described as being 'laws of local application', since they often apply only in a single locality.)

Finally, Orders in Council are primary legislation if they are made in the exercise of the royal prerogative, but subordinate legislation if they are made in the exercise of statutory powers.

Generally speaking, there is no legal limit to the areas of law in respect of which the power to legislate may be delegated but individual statutes may impose specific limitations. For example, the second schedule to the

[2] 'Report of the Committee on Ministers' Powers' (Cmd 4060, 1932).

European Communities Act 1972 specifies four cases in which the power (contained in section 2 of the Act) to implement Community obligations by means of Orders in Council cannot be used. The four cases are imposing or increasing taxation, doing anything with retroactive effect, conferring power to legislate other than by way of rules of court and creating criminal offences attracting penalties which exceed certain levels. By way of contrast, the Human Rights Act 1998 places no restrictions on the use of remedial orders (see page 52) which are made under section 4 of that Act in order to achieve compatibility between domestic law and the law of the European Convention on Human Rights.

Despite the general absence of legal limits on the use of subordinate legislation, there are three constraining influences on the exercise of the powers which it confers.

First, there is the possibility of political accountability. In its nature, the extent to which this is effective depends largely, if not entirely, on extra-legal factors, and nothing more need be said about it in the present context.

Secondly, there are some constitutional constraints on the content of subordinate legislation. The nature and extent of these constraints vary from one jurisdiction to another and in the context of written (or codified, or formal) constitutions, matters may be more straightforward than they are under the unwritten British constitution. However, even within the British context, some constitutional constraints are clearly identifiable. For example, article 4 of the Bill of Rights 1689, prohibits the 'levying of money' without parliamentary authority. The requirement of parliamentary authority as a condition precedent to the levying of money has shown itself to be particularly troublesome to government on a number of occasions. The leading case is *Attorney-General v Wilts United Dairies Ltd*,[3] where the Food Controller had a statutory duty to 'regulate the supply and consumption of food in such a manner as he thinks best for encouraging the production of food'. Despite the broad language in which this duty was couched, the House of Lords held that it was not effective to authorise the Controller to levy a 2d a gallon charge on milk. (In pre-decimal currency, 2d was the equivalent of 0.833p) (Also see *R v Richmond-upon-Thames London Borough Council ex parte McCarthy & Stone (Developments) Ltd*.[4])

Thirdly, there is the doctrine of ultra vires, which means *beyond the powers* and is the opposite of intra vires, which means *within the powers*. This doctrine enables the courts to keep those who exercise a wide range of governmental and quasi-governmental powers (including the power to make subordinate legislation) within the scope of their lawful authority. The wide applicability of the doctrine of ultra vires means that cases arising in one field

[3] *Attorney-General v Wilts United Dairies Ltd* (1921) 37 TLR 884.

[4] *R v Richmond-upon-Thames London Borough Council ex parte McCarthy & Stone (Developments) Ltd* [1992] 2 AC 48, discussed at p 163.

of law can be sound authority, at the level of principle, in relation to other fields. The discussion which follows, therefore, includes cases drawn from a range of fields of law

Although the phrase ultra vires is not generally used in the context of regulatory drafting, there is often a hierarchy in which a regulation-making body's constitution (whatever it may be called) authorises a whole range of committees to make regulations (again, whatever they may be called) dealing with specific aspects of the body's activities. The idea (if not the terminology) of ultra vires applies to this sort of hierarchy in the same way as it applies to subordinate legislation, so discussion of that doctrine is relevant to drafters working for regulation-making bodies.

The Doctrine of Ultra Vires

Introduction

The principles which underlie the doctrine of ultra vires may be used to control a wide variety of functions. Therefore, even such a brief overview as that which is offered here would be likely to be defective if it were to be restricted to authorities drawn from the field of subordinate legislation. Accordingly, the discussion in this section of this chapter is based on the most relevant authorities, whatever their detailed provenance, provided that the principles which they establish or illustrate are applicable to subordinate legislation.

The Drafters' Responsibilities

Essentially, the process of assessing the legality of subordinate legislation begins by applying the general principles of statutory interpretation (as discussed in chapter two) to the relevant provisions of both the parent Act and the relevant piece of subordinate legislation. Having established the meaning of both, the process concludes by comparing both meanings in order to answer the key question: intra vires or ultra vires?

It follows that primary legislation conferring power to make subordinate legislation should be drafted with sufficient precision to enable those who are responsible for drafting the subordinate legislation to know what they can and cannot lawfully do (assuming that different people draft primary and secondary legislation, although this is by no means always the case in all jurisdictions). It also follows that drafters of subordinate legislation should seek to achieve a similar level of precision, in order to create provisions which fall within the scope of the powers under which they purport to be made. Drafters of subordinate legislation should also constantly remind themselves that instruments may fall within the powers under which they purport to be made if the inquiry proceeds simply on the meanings of the relevant words, but may nevertheless fall outside those powers when viewed in the broader constitutional context.[5]

The purely technical skills required for drafting subordinate legislation are the same as those required for drafting statutes. However, since drafting and interpretation are opposite sides of the same coin, the following specific matters arise.

First, subordinate legislation is presumed to share the purpose or purposes of the Act under which it is made and will, therefore, be unlawful if it cannot be interpreted as doing so.[6]

Secondly, section 11 of the Interpretation Act 1978 provides that expressions which appear in both an Act and subordinate legislation made under it, 'have, unless the contrary intention appears, the meaning which they bear in that Act'.

Thirdly, the common law recognises that express powers conferred on corporate bodies carry with them implied powers to do anything which

> may fairly be regarded as incidental to or consequential upon those things which the legislature has authorised ought not (unless expressly prohibited) to be held, by judicial construction, to be ultra vires.[7]

This principle has been given statutory form in relation to local authorities by section 111 of the Local Government Act 1972:

> A local authority shall have power to do anything . . . which is calculated to facilitate, or is conducive or incidental to, the discharge of any of their functions.

Including similar provisions in Bills relating to other areas of law adds nothing of substance to the law (since, in the absence of any statutory provision, the common law would have the same effect), but it may have the advantage of making the law more accessible to readers who are not lawyers. However, it is easy to overstate the extent of this increased accessibility, since the full import of the reasonably incidental principle (whether in its common law or statutory form) cannot be appreciated without a good knowledge of the case law which explains and illustrates the limits of its applicability.

Inevitably, most of the case law on the reasonably incidental principle turns very much on a combination of the wording of each provision and the facts of each case, but one proposition of universal application is that the principle can operate only once in any given context. In other words, it cannot be used to justify doing something which is reasonably incidental to something which is itself lawful only because it is reasonably incidental to the exercise of an express power. For example, in *R v Richmond-upon-Thames London Borough*

[5] See, eg, the text to n 3 above.

[6] *Utah Construction and Engineering Pty Ltd v Pataky* [1966] AC 629.

[7] See the company law case of *Attorney-General v Great Eastern Railway* (1880) 5 App Cas 473, 478.

Council ex parte McCarthy & Stone (Developments) Ltd[8] the House of Lords held that, although a local planning authority had no specific power or duty to give advice to potential applicants for planning permission, section 111(1) of the 1972 Act did confer an implied power to do so. (Giving advice as to the kind of proposal which would be likely to be acceptable can be said to facilitate the performance of the local authority's planning functions in two ways. First, it reduces the amount of time which is wasted on assessing hopeless applications. Secondly, it reduces the number of appeals against refusals of permission in more borderline cases and, therefore, the amount of work which has to be put into preparing and presenting the local planning authority's case when resisting those appeals.) Furthermore, charging potential applicants for giving advice was reasonably incidental to giving the advice. However, the practice of charging for giving advice involved doing something which was reasonably incidental to something which was itself reasonably incidental to an authorised activity; and it was, therefore, one step removed from anything which was authorised by section 111(1). (An additional reason for the decision was that charging breached the prohibition, contained in article 4 of the Bill of Rights, on 'the levying of money' without the authority of Parliament.)

A drafter who decides to re-state the reasonably incidental principle could simply adopt the precedent of section 111(1), but it would be more in keeping with modern drafting style to replace *calculated* with *intended*.

Fourthly, there is the question of *severability*. A court which holds that only part of a piece of subordinate legislation is bad (on whatever ground) is immediately faced with a question: should it quash the whole of the subordinate legislation or should it cut away (or sever, to use the standard terminology) the bad part, leaving the good part in continued existence?

The starting point for considering the problem of severability lies in the doctrine of the separation of powers. More particularly, before deciding on severance coupled with partial quashing (in other words, quashing the unlawful parts while leaving the lawful parts extant) the court will bear in mind the danger of crossing the constitutional boundary which limits it to adjudicating and excludes it from legislating. In order to reassure itself in this respect, the court will ask itself whether the resulting text would, in substance, be one which a decision-maker who had been aware of the partial unlawfulness would nevertheless have made. The leading case on the tests for severance comes from the field of byelaws.

In *Director of Public Prosecutions v Hutchinson and Smith*,[9] the Secretary of State for Defence had power to make byelaws regulating the use of land appropriated for military purposes, provided that the byelaws did not 'take away or prejudicially affect any right of common'. When the Secretary of State made byelaws which did prejudicially affect certain rights of common, the House of Lords had to consider whether the byelaws could be severed. In

[8] [1992] 2 AC 48.

[9] *Director of Public Public Prosecutions v Hutchinson and Smith* [1990] 2 AC 783.

other words, could the byelaws be upheld as against anyone who did not claim rights of common, while being quashed as against anyone whose rights of common were prejudicially affected? The answer the House gave itself was that the residue of the byelaws, after severance and partial quashing, would be substantially different from those which the Secretary of State had actually made. The byelaws were, therefore, quashed in their entirety.

Lord Bridge, with whom three other Law Lords concurred, recognised that severability comes in two forms, namely *textual* and *substantial*, with the distinction being expressed thus:

> A legislative instrument is *textually* severable if a clause, a sentence, a phrase or a single word may be disregarded, as exceeding the lawmaker's power, and what remains of the text is still grammatical and coherent. A legislative instrument is *substantially* severable if the substance of what remains after severance is essentially unchanged in its legislative purpose, operation and effect.[10] (emphasis added)

Although Lord Bridge took the view that, generally speaking, both types of severability would need to be present before the court could undertake severance and partial quashing, he did acknowledge the possibility of exceptions, in which connection he emphasised *substantial* severability as the more important factor:

> A rigid insistence that the test of textual severability must always be satisfied . . . will in some cases . . . have the unreasonable consequence of defeating subordinate legislation of which the substantial purpose and effect was clearly within the lawmaker's power when, by some oversight or misapprehension of the scope of that power, the text, as written, has a range of application which exceeds that scope. It is important, however, that in *all* cases an appropriate test of substantial severability should be applied. (emphasis added)

In terms of textual severance, therefore, and assuming that part of a given piece of subordinate legislation will be held to be bad, the drafter has to decide whether half a legislative loaf is better than no legislative bread. In other words, is it better that the wording of an instrument should facilitate or obstruct severance? In terms of drafting technique, this amounts to choosing between a series of discrete provisions and such a closely interwoven whole that the failure of any one provision must cause the rest to unravel.

Facilitating textual severance will be much easier in some contexts than in others. For example, a set of byelaws regulating conduct in public parks will typically contain prohibitions on matters as diverse as skateboarding, trading from motor vehicles and flying model aeroplanes. Since it is natural to draft a separate byelaw for each of these activities, one byelaw may easily be quashed without affecting the integrity of the whole set. However, the question of severance may arise within the context of a single byelaw. For example, a byelaw which prohibits trading from motor vehicles may contain an exception permitting the sale of ice cream, soft drinks and confectionery, subject to a

[10] *Ibid*, 804.

condition that the trader must not advertise his business by the use of chimes or any other audible means. A court which decides that the condition is unlawful will also have to decide whether to quash either the whole of that byelaw, or the whole of the exception (leaving the basic prohibition standing), or the condition attached to the exception (leaving the basic prohibition and the basic exception to be effective without being fettered by the condition).

By way of contrast with byelaws, the nature of compulsory purchase orders means that they are likely to be single, integrated wholes, which almost certainly places the emphasis firmly on substantial severance alone. In this context, it is less likely that the person or authority making the compulsory purchase order will consider half a legislative loaf to be preferable to no legislative bread. However, something may still be preferable to nothing, in which case a drafter who is instructed to proceed with a scheme which he or she regards as being of doubtful legality when viewed as a whole, may choose to produce two or more separate instruments. If this can be done in a way which achieves a range of outcomes, but divides into separate instruments those which are clearly good and those which are open to challenge, the court will have the option of quashing only those which it finds to be bad, while leaving the others untouched.

When drafting in such a way as to facilitate severance is impracticable, the drafter will have to accept that the application of the tests for both textual and substantial severance are ultimately and inescapably matters of judgment for the court in all the circumstances of each case. However, it is worth observing that the general weight of the case law demonstrates a preference for severing that which is bad, in order to uphold that which is good where it is reasonably possible to do so. (This approach reflects the old common law maxim *ut res magis valeat quam pereat*, which may be translated as *it is better that a thing should be valid than that it should perish*.)

However, there will always be some cases in which the courts' preference for severance has to give way to other factors. For example, in *R v Secretary of State for Transport ex parte Greater London Council*,[11] the Secretary of State, acting in the exercise of a statutory power, made a direction requiring the GLC to pay London Regional Transport the sum of £281.5m. When it transpired that this figure was a substantial overpayment (having been calculated by reference to figures which were £10.2m adrift), the court took the view that it was dealing with a single and indivisible, lump sum, and therefore the direction as a whole should be quashed. In other words, the court was not willing to recalculate the amount which would have been due if the correct figures had been used, so that it could then sever the excess which had resulted from the defective calculation and uphold the balance.

Fifthly, and finally, there is the question of whether there is a special principle of interpretation, applicable only to byelaws, which increases the

[11] *R v Secretary of State for Transport ex parte Greater London Council* [1986] 1 QB 556.

likelihood of their being held to be intra vires. This question springs from the unambiguous and much quoted dictum of Lord Russell CJ that byelaws (or at least those made by local authorities for the good rule and government of their areas) should be construed 'benevolently'.[12] However, it is difficult to reconcile this view with the presumption that penal provisions should be interpreted strictly in favour of the defendant (see page 147) and, therefore, no prudent drafter (or prosecutor) should rely on it.

Classifying the Bases of Ultra Vires Action

Introduction

The traditional analysis of ultra vires action, so far as it is relevant to subordinate legislation, is into jurisdictional error, *Wednesbury* irrelevance, *Wednesbury* unreasonableness, and breach of either procedural fairness (or natural justice) at common law or express procedural requirements prescribed by statute. In *Council of Civil Service Unions v Minister for the Civil Service*,[13] (commonly known as the *GCHQ* case because it arose from a dispute involving the workforce at the Government Communication Headquarters), Lord Diplock recast[14] the traditional terminology thus:

> One can conveniently classify under *three heads* the grounds upon which administrative action is subject to control by judicial review. The first ground I would call *illegality*, the second *irrationality* and the third *procedural impropriety*. (emphasis added)

Although the traditional terminology is used in this book, in practice both versions are sufficiently widely used for the following table of equivalences to be useful:

Traditional	**GCHQ**
Jurisdictional error and *Wednesbury* irrelevance	Illegality
Wednesbury unreasonableness	Irrationality
Breach of procedural fairness at common law and Breach of express procedural requirements under statute	Procedural Impropriety

12 *Kruse v Johnson* [1898] 2 QB 91, 99.
13 *Council of Civil Service Unions v Minister for the Civil Service* [1985] AC 374.
14 *Ibid*, 410.

It is now appropriate to consider each category in turn.

Jurisdictional Error

Very occasionally, decision-makers purport to do things which they simply have no lawful power to do. For example, in *White & Collins v Minister of Health*,[15] a statute conferred power to make compulsory purchase orders, except where the land concerned was part of a park or garden belonging to a house. The court quashed a compulsory order which was made in breach of the exception. In situations giving rise to cases such as these, the drafter of the subordinate legislation has a clear professional duty to advise the instructing department that it is proposing to act unlawfully (and in a jurisdiction where the instructing department is short of professionally qualified legal staff, the drafter may even be said to bear the primary responsibility for avoiding jurisdictional errors).

In practice, the scope of jurisdictional error is significantly reduced by the *reasonably incidental* principle (see page 163) but this principle will not save a decision-maker whose abundance of enthusiasm results in a power which is conferred for one purpose being used in order to achieve another purpose. In *R (Richards and Another) v Pembrokeshire County Council*,[16] a local authority could lawfully make subordinate legislation for the operational purposes of a harbour. The Court of Appeal held that the authority acted ultra vires when it made subordinate legislation which affected pedestrian safety and traffic congestion over a large area but which only collaterally affected land held as part of the harbour estate. (This case could also be analysed as being an example of taking mixed considerations into account, but this is one aspect of the next sub-topic and is discussed there.)

Wednesbury Irrelevance

In *Associated Provincial Picture Houses Ltd v Wednesbury Corporation*,[17] Lord Greene MR made it clear that decision-makers err in law if, when exercising their statutory discretions, they fail to have regard to all relevant considerations and to disregard all irrelevant ones. The problem, of course, is to know which considerations are relevant and which are irrelevant in the context of any given discretion. For example, it is easy to state that planning authorities must have regard to policy matters and all other material considerations when determining applications for planning permission, but it is only through studying a mass of case law that any substantial degree of insight can be gained as to which considerations will rank as *material*. It follows that relatively little can be said in general terms but, nevertheless, two points may usefully be made.

[15] *White & Collins v Minister of Health* [1939] 2 KB 838.
[16] *R (Richards and Another) v Pembrokeshire County Council* [2005] LGR 105.
[17] *Associated Provincial Picture Houses Ltd v Wednesbury Corporation* [1948] 1 KB 223.

First, in *Padfield v Minister of Agriculture, Fisheries and Food*,[18] the House of Lords made it clear that a statutory discretion must not be used to frustrate the purpose of the statute which confers it. Another way of making the same point is that the purpose of the statute is always a relevant consideration. For example, the case of *Pilling v Abergele Urban District Council*[19] arose from the operation of the scheme for licensing sites for moveable dwellings under the Public Health Act 1936. The court held that amenity considerations are irrelevant to public health and, therefore, could not lawfully be used as the basis for exercising a discretion which was conferred for public health purposes.

Secondly, it is not uncommon in practice for decisions to be based on more than one consideration. The leading modern case on assessing the legality of the ensuing decision when some factors are relevant and others are not, is *R v Inner London Education Authority ex parte Westminster City Council*.[20] The education authority, which was funded by a number of London borough councils, proposed to spend £500,000 on an advertising campaign against the government's plan to exercise its control over local authorities' expenditure in such a way as to reduce the education authority's budget by £75,000,000. Westminster City Council, which was one of the local authorities which funded the education authority, argued that the expenditure on the advertising campaign was ultra vires. In the High Court, Glidewell J held that part of the motive for the expenditure was the provision of information, which was lawful under section 142(2)(a) of the Local Government Act 1972. However, he also held that another (and perhaps the major) purpose was to seek to persuade members of the public to accept the education authority's views as to the undesirability of the extent of the government's control of local government spending. The judge held that, on the facts, the education authority's decision was unlawful. However, the significance of the case in terms of legal principle is that he accepted that a decision based on a lawful consideration is not invalidated merely because it also achieves a subsidiary objective which would not, in itself, have been lawful. He stated the principle governing such cases in the following terms:

> It thus becomes a question of fact for me to decide, upon the material before me, whether in reaching its decision [the decision-maker] was pursuing an unauthorised purpose, namely that of persuasion, which has *materially influenced the making of the decision*.[21] (emphasis added.)

Wednesbury Unreasonableness

In the *Wednesbury* case itself,[22] Lord Greene MR formulated the test of unreasonableness for the purposes of the doctrine of ultra vires, as being

[18] *Padfield v Minister of Agriculture, Fisheries and Food* [1968] AC 997.
[19] *Pilling v Abergele Urban District Council* [1950] 1 KB 636.
[20] *R v Inner London Education Authority ex parte Westminster City Council* [1986] 1 WLR 28.
[21] *Ibid*, 49.
[22] See above, n 17.

'something so absurd that no sensible person could ever dream that it lay within the powers of the authority'.[23]

In the *GCHQ* case Lord Diplock not only re-labelled this kind of unreasonableness as *irrationality* but also reformulated the test as being whether the resulting decision 'is so outrageous in its defiance of logic or of accepted moral standards that no sensible person who had applied his mind to the question could have arrived at it.'[24] Two examples will suffice.

First, in *Backhouse v Lambeth London Borough Council*,[25] the Housing Finance Act 1972 required local housing authorities to choose between introducing a scheme of fair rents and increasing rents across the board by 50p per week. Because the local authority in this case did not wish to pursue either alternative, it identified one council house, which was not only vacant but was also in such poor condition that it was unlikely ever to be let. It then increased the rent of this house from £7 per week to £18,000 per week. When this increase was averaged out across the whole of the local authority's housing stock, it produced an arithmetical increase of 50p per property per week. Perhaps not surprisingly, the High Court had no difficulty in holding this to be *Wednesbury* unreasonable.

Secondly, a decision will be *Wednesbury unreasonable* if its terms are so uncertain that those who are affected by it are unable to identify what they can and cannot lawfully do. In *Bugg and Greaves v Director of Public Prosecutions*,[26] certain byelaws regulating the use of military land were unsatisfactory in a number of ways, including the fact that the relevant land was delineated on the plan annexed to the byelaws by means of a thick line. When this line was scaled up, there was real uncertainty as to the boundary of the land in question. The court held this to be *Wednesbury* unreasonable.

It is intrinsically unlikely that decision-makers (and perhaps especially politicians) who are acting in ways which the courts are likely to characterise as unreasonable or irrational (even if only in the *Wednesbury* or *GCHQ* senses of those terms) will recognise their own shortcomings spontaneously. This puts a special responsibility on those who draft subordinate legislation to give appropriate and unequivocal advice.

Breach of Procedural Fairness at Common Law

The common law's general principles of procedural fairness (or natural justice) require the provision of fair hearings. Both the elements of fairness and hearings are noted at pages 120–121 in the context of licensing cases, but where fair hearings are required before delegated legislation is made (as, for example, in the case of compulsory purchase orders), the practice is to enact specific schemes.

[23] *Ibid*, 229.
[24] See above, n 13 at 410.
[25] *Backhouse v Lambeth London Borough Council* (1972) 116 SJ 802.
[26] *Bugg and Greaves v Director of Public Prosecutions* (1993) 157 JP 675.

Taking a broader view of procedural fairness, in *R v Lord Chancellor ex parte the Law Society*,[27] the High Court held that, in principle, a professional body may legitimately expect to be consulted before subordinate legislation which adversely affects their members is made. Additionally, an established practice of consultation can give rise to a legitimate expectation that consultation will be forthcoming on future occasions.

Breach of Express Procedural Requirements under Statute

The range of possible procedural requirements under statutes is limited only by the scope of the imagination of drafters and of those who instruct them. However, in practice, requirements as to consultation are often among the most troublesome. (See page 118.)

Excluding and Restricting Challenges to the Validity of Subordinate Legislation

Introduction

One of the most important topics from the point of view of drafters is whether they can exclude or restrict challenges to the legality of subordinate legislation. Since judicial review is the most common means of challenging the legality of the exercise of public powers, including powers to make subordinate legislation, in the vast majority of cases this amounts to asking whether judicial review can be excluded or restricted. However, there are some situations in which the facts are such that challengers need not take the proactive route of applying for judicial review, but may simply wait for legal proceedings to be brought against them, so that they can raise the unlawfulness of the relevant piece of subordinate legislation by way of defence. One of the most obvious examples of this kind of situation arises where a defendant in a byelaw prosecution argues that the byelaw is ultra vires and, therefore, that whatever he or she has done cannot constitute a breach of the law.

In the regulatory context, judicial review may be available where regulation-making bodies are exercising what are essentially governmental functions, but legal challenges to the validity of regulations may also appear in private law proceedings arising from contractual disputes between regulation-making bodies and those who have agreed to be subject to their jurisdiction.

27 *R v Lord Chancellor ex parte the Law Society* (1994) 6 Admin LR 833.

The Leading Cases

Introduction

In practice, by far the most common way in which the legality of subordinate legislation is challenged is by way of a claim for judicial review. However, a defendant in legal proceedings (whether civil or criminal) which are based on an alleged breach of subordinate legislation may also succeed by challenging the legality of the subordinate legislation.[28]

The possibility of any challenge to the legality of subordinate legislation is, of course, a direct consequence of the fact that it is, by definition, not made by Parliament and, therefore, does not enjoy the protection of the doctrine of the legislative supremacy of Parliament. But a problem arises when Parliament enacts provisions which seek to exclude (the word 'oust' is frequently used), or at least restrict, the right of access to the courts by way of claims for judicial review. On the one hand, the legislative supremacy of Parliament requires the courts to implement whatever Parliament has enacted. On the other, the doctrine of the rule of law exerts a strong pull on the courts to assert their authority to adjudicate on legal disputes. The tension which results from this doctrinal conflict is resolved in different ways according to the form of words which Parliament has enacted, with the possibilities being total ouster clauses, time-limited ouster clauses, finality clauses, Henry VIII clauses, and provisions containing subjective tests.

Clearly, drafters have a responsibility to understand (and, where appropriate, advise on) the effect of each of these possibilities.

Total Ouster Clauses

A statutory provision which appears to oust the jurisdiction of the courts by totally precluding legal challenges to certain decisions must be read in the light of the presumption of statutory interpretation known as the *Anisminic* principle.[29] This principle limits the powers of administrative bodies to identifying what the law is, in order to apply it, but does not apply where they get the law wrong. It follows that an error of law means that the resulting decision (which may be a piece of subordinate legislation) is ultra vires and therefore the piece of subordinate legislation (or other decision) is void. Since something which is void has no legal effect, it cannot be a piece of subordinate legislation (or other decision), from which it follows that a statutory provision which puts questions of legality beyond the reach of the courts, is simply irrelevant.

The status of the *Anisminic* principle as a presumption of statutory interpretation emphasises that ultimately each case depends on the interpretation

[28] *Boddington v British Transport Police* [1999] 2 AC 143.

[29] After the leading case of *Anisminic v Foreign Compensation Commission* [1969] 2 AC 147.

of the relevant statutory provision, since a legislatively supreme Parliament may, if it so wishes, empower anyone to make definitive and unchallengeable findings on matters of law. From a drafting point of view, therefore, a total ouster clause should include something to the effect that the clause applies to

> any challenges to any decision or purported decision on whatever ground the challenge may be based, including the ground that [the decision-maker] had no lawful power to make the decision or purported decision.

This wording is likely to succeed in a constitutional context which includes the doctrine of the legislative supremacy of Parliament. However, in the context of a constitution which guarantees a right of access to the courts, a court could consider itself to be justified in striking down wording to this effect, on the ground of unconstitutionality.

Subject to two important differences, the idea underlying section 10 of the Tribunals and Inquiries Act 1992 (re-enacting an earlier provision dating from 1958) is similar to that which underlies the *Anisminic* principle. Section 10 provides:

> Any provision in an Act of Parliament passed before 1st August 1958 that any order or determination shall not be called into question in any court, or any provision in such an Act which by similar words excludes any of the powers of the High Court, shall not have effect so as to prevent the removal of the proceedings into the High Court by order of certiorari or to prejudice the powers of the High Court to make orders of mandamus.

(*Certiorari* and *mandamus* are now called quashing orders and mandatory orders respectively.) The first difference between the *Anisminic* principle and section 10 is that section 10 is expressed in absolute rather than presumptive terms, while the second difference is that section 10 applies only to statutes passed before 1 August 1958.

Time-limited Ouster Clauses

Where a statute specifically provides that a particular type of decision is subject to the jurisdiction of the High Court, either by way of an appeal on a point of law or a statutory application to quash, there is usually also a short time limit after which proceedings are time-barred. (These provisions are commonly found in statutes relating to land use matters, such as compulsory purchase orders and planning decisions, where the time limit is typically six weeks.)

It is usual to include a further provision expressly stating that once the specified time limit has expired, decisions are not open to challenge in any other legal proceedings. Since in the present context appeals on points of law and statutory applications to quash are, broadly speaking, variations on the common law concept of judicial review, the case law on the effect of time limited ouster clauses in relation to these applications may be applied with equal force to similar clauses in relation to judicial review.

It may seem obvious that the logic which underpins the *Anisminic* principle is equally applicable to time-limited ouster clauses. However, in *Smith v East Elloe Rural District Council*,[30] where the applicant came to the court several years after the expiry of a six-week time-limit for a statutory application to quash a compulsory purchase order, the House of Lords held that the ouster clause excluded even a challenge based on an allegation of bad faith. The drafting solution suggested in relation to total ouster clauses appears at first sight, therefore, to be superfluous in relation to time-limited ouster clauses. This appearance may be reinforced by the fact that, in *R v Secretary of State for the Environment ex parte Ostler*,[31] (which arose from a compulsory purchase order) the Court of Appeal decided to follow the *East Elloe* decision rather than extending the *Anisminic* principle to time-limited ouster clauses.

Finality Clauses

In *Re Gilmore's Application*,[32] the court held that a statutory provision to the effect that a tribunal's decision was 'final' was effective in relation to the findings of fact but did not prevent the court from entertaining a challenge to the decision in respect of a matter of law. The decision was based on the assumption that when Parliament gives a decision-maker the privilege of finality, there must have been an implied condition that its decisions would comply with the law, because it is not in the public interest that anyone below the level of the High Court should have the power to make final decisions on questions of law.

Henry VIII Clauses

The classic Henry VIII clause (so-called after the autocratic tendencies of that monarch) confers a power to make subordinate legislation which will then have effect 'as if enacted in this Act' (or words to that effect). Such clauses are effective to oust the jurisdiction of the courts, because the doctrine of the legislative supremacy of Parliament would have had this effect if the provisions of the subordinate legislation had actually been contained within the Act itself. For example, in *Institute of Patent Agents v Lockwood*,[33] where the Board of Trade had statutory power to make such rules 'as they think expedient' and the rules were stated to have effect as if enacted by Parliament, the House of Lords held that the wording of the Act was clear and that if it did not mean what it appeared to mean, it could not mean anything at all.

However, some cases are less straightforward. For example, in *Minister of Health v R ex parte Yaffé*,[34] a local authority had submitted an improvement scheme for the minister's confirmation. (Improvement schemes were schemes

[30] *Smith v East Elloe Rural District Council* [1956] AC 736.
[31] *R v Secretary of State for the Environment ex parte Ostler* [1977] QB 122.
[32] *Re Gilmore's Application* [1957] 1 QB 574.
[33] *Institute of Patent Agents v Lockwood* [1894] AC 347.
[34] *Minister of Health v R ex parte Yaffé* [1931] AC 494.

'for the rearrangement and reconstruction of the streets and houses in the area'.) However, as submitted, the scheme had exceeded the powers conferred by the parent Act and so, before confirming the scheme, the minister had exercised his power to amend it in such a way as to make it confirmable and had proceeded to confirm it. The House of Lords upheld the confirmation, but did say that if the invalid scheme had been confirmed, there would have been no immunity from challenge because confirmation could not cure the illegality which created the invalidity. Although technically this opinion was only an *obiter dictum*, it was made by way of express disapproval of an *obiter dictum* to the contrary by the Court of Appeal in *R v Minister of Health ex parte Davis*[35] and was no doubt very carefully considered.

Provisions containing Subjective Tests

It is not uncommon for statutes to give decision-makers power to do certain things provided they are satisfied as to specified matters. Such provisions raise the question of whether it is sufficient for the court to conclude that the decision-makers were actually satisfied as to the relevant matters, or whether the court must also consider the reasonableness (or otherwise) of the decision-makers' satisfaction. Briefly, the answer lies in the precise form of words which falls to be considered.

Where decision-makers are given statutory power to do X if they are satisfied as to Y, the problem which arises is whether the courts are entitled to inquire whether the decision-makers should have been satisfied, or are they bound to accept assertions that the decision-makers were, in fact, satisfied? Closer examination of the authorities shows that, in practice, there are two types of provision, one of which imports a test of reasonableness while the other does not.

The leading case on provisions which import a requirement of reasonableness is *R v Inland Revenue Commissioners ex parte Rossminster*,[36] where the Taxes Management Act 1970 authorised a revenue official who was executing a search warrant to seize anything 'which he [had] reasonable cause to believe may be required in evidence'. Lord Diplock said that 'the grounds on which the officer acted must have been sufficient to induce in a reasonable person the required belief', while Lord Wilberforce dealt with the question of proof by saying that 'the existence of [the] reasonable cause and of the belief founded upon it is ultimately a question of fact to be tried on the evidence'. In other words, this kind of provision does not make an honest but mistaken belief immune from challenge in the courts, unless the mistake is one which would also have been made by a hypothetical reasonable person in the position of the decision-maker. Although no lawyer should find this conclusion problematic, the clarity of the statutory provision could be improved by the following redraft:

35 *R v Minister of Health ex parte Davis* (1929) 93 JP 49.
36 *R v Inland Revenue Commissioners ex parte Rossminster* [1980] AC 952.

(1) A revenue official who is executing a search warrant may lawfully seize anything which he or she has reasonable cause to believe may be required in evidence.
(2) A revenue official's belief is to be treated as having been reasonably caused only if it is proved that the facts which gave rise to that belief

(a) existed when the official's belief was formed;
(b) were present to the official's mind when the belief was formed; and
(c) were such that a reasonable person, being aware of those facts at that time, could have formed the same belief.

The leading case on provisions which do not import a requirement of reasonableness is *Secretary of State for Education and Science v Tameside Metropolitan Borough Council*.[37] Lord Wilberforce said[38] that a provision conferring a decision-making power without importing a test of reasonableness

> may, no doubt, exclude judicial review on what is or has become a matter of pure judgment. But I do not think that they go further than that. If a judgment requires, before it can be made, the existence of some facts, then, although the evaluation of those facts is a matter for [the decision-maker] alone, the court must inquire whether those facts exist, and have been taken into account, whether the judgment has been made on a proper self-direction as to those facts, whether the judgment has not been made upon other facts which ought not to have been taken into account. If these requirements are not met, then the exercise of judgment, however bona fide, becomes capable of challenge.

The case of *R v Secretary of State for the Environment ex parte Norwich City Council*[39] arose from a statutory scheme which gave local authority tenants the right to buy their houses at substantial discounts from the prices they would fetch on the open market. The scheme was introduced by a Conservative government and was deeply unpopular with many Labour-controlled local authorities. The possibility of such unpopularity had, of course, been foreseen. Accordingly, the Secretary of State had been given statutory power to take over the functions of local authorities in relation to the sale of council houses to sitting tenants 'where it appears to [him] that tenants . . . have or may have difficulty in exercising the right to buy effectively and expeditiously'.[40] Despite the purely subjective nature of the test which the secretary of state was required to apply, the Court of Appeal insisted that judicial review of the exercise of the power would still be possible if the secretary of state acted in bad faith, or by reference to irrelevant considerations, or if he misdirected himself in relation to matters of fact or law.

[37] *Secretary of State for Education and Science v Tameside Metropolitan Borough Council* [1977] AC 1014.
[38] *Ibid*, 1047.
[39] *R v Secretary of State for the Environment ex parte Norwich City Council* [1982] QB 808.
[40] See s 23(1) Housing Act 1980.

Appendix One

Extracts from the Interpretation Act 1978

Note that although this Act applies only to legislation, regulatory drafters may incorporate any of its provisions into the instruments they produce. However, the interests of accessibility suggest that any incorporation should be done by inclusion of provisions based on those of the Act, rather than simply by reference to the relevant section or sections of the Act. Whatever drafting technique is adopted, incorporating the entire Act will result in overkill.

An Act to consolidate the Interpretation Act 1889 and certain other enactments relating to the construction and operation of Acts of Parliament and other instruments, with amendments to give effect to recommendations of the Law Commission and the Scottish Law Commission.

[20th July 1978]

General Provisions as to Enactment and Operation

1 Words of Enactment

Every section of an Act takes effect as a substantive enactment without introductory words.

2 Amendment or Repeal in same Session

Any Act may be amended or repealed in the Session of Parliament in which it is passed.

3 Judicial Notice

Every Act is a public Act to be judicially noticed as such, unless the contrary is expressly provided by the Act.

4 Time of Commencement

An Act or provision of an Act comes into force—

(a) where provision is made for it to come into force on a particular day, at the beginning of that day;
(b) where no provision is made for its coming into force, at the beginning of the day on which the Act receives the Royal Assent.

Interpretation and Construction

5 Definitions

In any Act, unless the contrary intention appears, words and expressions listed in Schedule 1 to this Act are to be construed according to that Schedule.

6 Gender and Number

In any Act, unless the contrary intention appears,—

(a) words importing the masculine gender include the feminine;
(b) words importing the feminine gender include the masculine;

words in the singular include the plural and words in the plural include the singular.

7 References to Service by Post

Where an Act authorises or requires any document to be served by post (whether the expression 'serve' or the expression 'give' or 'send' or any other expression is used) then, unless the contrary intention appears, the service is deemed to be effected by properly addressing, pre-paying and posting a letter containing the document and, unless the contrary is proved, to have been effected at the time at which the letter would be delivered in the ordinary course of post.

8 References to Distance

In the measurement of any distance for the purposes of an Act, that distance shall, unless the contrary intention appears, be measured in a straight line on a horizontal plane.

9 References to Time of Day

Subject to section 3 of the Summer Time Act 1972 (construction of references to points of time during the period of summer time), whenever an expression of time occurs in an Act, the time referred to shall, unless it is otherwise specifically stated, be held to be Greenwich mean time.

10 References to the Sovereign

In any Act a reference to the Sovereign reigning at the time of the passing of the Act is to be construed, unless the contrary intention appears, as a reference to the Sovereign for the time being.

11 Construction of Subordinate Legislation

Where an Act confers power to make subordinate legislation, expressions used in that legislation have, unless the contrary intention appears, the meaning which they bear in the Act.

Statutory Powers and Duties

12 Continuity of Powers and Duties

(1) Where an Act confers a power or imposes a duty it is implied, unless the contrary intention appears, that the power may be exercised, or the duty is to be performed, from time to time as occasion requires.
(2) Where an Act confers a power or imposes a duty on the holder of an office as such, it is implied, unless the contrary intention appears, that the power may be exercised, or the duty is to be performed, by the holder for the time being of the office.

13 Anticipatory Exercise of Powers

Where an Act which (or any provision of which) does not come into force immediately on its passing confers power to make subordinate legislation, or to make appointments, give notices, prescribe forms or do any other thing for the purposes of the Act, then, unless the contrary intention appears, the power may be exercised, and any instrument made thereunder may be made so as to come into force, at any time after the passing of the Act so far as may be necessary or expedient for the purpose—

(a) of bringing the Act or any provision of the Act into force; or
(b) of giving full effect to the Act or any such provision at or after the time when it comes into force.

14 Implied Power to Amend

Where an Act confers power to make—

(a) rules, regulations or byelaws; or
(b) Orders in Council, orders or other subordinate legislation to be made by statutory instrument,

it implies, unless the contrary intention appears, a power, exercisable in the same manner and subject to the same conditions or limitations, to revoke, amend or re-enact any instrument made under the power.

Repealing Enactments

15 Repeal of Repeal

Where an Act repeals a repealing enactment, the repeal does not revive any enactment previously repealed unless words are inserted reviving it.

16 General Savings

(1) Without prejudice to section 15, where an Act repeals an enactment, the repeal does not, unless the contrary intention appears,—

  (a) revive anything not in force or existing at the time at which the repeal takes effect;
  (b) affect the previous operation of the enactment repealed or anything duly done or suffered under that enactment;
  (c) affect any right, privilege, obligation or liability acquired, accrued or incurred under that enactment;
  (d) affect any penalty, forfeiture or punishment incurred in respect of any offence committed against that enactment;
  (e) affect any investigation, legal proceeding or remedy in respect of any such right, privilege, obligation, liability, penalty, forfeiture or punishment;

  and any such investigation, legal proceeding or remedy may be instituted, continued or enforced, and any such penalty, forfeiture or punishment may be imposed, as if the repealing Act had not been passed.

(2) This section applies to the expiry of a temporary enactment as if it were repealed by an Act.

17 Repeal and Re-enactment

(1) Where an Act repeals a previous enactment and substitutes provisions for the enactment repealed, the repealed enactment remains in force until the substituted provisions come into force.
(2) Where an Act repeals and re-enacts, with or without modification, a previous enactment then, unless the contrary intention appears,—
   (a) any reference in any other enactment to the enactment so repealed shall be construed as a reference to the provision re-enacted;
   (b) in so far as any subordinate legislation made or other thing done under the enactment so repealed, or having effect as if so made or done, could have been made or done under the provision re-enacted, it shall have effect as if made or done under that provision.

Miscellaneous

18 Duplicated Offences

Where an act or omission constitutes an offence under two or more Acts, or both under an Act and at common law, the offender shall, unless the contrary intention appears, be liable to be prosecuted and punished under either or any of those Acts or at common law, but shall not be liable to be punished more than once for the same offence.

19 Citation of other Acts

(1) Where an Act cites another Act by year, statute, session or chapter, or a section or other portion of another Act by number or letter, the reference shall, unless the contrary intention appears, be read as referring—
   (a) in the case of Acts included in any revised edition of the statutes printed by authority, to that edition;
   (b) in the case of Acts not so included but included in the edition prepared under the direction of the Record Commission, to that edition;
   (c) in any other case, to the Acts printed by the Queen's Printer, or under the superintendence or authority of Her Majesty's Stationery Office.
(2) An Act may continue to be cited by the short title authorised by any enactment notwithstanding the repeal of that enactment.

20 References to other Enactments

(1) Where an Act describes or cites a portion of an enactment by referring to words, sections or other parts from or to which (or from and to which)

the portion extends, the portion described or cited includes the words, sections or other parts referred to unless the contrary intention appears.

(2) Where an Act refers to an enactment, the reference, unless the contrary intention appears, is a reference to that enactment as amended, and includes a reference thereto as extended or applied, by or under any other enactment, including any other provision of that Act.

20A References to Community Instruments

Where an Act passed after the commencement of this section refers to a Community instrument that has been amended, extended or applied by another such instrument, the reference, unless the contrary intention appears, is a reference to that instrument as so amended, extended or applied.

Supplementary

21 Interpretation Etc

(1) In this Act 'Act' includes a local and personal or private Act; and 'subordinate legislation' means Orders in Council, orders, rules, regulations, schemes, warrants, byelaws and other instruments made or to be made under any Act.

(2) This Act binds the Crown.

22 Application to Acts and Measures

(1) This Act applies to itself, to any Act passed after the commencement of this Act [(subject, in the case of section 20A, to the provision made in that section)] and, to the extent specified in Part I of Schedule 2, to Acts passed before the commencement of this Act.

(2) In any of the foregoing provisions of this Act a reference to an Act is a reference to an Act to which that provision applies; but this does not affect the generality of references to enactments or of the references in section 19(1) to other Acts.

(3) This Act applies to Measures of the General Synod of the Church of England (and, so far as it relates to Acts passed before the commencement of this Act, to Measures of the Church Assembly passed after 28th May 1925) as it applies to Acts.

23 Application to other Instruments

(1) The provisions of this Act, except sections 1 to 3 and 4(b), apply, so far as applicable and unless the contrary intention appears, to subordinate

legislation made after the commencement of this Act and, to the extent specified in Part II of Schedule 2, to subordinate legislation made before the commencement of this Act, as they apply to Acts.

(2) In the application of this Act to Acts passed or subordinate legislation made after the commencement of this Act, all references to an enactment include an enactment comprised in subordinate legislation whenever made, and references to the passing or repeal of an enactment are to be construed accordingly.

(3) Sections 9 and 19(1) also apply to deeds and other instruments and documents as they apply to Acts and subordinate legislation; and in the application of section 17(2)(*a*) to Acts passed or subordinate legislation made after the commencement of this Act, the reference to any other enactment includes any deed or other instrument or document.

(4) Subsections (1) and (2) of this section do not apply to Orders in Council made under section 5 of the Statutory Instruments Act 1946, section 1(3) of the Northern Ireland (Temporary Provisions) Act 1972 or Schedule 1 to the Northern Ireland Act 1974.

[Sections 23A and 23B deal with Acts of the Scottish Parliament and Measures and Acts of the National Assembly for Wales.]

25 Repeals and Savings

(1) The enactments described in Schedule 3 are repealed to the extent specified in the third column of that Schedule.

(2) Without prejudice to section 17(2)(a), a reference to the Interpretation Act 1889, to any provision of that Act or to any other enactment repealed by this Act, whether occurring in another Act, in subordinate legislation, in Northern Ireland legislation or in any deed or other instrument or document, shall be construed as referring to this Act, or to the corresponding provision of this Act, as it applies to Acts passed at the time of the reference.

(3) The provisions of this Act relating to Acts passed after any particular time do not affect the construction of Acts passed before that time, though continued or amended by Acts passed thereafter.

26 Commencement

This Act shall come into force on 1st January 1979.

27 Short Title

This Act may be cited as the Interpretation Act 1978.

SCHEDULE 1

Words and expressions defined (s 5)

Note: The years or dates which follow certain entries in this Schedule are relevant for the purposes of paragraph 4 of Schedule 2, which provides that the provisions of this Act apply to enactments passed on or after a specified date or after a specified year.

Definitions

'Act' means an Act of Parliament.

. . .

British Islands' means the United Kingdom, the Channel Islands and the Isle of Man. [1889]

'British overseas territory' has the same meaning as in the British Nationality Act 1981.

'British possession' means any part of Her Majesty's dominions outside the United Kingdom; and where parts of such dominions are under both a central and a local legislature, all parts under the central legislature are deemed, for the purposes of this definition, to be one British possession. [1889]

. . .

'Central funds', in an enactment providing in relation to England and Wales for the payment of costs out of central funds, means money provided by Parliament.

'Civil partnership' means a civil partnership which exists under or by virtue of the Civil Partnership Act 2004 (and any reference to a civil partner is to be read accordingly).

'Colonial legislature', and 'legislature' in relation to a British possession, mean the authority, other than the Parliament of the United Kingdom or Her Majesty in Council, competent to make laws for the possession.

'Colony' means any part of Her Majesty's dominions outside the British Islands except—

(a) countries having fully responsible status within the Commonwealth;
(b) territories for whose external relations a country other than the United Kingdom is responsible;
(c) associated states;

and where parts of such dominions are under both a central and a local legislature, all parts under the central legislature are deemed for the purposes of this definition to be one colony. [1889]

'Commencement', in relation to an Act or enactment, means the time when the Act or enactment comes into force.

. . .

'The Communities', 'the Treaties' or 'the Community Treaties' and other expressions defined by section 1 of and Schedule 1 to the European Communities Act 1972 have the meanings prescribed by that Act.

. . .

'England' means, subject to any alteration of boundaries under Part IV of the Local Government Act 1972, the area consisting of the counties established by section 1 of that Act, Greater London and the Isles of Scilly. [1st April 1974]

'Financial year' means, in relation to matters relating to the Consolidated Fund, the National Loans Fund, or moneys provided by Parliament, or to the Exchequer or to central taxes or finance, the twelve months ending with 31st March. [1889]

'Governor-General' includes any person who for the time being has the powers of the Governor-General, and 'Governor', in relation to any British possession, includes the officer for the time being administering the government of that possession. [1889]

'Her Majesty's Revenue and Customs' has the meaning given by section 4 of the Commissioners for Revenue and Customs Act 2005.

. . .

'Land' includes buildings and other structures, land covered with water, and any estate, interest, easement, servitude or right in or over land. [1st January 1979]

. . .

'Month' means calendar month. [1850]

. . .

'Oath' and 'affidavit' include affirmation and declaration, and 'swear' includes affirm and declare.

. . .

'Person' includes a body of persons corporate or unincorporate. [1889]

. . .

'Secretary of State' means one of Her Majesty's Principal Secretaries of State.

'Statutory declaration' means a declaration made by virtue of the Statutory Declarations Act 1835.

'Trust of land' and 'trustees of land', in relation to England and Wales, have the same meanings as in the Trusts of Land and Appointment of Trustees Act 1996.

'United Kingdom' means Great Britain and Northern Ireland. [12th April 1927]

. . .

'Writing' includes typing, printing, lithography, photography and other modes of representing or reproducing words in a visible form, and expressions referring to writing are construed accordingly.

. . .

Construction of Certain Expressions relating to Offences

In relation to England and Wales—

(a) 'indictable offence' means an offence which, if committed by an adult, is triable on indictment, whether it is exclusively so triable or triable either way;
(b) 'summary offence' means an offence which, if committed by an adult, is triable only summarily;
(c) 'offence triable either way' means an offence[, other than an offence triable on indictment only by virtue of Part V of the Criminal Justice Act 1988] which, if committed by an adult, is triable either on indictment or summarily;

and the terms 'indictable', 'summary' and 'triable either way', in their application to offences, are to be construed accordingly.

In the above definitions references to the way or ways in which an offence is triable are to be construed without regard to the effect, if any, of [section 22 of the Magistrates' Courts Act 1980] on the mode of trial in a particular case.

Construction of Certain References to Relationships

In relation to England and Wales—

(a) references (however expressed) to any relationship between two persons;
(b) references to a person whose father and mother were or were not married to each other at the time of his birth; and
(c) references cognate with references falling within paragraph (b) above,

shall be construed in accordance with section 1 of the Family Law Reform Act 1987. [The date of the coming into force of that section.]

Appendix Two

Extracts from the European Convention for the Protection of Human Rights and Fundamental Freedoms

Articles 2–12 and 14 of, and Articles 1–3 of the First Protocol, and Articles 1 & 2 of the Sixth Protocol to, the European Convention for the Protection of Human Rights and Fundamental Freedoms 1950

Section 1

Article 2

1. Everyone's right to life shall be protected by law. No one shall be deprived of his life intentionally save in the execution of a sentence of a court following his conviction of a crime for which this penalty is provided by law.
2. Deprivation of life shall not be regarded as inflicted in contravention of this Article when it results from the use of force which is no more than absolutely necessary:
   (a) in defence of any person from unlawful violence;
   (b) in order to effect a lawful arrest or to prevent the escape of a person lawfully detained;
   (c) in action lawfully taken for the purpose of quelling a riot or insurrection.

Article 3

No one shall be subjected to torture or to inhuman or degrading treatment or punishment.

Article 4

1. No one shall be held in slavery or servitude.
2. No one shall be required to perform forced or compulsory labour.

3. For the purpose of this Article the term 'forced or compulsory labour' shall not include:

   (a) any work required to be done in the ordinary course of detention imposed according to the provisions of Article 5 of this Convention or during conditional release from such detention;
   (b) any service of a military character or, in case of conscientious objectors in countries where they are recognized, service exacted instead of compulsory military service;
   (c) any service exacted in case of an emergency or calamity threatening the life or well-being of the community;
   (d) any work or service which forms part of normal civic obligations.

Article 5

1. Everyone has the right to liberty and security of person. No one shall be deprived of his liberty save in the following cases and in accordance with a procedure prescribed by law:

   (a) the lawful detention of a person after conviction by a competent court;
   (b) the lawful arrest or detention of a person for non-compliance with the lawful order of a court or in order to secure the fulfilment of any obligation prescribed by law;
   (c) the lawful arrest or detention of a person effected for the purpose of bringing him before the competent legal authority on reasonable suspicion of having committed an offence or when it is reasonably considered necessary to prevent his committing an offence or fleeing after having done so;
   (d) the detention of a minor by lawful order for the purpose of educational supervision or his lawful detention for the purpose of bringing him before the competent legal authority;
   (e) the lawful detention of persons for the prevention of the spreading of infectious diseases, of persons of unsound mind, alcoholics or drug addicts, or vagrants;
   (f) the lawful arrest or detention of a person to prevent his effecting an unauthorized entry into the country or of a person against whom action is being taken with a view to deportation or extradition.

2. Everyone who is arrested shall be informed promptly, in a language which he understands, of the reasons for his arrest and of any charge against him.
3. Everyone arrested or detained in accordance with the provisions of paragraph 1(c) of this Article shall be brought promptly before a judge or other officer authorized by law to exercise judicial power and shall be entitled to trial within a reasonable time or to release pending trial. Release may be conditioned by guarantees to appear for trial.

4. Everyone who is deprived of his liberty by arrest or detention shall be entitled to take proceedings by which the lawfulness of his detention shall be decided speedily by a court and his release ordered if the detention is not lawful.
5. Everyone who has been the victim of arrest or detention in contravention of the provisions of this Article shall have an enforceable right to compensation.

Article 6

1. In the determination of his civil rights and obligations or of any criminal charge against him, everyone is entitled to a fair and public hearing within a reasonable time by an independent and impartial tribunal established by law. Judgment shall be pronounced publicly but the press and public may be excluded from all or part of the trial in the interest of morals, public order or national security in a democratic society, where the interest of juveniles or the protection of the private life of the parties so require, or to the extent strictly necessary in the opinion of the court in special circumstances where publicity would prejudice the interests of justice.
2. Everyone charged with a criminal offence shall be presumed innocent until proved guilty according to law.
3. Everyone charged with a criminal offence has the following minimum rights:

   (a) to be informed promptly, in a language which he understands and in detail, of the nature and cause of the accusation against him;
   (b) to have adequate time and facilities for the preparation of his defence;
   (c) to defend himself in person or through legal assistance of his own choosing or, if he has not sufficient means to pay for legal assistance, to be given it free when the interests of justice so require;
   (d) to examine or have examined witnesses against him and to obtain the attendance and examination of witnesses on his behalf under the same conditions as witnesses against him;
   (e) to have the free assistance of an interpreter if he cannot understand or speak the language used in court.

Article 7

1. No one shall be held guilty of any criminal offence on account of any act or omission which did not constitute a criminal offence under national or international law at the time when it was committed. Nor shall a heavier penalty be imposed than the one that was applicable at the time the criminal offence was committed.

2. This Article shall not prejudice the trial and punishment of any person for any act or omission which, at the time when it was committed, was criminal according to the general principles of law recognized by civilized nations.

Article 8

1. Everyone has the right to respect for his private and family life, his home and his correspondence.
2. There shall be no interference by a public authority with the exercise of this right except such as is in accordance with the law and is necessary in a democratic society in the interests of national security, public safety or the economic well-being of the country, for the prevention of disorder or crime, for the protection of health or morals, or for the protection of the rights and freedoms of others.

Article 9

1. Everyone has the right to freedom of thought, conscience and religion; this right includes freedom to change his religion or belief, and freedom, either alone or in community with others and in public or private, to manifest his religion or belief, in worship, teaching, practice and observance.
2. Freedom to manifest one's religion or beliefs shall be subject only to such limitations as are prescribed by law and are necessary in a democratic society in the interests of public safety, for the protection of public order, health or morals, or for the protection of the rights and freedoms of others.

Article 10

1. Everyone has the right to freedom of expression. This right shall include freedom to hold opinions and to receive and impart information and ideas without interference by public authority and regardless of frontiers. This Article shall not prevent States from requiring the licensing of broadcasting, television or cinema enterprises.
2. The exercise of these freedoms, since it carries with it duties and responsibilities, may be subject to such formalities, conditions, restrictions or penalties as are prescribed by law and are necessary in a democratic society in the interests of national security, territorial integrity or public safety, for the prevention of disorder or crime, for the protection of health or morals, for the protection of the reputation or rights of others, for preventing the disclosure of information received in confidence, or for maintaining the authority and impartiality of the judiciary.

Article 11

1. Everyone has the right to freedom of peaceful assembly and to freedom of association with others, including the right to form and to join trade unions for the protection of his interests.
2. No restrictions shall be placed on the exercise of these rights other than such as are prescribed by law and are necessary in a democratic society in the interests of national security or public safety, for the prevention of disorder or crime, for the protection of health or morals or for the protection of the rights and freedoms of others. This Article shall not prevent the imposition of lawful restrictions on the exercise of these rights by members of the armed forces, of the police or of the administration of the State.

Article 12

Men and women of marriageable age have the right to marry and to found a family, according to the national laws governing the exercise of this right.

Article 14

The enjoyment of the rights and freedoms set forth in this Convention shall be secured without discrimination on any ground such as sex, race, colour, language, religion, political or other opinion, national or social origin, association with a national minority, property, birth or other status.

Note: Articles 16, 17 and 18 respectively provide that arts.10, 11 and 14 do not prohibit restrictions on the political activities of aliens; nothing in the Convention gives any right to do anything which would harm the rights which it protects; and the restrictions contained in the Convention may be applied only for the purposes for which they are prescribed.

Articles 1–3 of Protocol 1—Enforcement of Certain Rights and Freedoms not included in Section 1 of the Convention

Article 1

Every natural or legal person is entitled to the peaceful enjoyment of his possessions. No one shall be deprived of his possessions except in the public interest and subject to the conditions provided for by law and by the general principles of international law.

The preceding provisions shall not, however, in any way impair the right of a State to enforce such laws as it deems necessary to control the use of property in accordance with the general interest or to secure the payment of taxes or other contributions or penalties.

Article 2

No person shall be denied the right to education In the exercise of any functions which it assumes in relation to education and to teaching, the State shall respect the right of parents to ensure such education and teaching in conformity with their own religious and philosophical convictions.

Article 3

The High Contracting Parties undertake to hold free elections at reasonable intervals by secret ballot, under conditions which will ensure the free expression of the opinion of the people in the choice of the legislature.

Articles 1 and 2 of Protocol 6—Concerning the Abolition of the Death Penalty

Article 1

The death penalty shall be abolished. No one shall be condemned to such penalty or executed.

Article 2

A state may make provision in its law for the death penalty in respect of acts committed in time of war or of imminent threat of war; such penalty shall be applied only in the instance laid down in the law and in accordance with its provisions. The State shall communicate to the Secretary General of the Council of Europe the relevant provisions of that law.

Appendix Three

The Better Regulation Executive's Code of Practice on Guidance on Regulation

Introduction

This code of practice sets out the golden rules for guidance on legislation which will have a significant effect on business and the third sector. They have been created following views expressed by businesses, the third sector and other organisations and by a formal consultation process.

Who this Code applies to

UK Government Departments and their Agencies.

Status of the Code

The Code is a non-statutory code of practice. It sets out what you can expect from Government guidance. It is not legally binding and cannot prevail over statutory or mandatory external requirements (e.g. under European Community law). Government departments and their agencies will, however, abide by this Code of Practice unless there are good reasons to depart from it.

The Government is committed to reviewing the effectiveness of this code. Feedback is welcome to guidance@berr.gov.uk.

The Golden Rules of Good Guidance

The guidance you receive should be . . .

1 Based on a Good Understanding of Users

Effective guidance requires a good understanding of the target audience and their needs. Different types of organisations may have different needs for guidance.

2 Designed with Input from Users and their Representative Bodies

Input from the users and their representative organisations is important to ensure that the guidance is designed and communicated effectively.

3 Organised around the User's Way of Working

As far as possible, guidance will be aimed at helping businesses understand how the law applies to common business processes.

4 Easy for the Intended Users to Understand

Guidance will be written in clear language appropriate to the intended audience. It will be as concise as possible and avoid unnecessary acronyms and jargon.

5 Designed to provide an Appropriate Understanding of how to Comply with the Law

Businesses should be confident that the guidance will help them understand how to comply with the law by providing a clear explanation of the law. While many regulations have exceptions or complexities, and their application will depend on particular facts, the guidance will give a clear understanding of how to comply in most cases. Simple checklists will be used wherever possible.

6 Issued in Good Time

To give organisations time to prepare for regulations, guidance will be issued at least 12 weeks before a regulation comes into effect, with some necessary exceptions, e.g. emergencies. Sometimes more than 12 weeks will be needed, for example if a regulation is complex or costly to implement.

7 Easy to Access

Guidance will be easily available to the user. It will be accessible via businesslink.gov.uk. Other forms of communication, including sending guidance directly to businesses or communicating through intermediaries, will also be used where they will be effective.

8 Reviewed and Improved

Guidance will be reviewed to check it is up-to-date and allow direct feedback to check it works for the users. Guidance will be designed so that users can be confident that they are using the current version.

> 1 Based on a Good Understanding of Users
>
> Effective guidance requires a good understanding of the target audience and their needs. Different types of organisations may have different needs for guidance. We will establish the intended audience for the guidance. We will consider what types of organisation may be interested and whether we have covered all appropriate sectors.

- A good understanding of the audience will help to ensure that guidance is in the most appropriate format and language, and, once written, that it is distributed and publicised so that it has a good chance of reaching the target audience.

2 Designed with input from Users and their Representative Bodies

Input from the users and their representative organisations is important to ensure that the guidance is designed and communicated effectively.

- Guidance should be designed to meet the needs of the end-user and provides information that helps the organisation to comply with the law. When designing guidance, end-users should be involved at an early stage. This could be through a stakeholder panel or user-testing of specific pieces of draft guidance. Representative groups, such as trade associations, can be useful sources of knowledge and advice on how to make guidance work well for the target audience and should be approached when possible.
- Input sought as early as possible will help ensure that the policy and guidance will work in practice.

3 Organised around the User's Way of Working

As far as possible, guidance will be aimed at helping businesses understand how the law applies to common business processes.

- Guidance has often focused on specific legislation or the work of a particular Government Department that created the regulation. We understand that for a business trying to follow regulation, this approach can be unhelpful. We recognise that businesses and third sector organisations often think in terms of their own processes rather than legislative structures, and so may not realise some pieces of regulation apply in some circumstances.
- For common business processes such as hiring new staff a number of areas of regulation must be considered and it can be confusing for organisations to try to bring together different sources of guidance and apply them.
- As far as possible, guidance will be organised around common business processes, making it clear what actions should be taken at each stage.

4 Easy for the Intended Users to Understand

Guidance will be written in clear language appropriate to the intended audience. It will be as concise as possible and avoid unnecessary acronyms and jargon. The easier guidance is to understand the more likely it is to be followed correctly. The language used should be as clear as possible. We will avoid jargon and acronyms which are not familiar to the end user. Clear communication is not restricted to text. When appropriate we will use graphics, flowcharts and videos to help to make guidance easier to understand.

- Users should be able to tell quickly whether the regulation is likely to apply to their
- organisation, so they can decide whether to continue reading the guidance.
- Guidance should be as concise as possible so that users do not have to spend too much time reading it.
- As far as possible guidance should stand alone—most users should not need to consult other documents to understand it (although there should be clear links to more detailed or technical guidance for those that need it).

5 Designed to provide an Appropriate Understanding of how to Comply with the Law

Businesses should be confident that the guidance will help them understand how to comply with the law by providing a clear explanation of the law. While many regulations have exceptions or complexities, and their application will depend on particular facts, the guidance will give a clear understanding of how to comply in most cases. Simple checklists will be used wherever possible.

- If guidance is to be effective it should help most businesses understand how to comply with the regulations. This does not mean that guidance should aim to cover every possible scenario for compliance, as that would make it too complicated and unwieldy. It also does not remove the responsibility of businesses and third sector organisations to comply with the law, or the fact that interpretation of the law is ultimately a matter for the courts.
- Nonetheless, giving businesses a good idea of how to comply is essential. The *Regulation and Business Advice* report found that uncertainty and lack of confidence make businesses more likely to pay for external advice, increasing the costs of complying legislation. The Hampton Report also stressed the need for guidance to be authoritative.
- Users of guidance will be advised how to seek further advice if they are not sure, from the regulator in the first instance.

6 Issued in Good Time

To give organisations time to prepare for regulations, guidance will be issued at least 12 weeks before a regulation comes into effect, with some necessary exceptions, e.g. emergencies. Sometimes more than

12 weeks will be needed, for example if a regulation is complex or costly to implement.

- If guidance is not issued in good time it can greatly increase the costs of regulation for businesses and third sector organisations. Late guidance can mean that organisations do not have time to get their systems ready to meet the regulation and so compliance is affected. Late guidance can also cause over-compliance, as businesses take a 'better safe than sorry' approach because of the uncertainty about the regulation.
- Guidance issued at least 12 weeks before a regulation comes into force gives businesses a reasonable amount of time to prepare for that legislation. If the legislation is particularly complex or expensive, we will consider whether a longer period to prepare may be appropriate. However, there will be also be a limited number of occasions, such as emergencies, some taxation changes, and some European law, where legislation has to come into force quickly and it may not be possible to meet the 12 week limit.[1]
- There are two 'Common Commencement Dates' (6th April and 1st October) when the government is committed to bringing in regulation affecting businesses (unless the regulation is covered by an exemption). As far as possible, guidance will be issued 12 weeks before these dates.

7 Easy to Access

Guidance should be easily available to the user. It should always be accessible via businesslink.gov.uk. Other forms of communication, including sending guidance directly to businesses or communicating through intermediaries, will also be used where they will be effective.

- We recognise that high quality guidance will be ineffective if no-one reads it. Having understood our audience, we will produce guidance working with the audience and then ensure that it is made available in the most appropriate fashion. Input on how best to communicate guidance should be sought when gaining input on designing the guidance.
- Guidance will be accessible through businesslink.gov.uk,[2] either by hosting on businesslink.gov.uk or by providing links to guidance sources.
- Businesses like government to be active in informing them about new regulation. We will consider direct communication of guidance where this is likely to be effective.

[1] See Small Business Service, 'Guidance on implementation periods: timing of the issue of guidance to business on compliance with new regulation' (London, 2000).

[2] Except in exceptional circumstances such as where guidance is subject to national security restrictions.

8 Reviewed and Improved

Guidance will be reviewed to check it is up-to-date and allow direct feedback to check it works for the users. Guidance will be designed so that users can be confident that they are using the current version.

- Even guidance that has been well designed and tested before publication may not work perfectly. We will work to ensure that guidance is tested after it has been issued to see whether it is effective in informing users. If we identify problems, we will revise the guidance. Guidance should include the facility to provide feedback from users.
- We will ensure that guidance is clearly dated and marked with a review date.
- Guidance will also be withdrawn or archived when it no longer applies.
- Guidance should also make it clear when it was issued and how long it applies for, so that users can be sure they are using the most up-to-date version.

Index

In this Index the following abbreviations are used:

ECHR European Convention for Protection of Human Rights and Fundamental Freedoms
ECtHR European Court of Human Rights
HRA Human Rights Act 1998

Abeysekere, N, 39, 42
absolute liability, 152
absurdity, presumption against, 28, 29
Acts, *see* legislation; statutes
actus reus, 148, 151
adult literacy, 6, 7–8
Allen, Sir Carleton Kemp, 64
ambiguities, 2, 3–4
  courts, and, 45, 51
  Hansard, use of, 27
  international obligations, and, 57–58
  preambles, and, 23
amendments and amending legislation, 22, 36, 51, 52
  amending provisions, drafting, 92–94
  consequential amendments and repeals, 99–100
Anderson, Sir John, 4
Anisminic principle, 172–73, 174
anticipatory exercise of powers, 114
apostrophes, 88
appeals, 12
  courts, 9, 37
  creation of right, 37–38
  decision-making function, and, 36–38
  licensing schemes, 120–21
  ministers to, 37
  penal provisions, 139
application procedures for licensing schemes 116-20
application, statutes, of, 96–97
Asquith LJ, 30

Barak, A, 44
Bennion, F, 11, 15, 87
Better Regulation Executive *see Code of Practice on Guidance on Regulation*
bias, 121
Bill of Rights 1689, 161, 164
Bills, 3, 4, 5, 60, 66
  academic criticism, 6
  amendments, 83, 91
  compatibility, statements of, 53
  debating, 27
  legislative programme, 35
  Money, 91
  readings, 87
  statements of purpose, 17
see also general principles of drafting
Bills of Right, 143
binding precedent *see* precedent
Bingham, Lord. 13, 31, 50
bodies corporate and unincorporated associations, 59, 78, 80, 118
Bowman, Sir Geoffrey, 63
brackets, 87–88
Bridge LJ, 32, 57, 165
British Constitution *see under* constitutional considerations
Brown, Simon LJ, 47
Browne-Wilkinson, Lord, 27
Burchfield, RW, 77
Butt, P, 72
byelaws, 159, 160, 164–67, 170, 171

Cabinet Office, 66
Cairns, Lord, 104
Castle, R, 72
certainty, 43, 45, 100
certiorari, 173
civil and criminal liability, 140–43
Civil Service Department, 66
clarity *see under* language
clients:
  departments *see* departments
  drafters as, 5, 33–34
  lawyers, and, *see* under lawyers
see also drafting instructions
Clyde, Lord, 55
Code of Practice on Guidance on Regulation (BERR), 83, 193–98
Coleridge J, 105
commas, 88–90
commencement and coming into force sections, 24, 94–96

common law, 6, 7, 20, 36, 102
  conditional licences, 122
  consultation requirements, 119
  continuing offences, 146
  corporations, 135, 163
    human rights, and, 43, 48
  offences, 148
  powers, 59
    duties, and, 104
  principles of interpretation, and, 148
  procedural fairness *see* procedural fairness
  statutory duty, damages for breach of, 107
  Wednesbury principle *see Wednesbury* principle
communication and drafting, 1–10
see also drafting instructions; general principles of drafting; language
companies, 133, 134
compatibility, statements of, 53
compulsory purchase orders, 160, 166, 168, 170, 173
conditional licences, 122–25
conjunctive and disjunctive words, 79–80, 83
consent and *mens rea*, 154–55
consequential amendments and repeals, 99–100
considerations, relevant *see* relevant considerations
constitutional considerations, 36, 37, 43–46
  British Constitution, 41, 43, 44, 46, 161
  constitutional context of drafting, 44–46
    courts, and, 41, 44–46, 172–73
    drafters, and, 41–42
    executive powers and titles, 43, 60
  human rights, and *see* human rights
  interpreting constitutions, 44–46
  ouster clauses, total, 172–73
  paving legislation *see* paving legislation
  unconstitutional proposals, 41–42, 172–73
construction:
  principles *see under* principles of interpretation
  purposive, 16–20
  updating *see* updating construction
consultation requirements, 116, 118–20, 171
contextual approach, 15–28
  context, meaning of words, and, 11, 14, 16
  provisions, objective as purpose, 16
  purpose, part of context, as, 16–20, 45
    identifying purpose, 16–17
    illustrated, 17–20
    legislative intention, 19–20
  purposive approach defined, 16
continuing offences, 145–47
conventions, 41
  Convention rights under HRA *see under* HRA
  international, 57–58
Coode, G, 75
corporations, 133, 163
  mens rea, and, 155
  statutory *see* statutory corporations
costs, 36, 139
Cotton LJ, 104
Council of Europe, 48
courts:
  access to, 38, 47, 172–73
  ambiguities, and, 45, 51
  appeals, 9, 37
  constitutional doctrines, and, 41, 44–46
  criminal, 141, 143
  discretion, 100, 106, 114, 124
  disputes, 9
  European community law, and, *see under* European community law
  extra-territorial legislation, 97–98
  Hansard, and, 27
  hearings, right to, limited, 121
  human rights, *see under* human rights
  international obligations, and, 57–58
  judicial review *see* judicial review
  legislative:
    intention, 19–20
    licensing schemes, 118, 121, 124
    supremacy of Parliament, 45, 46, 172
  magistrates *see* magistrates
  matters of law and fact, and, 12–14
  'may' and 'shall', powers and duties, and, 104–107
  ouster clauses *see* subordinate legislation *under* judicial review
  precedent, 19
  principles of interpretation, 6, 16, 45, 102
  public authority, as, 52–53, 54
  punctuation, and, 87
  role, 5, 7, 31, 41, 45
  rule of law, and, 172
  separation of powers, doctrine of, and, 45
  severability *see* severability
  unconstitutional legislation, 41, 44
  updating construction *see* updating construc tion
  voidness, 123–24, 172–73
  weighing and balancing factors, 15
see also decision-makers; judges; juries; tribunalCrabbe, VCRAC, 143–44
criminal liability and offences *see under* penal provisions
cross-headings *see* headings
Crown, the, 58, 133
  Acts binding, 97
see also royal prerogative

Dale, Sir William, 65
decision-makers, 105
  bias, 121

control of, 45
courts, and, 55–56
creation of decision-making function *see under* drafting instructions
discretion, 45, 100, 106
judicial review *see* judicial review
non-lawyers as, 28
principles of interpretation, 45
see also courts; judges; juries; tribunals
declarations of incompatibility, 52
definition sections, 24, 100–102
delegated legislation *see* subordinate legislation
democratic societies and democracy, 37, 48, 54–57, 121
Denning MR, Lord, 26, 111
departments, 66
clients, as, 5
executive functions and titles, reallocation of, 60
guidance *see under* guides and guidance
instructing *see under* drafting instructions
savings and transitional provisions, 98–99
developing countries, 34, 39
Dickerson, Reed, 17, 85
dictionaries, 20, 21, 25, 26
Diplock, Lord, 13–14, 16, 18, 19, 80, 149, 154, 170, 175
disapplying definitions, 102
disciplinary provisions, 139
discretion:
decision-makers, and *see under* decision-makers
ministers', 107
statutory, 105
disjunctives and conjunctives, 79–80
Donoughmore Report, 160
Donovan J, 151–52
drafters:
amending legislation, 22
clients:
own, as, 5, 33–34
lawyer-client relationships, 40
duties, 35, 37, 38, 45
ejusdem generis principle, 22
employment terms, 40
ethical considerations, and *see under* ethical dimension of drafting
government employees, as, 39–40
headings and marginal notes, 24
HRA, implications of, *see* HRA *under* human rights
independence, 39–40, 42
instructions *see* drafting instructions
intention, 20
lawyers, as, 34, 40
code of professional conduct, 40
licensing and registration *see* licensing and registration
objectives *see* objectives of drafting
parliamentary counsel, 3, 17, 42, 63, 72, 87, 159, 160
Drafting Technique Group *see* Drafting Technique Group
history, 66
penal provisions *see* penal provisions
powers and duties *see* powers and duties
principles of interpretation, 2, 9, 11, 16
problems, drafting *see* problems of drafting
public office, as holders of, 39, 40, 42
punctuation, 87
readership, 4–8
regulatory drafting *see* regulatory drafting
savings and transitional provisions, 98–99
specialist expertise, 38–39
statements of purpose, 17
subordinate legislation *see* subordinate legislation
updating construction, and, 32
drafting instructions, 33–42, 112, 113, 116
content, 35–38
decision-making function, creation of, 36–38
drafters acting on, 5, 8
own clients as, 5, 33–34
ethical dimension of drafting *see* ethical dimension of drafting
form, 38–39
instructing departments, 34–35, 39
iterative process, 35
jurisdictional errors, drafter's responsibility in respect of, 168
meaning of, 33
nature of, 34–35
policy, 34–35, 37
precedents, insertion of, 38–39
regulatory drafting, 33–34
see also communication and drafting; general principles of drafting
Drafting Technique Group, 67, 69, 79, 80, 92–93, 94, 95, 107, 134
Driedger, EA, 38, 39, 83
du Parcq, Lord, 111, 112
duration of licences, 125–26
duties *see* powers and duties
Dworkin, R, 31
Dyson J, 58

Easter Act 1928, 95–96
ECHR, 6, 43, 48–49, 58, 139, 187–92, 161
concepts, interpretation of, 54–57
HRA, and, 47
law of, 48

ECtHR, 48–49, 50, 52, 57
  margin of appreciation, 56, 57
  purposive approach to interpretation, 48
ejusdem generis principle, 21–22
electronic signatures, 116–17, 118
email, 118
enacting formulas, 90, 91
enforcement:
  licensing regime, of, 127–29
  penalties, of, 140–43
English language, 30
  literal meaning, 11, 14–15, 16, 18, 20, 57
  ordinary words, 11–14, 100–101
equality *see under* human rights
equity, 6
ethical dimension of drafting, 39–42
  drafters' ethical considerations, 40–42
    European:
  Community and Union, 48
  Court of Justice, 48
  Community law, 6, 130
    courts, and, 45, 48–49, 51
evidence, rules of, 139
executive powers and titles, 43, 60
exemplary damages, 140
expressio unius exclusio alterius, 101
extent of a statute, 97–98
extra-territorial legislation, 97–98
extrinsic materials, 16, 25–29
  dictionaries, 20, 21, 25, 26
  legal textbooks, 25–26
  parliamentary materials, 16, 27
  post-parliamentary materials, 16, 27–28
  pre-parliamentary materials, 16, 26–27

fact, matters of, 12–14, 100–101
  fairness *see* hearings; procedural fairness
fees, 117
Fiennes, Sir John, 72
finality clauses, 174
fines, standard scale of, 156–57
first-time licensing applications, 120–21
fixed-time Acts, 30
footnotes, 3
foreign jurisdictions:
  experience, 36
  qualifications from, 130–31
fundamental rights and freedoms *see* human rights
fundamentality, 123–24

gender-neutral drafting, 76–78, 94
general principles of drafting, 61–102
  amending provisions, 92–94
  application and extent, 96–98
  art or science, as, 62–63
  bodies corporate, 80
  commencement, 94–96
  consequential amendments and repeals, 99–100
  definition sections, 100–102
  enacting formulas, titles and preambles, 90–92
  gender-neutral drafting, 76–78, 94
  Interpretation Acts, 102
  layout, 71–73
  modifiers, 78, 79
  mongoose principle, 61–62
  nature of, 61–63
  nominalisations, avoiding, 80
  objectives *see* objectives of drafting
  plain language drafting, 63–65, 116
    guides, 83
    historical context, 64
    limitations, 64–65
  positive drafting, 74–75
  problems of drafting *see* problems of drafting
  provisos, 83–84
  ranges of items, 84–85
  restrictive and non-restrictive phrases and clauses, 89–90
  savings and transitional provisions, 98–99
  sentences:
    constructing legislative, 75
    length, 72–73
  structuring instruments, 65–71
    principal and subordinate provisions, 65–66
    subordinate provisions, placing, 69–71
    Thring's rules, 67–69
    uniformity, 66–71, 73
  tenses, 79
  words:
    active and passive use, 73–74
    conjunctive and disjunctive, 79–80, 83
    consistent use of, 73
    ordinary, use of, 81–83
see also drafting instructions; penal provisions; powers and duties; subordinate legislation
general public:
  adult literacy, 6, 7–8
  guidance for, 27
  interests of, 106, 110–11, 174
  legislation, and, 1, 3, 4,6
  licensing schemes, 117
  non-lawyers and lay people *see* non-lawyers
  public opinion, 30–31
  strict liability offences, 153
Glidewell J, 169
Goddard, Lord, 25
Goff, Lord, 152
Goldsworthy, J, 44
government departments *see* departments

grandparenting, 130
Gray, John Chipman, 19
Greenberg, D, 159
Greene MR, Lord, 168, 169–70
group section headings *see* headings
grundnorm, 41
guides and guidance:
  departmental, 27–28, 83
  Drafting Technique Group *see* Drafting Technique Group
  interpreting legislation, 7, 15
  general public for, 27
  plain language, 83
  Thring's rules, 67–69

Hailsham LC, Lord, 26, 116
Halsbury LC, Lord, 26
Hansard, 27
headings, 16, 24
hearings, licensing, right to, 120–21, 170
Henry VIII clauses, 174–75
Hoadley, Bishop, 65
Hoffman, Lord, 27
Hope, Lord, 53
House of Lords' jurisdiction, 12, 14
HRA *see under* human rights
human rights, 6, 36, 46–58
  common law, and, 43, 48
  courts, and, 46–47, 50–53, 55–56
  ECHR *see* ECHR
  equality, homosexual, 30–31, 54, 56
  HRA, 43, 46, 47, 49–57, 74, 91, 139
    Convention rights under, 49–53
    implications for drafters, 46
    incompatibility, declarations of, 52
    legal protection before, 46–47, 56
    retrospectivity, 53–54
    statements of compatibility, 53
    subordinate legislation, 161
  international law, presumption of compliance with, 57–58
  interpretation and validity of legislation, 50–52
  public authorities, duty on, 52–53

illegality, 122, 124
impact assessments, 36
'includes' and 'means', 100–101
incompatibility, declarations of, 52
indentations, 3
inheritance, 7
injustice, presumption against, 28–29
innocence, presumption of, 144
instructing departments *see under* drafting instructions
instructions, drafting *see* drafting instructions
instruments, reading *see* reading provisions and instruments as a whole
intelligibility, 3–4
interest groups, 5, 9, 71
international:
  law, 48, 57–58
  obligations, 36
Internet, 116
interpretation *see under* constitutional considerations; *see* principles of interpretation
Interpretation Act 1850, 102
Interpretation Act 1889, 91
Interpretation Act 1978, 9, 91, 95, 99, 102, 177–86
  anticipatory exercise of powers, 114
  powers and duties, 103, 113–14
  service by post, 118
  subordinate legislation, 159, 163
Interpretation Acts, 102, 103, 148
interpretative obligation, 50–52, 53
intestacy, 7
irrationality, 122, 170
irrelevance, *Wednesbury see under* relevant considerations

Jessell MR, Sir George, 25
judges, 3, 9, 12, 105
  discretion, 100
  extra-judicial opinions, 25–26
  grundnorm concept, 41
  guidance, and, 27
  headings and marginal notes, 24
  independence, 42
  legislative intention, 19–20
  'may' and 'shall', powers and duties, and, 104–107
  punctuation, and, 87
  statements of purpose, 17
see also courts; decision-makers; juries; tribunals
judicial review, 5, 38, 56, 57
  duties, enforcing, 103, 107–10
  excluding, 38
  subordinate legislation, and, 171–76
    finality clauses, 174
    Henry VIII clauses, 174–75
    time-limited ouster clauses, 173–74
    total ouster clauses, 172–73
    subjective tests, provisions containing, 175–76
juries, 12, 100
see also courts; decision-makers; judges; tribunals
jurisdictional error, 167, 168
justice:
  barring access to, 38, 47, 172–73
  interests of, 46, 106, 112, 121
  natural *see* procedural fairness
  presumption against injustice, 28–29

Keeling schedules, 93
Keith, Lord, 58
Kelsen, Hans, 41, 42
Kent, Sir Harold, 3

language:
  advantages, 2
  clarity, 3–4
    meaning, 3–4, 45
    objectivity, 4–8
  'drafting', 81
  English, *see* English language
  imprecision, 2
  oral language compared, 2–3
  plain language drafting, 63–65, 116
see also communication and drafting
law:
  British constitution *see under* constitutional considerations
  matters of, 12–14, 100–101
  predictability, 1
  rule of *see* rule of law
Law Commission, 26, 111–12, 113, 153
Laws, LJ, 50
lawyers, 7, 71
  academic, 6, 17
    opinions, 36
  clients, and, 5, 8, 16
  described, 8, 16
  drafters, as, 34, 40
    code of professional conduct, 40
  lawyer-client relationships, 40
  legal profession, 3, 5, 9
    statements of purpose, 17
  legal textbooks, 25
  non-lawyers *see* non-lawyers
lay people *see* general public
layout, 71–73
  sentence length, 72–73
legal:
  profession *see under* lawyers
  representation, 121
  textbooks, 25–26
legality, presumption of, 41
legislation:
  ambiguous *see* ambiguity
  certainty *see* certainty
  commencement sections *see* commencement sections
  constitutional considerations *see* constitutional considerations
  definition sections *see* definition sections
  European community law, and, *see* European community law
  extra-territorial, 97–98
  headings and marginal notes, 16, 24
  HRA *see under* human rights
  instructions for *see* drafting instructions
  interpretation by courts, 6, 102
  legislative:
    intention, 19–20
    programme, 35
  objectives *see* objectives of drafting
  paving *see* paving legislation
  preambles and long titles, 16, 23
  presumptions of interpretation, 28–29
  problems of drafting *see* problems of drafting
  purpose and mischief, 16–20, 23, 24, 26, 44
  readership, 4–8
  reference, by, 93
  schedules *see* schedules
  short titles, 16, 23–24
  statements of purpose, 17
  structure, 6
  subordinate *see* subordinate legislation
see also statutes
legislative:
  drafting *see* constitutional considerations; drafting instructions
  intention, 19–20
  licensing schemes *see* licensing and registration
  programmes, 35
legitimate expectation:
  consultation, 171
  guidance, and, 28
    protection of, 43
  licences, and, 120, 122
licensing and registration, 115–31
  application procedures, 116-20
    consultation requirements, 116, 118–20
    disputed matters of fact, 121
    notice of applications, giving, 116, 117–18
    standard application forms, 116–17
  conditional licences, 122–25
  criteria for granting and withholding licences, 121–22
  duration of licences, 125–26
  enforcement of licensing regime, 127–29
  first-time applications, renewals, revocations and appeals, 120–21
  qualifications from other jurisdictions, 130–31
  transitional provisions, 130
literal meaning and rule, 11, 14–15, 16, 18, 57
literary writing, 8, 9
local authorities, 78, 80, 108, 127, 133, 159, 163, 167, 176
long titles, 16, 23, 90, 91–92
Lowry, Lord, 56, 87

Mackay LC, Lord, 27
Mackay J, 50
magistrates, 100, 128, 140, 141

see also courts; decision-makers; judges; juries; tribunals
mandatory orders *and mandamus*, 173
margin of appreciation, doctrine of, 55, 56–57
marginal notes, 16, 24
material considerations *see* relevant considerations
matters of fact and law, 12–14, 100–101
'may' and 'shall', 104–107
McCardie J, 21–22
meaning:
  communication *see* communication
  context *see under* principles of interpretation
  fact or law, as, *see under* principles of interpretation
  language *see* language
  literal *see under* principles of interpretation
  legislation, 3
'means' and 'includes', 100–101
Megarry V-C, Sir Robert, 46–47, 120
mens rea, 36
  consent, and, 154–55
  necessary element of statutory offences, 148–54
  offences by corporations, and, 155–56
Millett, Lord, 108–109
ministers, 27, 53, 160
  appeals to *see under* appeals
  discretion, 107
  drafters's advice, and, 40
  executive functions and titles, reallocation of, 60
mischief, 24, 26
modifiers, 78, 79
monarchs, 58–59, 60
Money Bills, 91
mongoose principle, 61–62
Moulton, Lord, 91

natural justice *see* procedural fairness
Neill LJ, 47
Nicholls, Lord, 20
nominalisations, 80
non-human actors *see* bodies corporate and unincorporated associations
non-lawyers, 6, 7, 9, 65
  decision-makers, 28
see also general public
non-textual amendments, 92–93
Normand, Lord, 23
notice of applications, giving, 116, 117–18
numbering newly-inserted provisions, 94

objectives, drafting, of, 1, 3, 4, 8, 23
objective legislative purposes, 44
official reports, 26, 36
Oliver, Lord, 29
ombudsmen, 37–38
omissions from instruments, 22
omnia praesumuntur rite esse acta, 41
oral:
  hearings, 120–21
  language, 2
orders, 160
Orders in Council, 52, 60, 160
ordinary words *see under* English language
ouster clauses, 172–75
Oxford Dictionary, 26

paragraphing, 3
parentheses, 87–88
parish councils, 80
Parker CJ, Lord, 23, 149
Parliament, 3, 5, 91
  amending legislation, 14
  Bills *see* Bills
  common law, and, 148
  extra-territorial legislation, 97–98
  Hansard, 27
  headings and marginal notes, 24
  intention, 19–20, 30, 31, 37, 53, 57, 111
  international obligations, and, 57–58
  legislative supremacy, 43, 44, 45, 46, 51, 52, 65
    ouster clauses, and, 172–74
    subordinate legislation, 45, 119, 172
  Members, 27, 71, 93
    intention, 20
    mischiefs, and, 26
  parliamentary materials, 16, 27
  post-parliamentary materials, 16, 27–28
  successors not binding, 48
parliamentarians, 27, 71
parliamentary counsel *see under* drafters
passage of time, effect of *see* updating construction
paving legislation, 24, 58–60, 138
  constitutional considerations, 43
penal provisions, 139–57
  civil and criminal liability, 140–43
  continuing offences, 145–47
  criminal liability, nature of, 139–47
  criminal offences, 36, 118, 127, 139, 141, 142
    creating, drafting techniques for, 143–45
  fines, standard scale of, 156–57
  interpretation, 147–56
    consent and *mens rea*, 154–55
    mens rea as necessary element 148–54
    offences by corporations and *mens rea*, 155–56
  penalties:
    enforcement, and 140–43, 151
    remedies, and, 112–113
plain language *see under* language

plurals, 77, 80
political parties, 51, 71
Poole J, 50
positive drafting, 74–75
post-parliamentary materials, 16, 27–28
powers and duties, 103–114
  anticipatory exercise of powers, 114
  continuity of, 113–14
  distinction between 103–107
  judicial review, enforcing duties by, 107–10
  'may' and 'shall', 104–107
    prohibitions, 105–106
  statutory duty, damages for breach of, 110–12
    remedies and penalties, 112–13
    vicarious liability, 113
preambles, 16, 23, 91–92
precedent, 12, 19, 100
  decided cases, 20, 25, 36, 44
Preparation of Legislation, The (Renton Report), 17
preparatory work *see* paving legislation
pre-parliamentary materials, 16, 26–27
presumptions:
  Anisminic, statutory interpretation, and, 172–73, 174
  innocence, of, 144
  interpretation, of, 11, 28–29, 73
    absurdity, against 28, 29
    injustice, against, 28–29
  legality, of, 41
  licences, indefinite validity of, 125
  mens rea, need for *see mens rea*
  penal provisions construed in defendant's favour, 147, 167
  penalties and remedies, and, 112
  retrospectivity, against, 54
principal provisions, 65–66
principles of drafting *see* general principles
principles of interpretation, 11–32, 103
  amending legislation, 22
  commencement sections *see* commencement sections
  common law, and, 148
  construction, and, 11–12
  contemporary standards, 12
  context *see* context and contextual approach
  courts applying *see under* courts
  definition sections *see* definition sections
  drafters, and, 2, 9, 11, 16
  ejusdem generis principle, 21–22
  extrinsic materials *see* extrinsic materials
  guides to *see* guides and guidance
  headings and marginal notes, 16, 24
  importance of, 2
  literal rule meaning, 11, 14–15, 16, 18
  matters of fact or law, 11
  omissions from instruments, 22
  penal provisions, 147
  preambles and long titles, 16, 23
  presumptions *see* presumptions of interpretation
  purpose as part of context *see under* contextual approach and context
  reading provisions *see* reading provisions and instruments as a whole
  rule of rank, 21
  same meaning to same words, 22
  schedules *see* schedules
  short titles, 16, 23–24
  tribunals, and, 5
  updating construction *see* updating construction
  weighing and balancing factors, 15
private:
  law proceedings, 171
  practitioners as drafters, 39
  sector, 36
private interests, 111
problems of drafting, 1, 3, 16, 35–38
procedural:
  fairness, 167, 170–71
  requirements, 116–20, 171
professional bodies, 5, 60, 119, 171
professions, members of, 5, 6
prohibitions, 105–106
pronouns, 76–77
proof:
  burden of, 144
  standards of, 139, 147
proportionality, doctrine of, 43, 55, 56
provisions:
  purpose *see* purpose *under* legislation
  reading *see* reading provisions and instruments as a whole
provisos, 83–84
public:
  general *see* general public
  law, 7
    duties *see* powers and duties
  office, drafters as holders of, 39, 40, 42
  officials, 5, 27
  opinion *see under* general public
  services, 36
public authorities, duty on, 52–53, 54
punctuation, 3, 85–89
punitive damages, 140
purpose:
  legislation, of *see under* legislation
  purposive construction, 16–20, 45, 48–49
  statements of, 17

quashing orders, 173

ranges of items, 84–85
rank principle, 21
readership of legislation, 4–8
  co-operation, and, 8–9
reading provisions and instruments as a whole, 20–25
reasonableness, 55–56, 108, 122
  subjective tests, and, 175–76
  Wednesbury unreasonableness, 167, 169–70
reasonably incidental principle, 135, 163–64, 168
re-enactment, amending by, 93–94
registration *see under* licensing and registration
regulations, 160
regulatory drafting, 43–44
  certainty *see* certainty
  drafting instructions, 33–34
    drafters as own client, 5, 33–34
  executive functions and titles, reallocation of, 60
  objectives *see* objectives of drafting
  penal provisions *see* penal provisions
  problems of drafting *see* problems of drafting
  readership, 4–8
  regulatory regime, 44
see also subordinate legislation
regulatory impact assessments, 36
regulatory offences, 142
Reid, Lord, 12, 19–20, 86, 152
relevant and irrelevant considerations, 7, 105, 108, 122, 123, 167, 168-69
remedial orders, 52
remedies and penalties, 112–13
renewals, licensing schemes in, 120–21
Renton Committee, 5, 17, 71, 72, 93
repeals, 36, 52
  amending by, 93–94
  consequential amendments and repeals, 99–100
Report of the Committee on Ministers' Powers, 160
restrictive and non-restrictive phrases and clauses, 89–90
retrospectivity, 28, 46, 59, 106
  HRA, and, 51, 53–54
revocations, licensing schemes in, 120–21
revolutionary situations, 41–42
Roch LJ, 30
Rodger, Lord, 50–51, 74
Rowlatt, Sir John, 4
Royal:
  Assent, 59, 86, 90, 95
  Charters, 133
  Commissions, 26
  prerogative, 51, 52, 58–59, 160
rule of law, 1, 14, 41, 44–45
  ouster clauses, and, 172
  predictability in interpretation, 44
rule of rank, 21
rules, 160
Russell CJ, Lord, 167

savings, 98–99
schedules, 24
Scott, Lord, 109–10
secondary legislation *see* subordinate legislation
secretaries of state, 58–59, 133
section headings *see* marginal notes
Seidman, A, 39, 42
Seidman, RB, 39, 42
sentences:
  constructing legislative, 75
  length, 72–73
separation of powers, doctrine of, 41, 44, 45–46, 124–25, 164
service by post, 118
severability, 123–24, 164–67
Sheen J, 29
short titles, 16, 23–24, 90, 91–92
shoulder-notes *see* marginal notes
side-notes *see* marginal notes
signatures, electronic, 116–17, 118
Simon LC, Lord, 23, 80
Simonds, Lord, 45
Slynn, Lord, 50
social attitudes *see under* updating construction
Speaker of House of Commons, 91
Stamp, J, 20–21
standard application forms, 116–17
standards of proof *see under* proof
standing, 107
statements:
  compatibility, of, 53
  purpose, of, 17
statutes, 5
  'always speaking', 30, 79
  fixed-time Acts, 30
  skeleton Acts, 159
  subordinate legislation *see* subordinate legislation
see also legislation
statutory corporations, 99, 133–38
  creating, 134–38
    dissolution, 137–38
    employees, 137
    meetings, 136–37
    members, 135–36
    names, 134
    objects, 135
  nature of, 133
  paving legislation, 138

statutory:
  discretion *see under* discretion
  duty, breach of *see under* powers and duties
  instruments, 160
  offences, *mens rea*, and, 148–54
Staughton LJ, 112
Stephen J, 8
Steyn, Lord, 51, 54, 55, 153
Strasbourg jurisprudence, 48, 50
strict liability offences, 148–54
subjective:
  legislative purposes, 44
  tests, provisions containing, 175–76
subordinate legislation, 6, 9, 60, 159–76
  challenges, excluding and restricting, 171–76
    finality clauses, 174
    Henry VIII clauses, 174–75
    subjective tests, provisions containing, 175–76
    time-limited ouster clauses, 173–74
    total ouster clauses, 172–73
  constraints on, 161–62
  consultation requirements, 119, 171
  corporations, 137
  executive functions and titles, reallocation of, 6
  extent, 160–61
  fees, 117
  forms of, 160
  quashing, 45, 51
  legislative supremacy, and, 45, 119, 172
  licensing applications, 117–18, 119, 121
  nature of, 159–60
  remedial orders, 52
  savings and transitional provisions, 98, 99, 102
  ultra vires *see under* ultra vires
  void, 123
see also regulatory instruments
subordinate provisions, 65–66
  placing, 69–71
substantial severability *see* severability
Sullivan R, 103–104
sunset clauses, 98
supremacy of Parliament *see* legislative supremacy *under* Parliament

technological developments *see under* updating construction
teleological approach *see* purposive construction *under* purpose
clauses, 79, 104
textual:
  amendments, 92
  severability *see* severability
third sector, 36, 83
Thornton, GC, 33–34, 35, 98, 143
Thring, Baron, 66–69
  rules, 67–69
time, effects of passage *see* updating construction
time-limited ouster clauses, 173–74
titles *see* executive powers and titles; long titles; short titles
total ouster clauses, 172–73
trade associations, 60, 119
trade unions, 5, 9
transitional provisions, 98–99, 130
Treasury, the, 27, 66
treaties, 48
tribunals, 5, 139
  discretion, 100
  judicial review *see* judicial review
  matters of fact or law, and, 12
  non-lawyer decision-makers, 28
  public authority, as, 52–53, 54
see also courts; decision-makers; judges; juries
typography, 101

ultra vires, 108, 121, 135
  Anisminic principle, and, 172–73, 174
  subordinate legislation, and, 161–71
    actions, classifying bases of, 167–71
    drafters' responsibilities, 162–67
    reasonably incidental principle *see* reasonably incidental principle
    severability *see* severability
unconstitutional proposals, 41–42, 44
uniformity, 66–71, 73
unincorporated associations *see* bodies corporate and unincorporated associations,
United Kingdom, 8, 76, 96, 97
unreasonableness, *Wednesbury see under* reasonableness
updating construction, 11, 29–32
  courts, 16
  drafters, and, 32
  social attitudes, 12, 16
    social change, problem of, 31–31
  technological developments, 12, 16
    problem of, 32
unius inclusio alterius exclusio, 101
Upjohn LJ, 24

vicarious liability, 113
Vienna Convention on the Law of Treaties 1969, 48
voidness, 123–24, 172–73

Waite LJ, 30, 47
Ward LJ, 31, 32
Webster J, 118–19
Wednesbury principles, 7, 122, 123
  irrelevance, 167, 168–69

unreasonableness, 167, 169–70
see also reasonableness; relevant considerations;
White Papers, 59
Widgery CJ, Lord, 114
Wilberforce, Lord, 175, 176
witnesses, 121
words:
active and passive, 73–74
conjunctive and disjunctive, 79–80, 83
consistent use of, 73
ordinary:
meaning, 11–14, 100–101, 102
interpretation *see* principles of interpretation
use in drafting, 82–83
Wright J, 148
written:
constitutions, 46, 161
language *see* language
representations, 121